MW01251413

I DIDN'T COME HERE TO STAY

I DIDN'T COME HERE TO STAY

THE MEMOIRS OF ED PARKER

With the compliments of Frank R. Joubin

Dec 1993

NATURAL HERITAGE / NATURAL HISTORY INC.

The material contained within these published memoirs reflects the views and experiences of the late Edward Parker. The copyright holder and/or Natural Heritage/Natural History Inc. will be pleased to correct any erroneous information in future editions.

I Didn't Come Here to Stay
by Ed Parker

Published by Natural Heritage / Natural History Inc.
P.O. Box 95, Station "O", Toronto, M4A 2M8

Editorial Consultant: David McCorquodale
Design and typesetting: Robin Brass Studio
Printed and bound in Canada by Hignell Printing Limited, Winnipeg, Manitoba

Canadian Cataloguing in Publication Data

Parker, Ed, 1918–1988
    I didn't come here to stay : the memoirs of Ed Parker

ISBN 0-920474-86-1

1. Parker, Ed, 1918–1988. 2. Journalism – Canada – Biography. 3. Public relations consultants – Canada – Biography. I. Title

PN4913.P37A3 1993   070'.92   C93-095282-0

Contents

Dedicated to those assistants who kept the words coming, the manuscript legible, and the project insistent on its own completion.

A particular Hosannah to wife Ilene who cheered me to the finish line.

CHAPTER **1**

FAMILY
ROOTS

The Winnipeg to which my father and my uncle Joe, my mother's brother, came, somewhere around 1911 or 1912, was a community reflecting a multi-varied folk motif.

Apart from the colony of Scots dating back to the Selkirk settlers, there were people from Iceland, Germany, the Ukraine, and Poland. Jews who settled here came mostly from the villages and ghettos in Russia, unlike Toronto Jews who originally came from Poland.

What brings people to a specific area? Usually it's a lead man, a pioneer who finds a spot to settle and then arranges to bring out more people of his own language group. In the case of Jewish immigrants, Yiddish was the common denominator.

My father and my uncle Joe were encouraged to emigrate to Canada by one of the titans of the Jewish pioneer community in Winnipeg, Abraham Berg. He was one of the earliest immigrants from Central Europe arriving around the turn of the century and came under the acceptable disguise of a seemingly illiterate peasant. He explained it this way. Canada, at that time, didn't want foreign-speaking intellectuals nor the revolutionaries of Czarist Russia or Kaiser Germany. These were seen as "disruptive" elements – malcontents. Besides, would immigrants who once had been part of the bourgeoisie of Europe or who were proletarian intellectuals be content to break the land in an undeveloped rocky part of the prairies?

Removing boulders from marginal agricultural land was backbreaking work. To get people to do that, Canada would need immigrants without reading and writing skills. They would need to be dispossessed in the sense that they wouldn't have much or any capital. If they were healthy but indigent, so much the better; that would keep them on the land near Selkirk, Manitoba, once they were there. Without knowledge of English as a working language, they would have no mobility and would become rooted wherever they were deposited.

Jewish people, by and large, were not illiterate, however. The dictates of religion saw to that. Hebraism places high spiritual value on the ability to read the Torah. One best worships God by reading, studying his wisdom and by ingesting the words of the prophets. The Talmud could be learned by listening, but the highest pursuit, "insight", came through reading books.

So, to immigration officers in Canada at the turn of the century all that mattered was that a candidate appear to be a peasant in a sheepskin. He could be a Jew, but they probably wouldn't ask that. Thus, East European Jews trickled into Canada as part of the mix of Ukrainians, Poles and other Slavic people then being recruited by immigration officers.

Abraham Berg would have arrived in such a mélange. Not content with the government's gifts of a wheelbarrow, hoe and sack of seed to begin a life of farming marginally economic land, he quickly migrated to the city of Winnipeg. Here he found someone to whom he could sell a bag of seed for cash or trade. Small merchants offered him their odds and ends, goods they couldn't sell to their customers. Berg made these "seconds" available to immigrant farmers in exchange for their produce. It didn't take Berg long to assume the role as middleman trader, serving the Ukrainians and other immigrants who couldn't read and write.

It is my theory that after 1870, many of the early Jewish immigrants turned from marginal farming to bartering in rags, bottles, scrap material and secondhand goods. Exposed to taunts and prejudices, they nevertheless felt above the role they projected. They were secure in their religion and this gave them inner dignity. They were God's men. On Fridays, on the eve of the Sabbath, they washed, were kings in their homes and were revered by their families. Being orthodox, they did not work on Saturdays. This spirit helped these early pioneers survive and thrive in remote places like Winnipeg.

Eventually, Abraham Berg became affluent and acquired a mansion on the bank of the Red River. His European relatives wrote to him and asked him to help their children settle in Canada. The first relative he brought out was my mother's brother, Joe Perlmutter.

In Russia, Joe was a wanderer and a scalawag. In his travels, he had met my father; a tall, good-looking, curly black-haired poetic guy, Harry Pachter. Harry's father was a non-secular Jew who belonged to a group of "veltmenshen" which the Czar put to use and abuse. Grandpa Pachter, like Abraham Berg, was enterprising enough to be have been given an overseer's job in the Czarist forest reserves. He was granted a concession where he could enjoy a percentage of the profits. The Czarist system would give a man 60 per cent of the profits the first year, 40 per cent the next, 20 per cent the next, 5 per cent the next, and then so little that such an official would be pressing pretty hard to make his own living.

Overseers utilized many serfs to achieve productivity. People were worked hard, so an overseer wasn't very popular. For this reason, the Czar's found the technique of using middlemen very convenient. Many middlemen were Jews. When grievances mounted against the system, troublemakers would go around and say that a Christian child had been killed; its blood was being drunk at Passover. This would arouse and divert the passions of the peasantry from the real issues of the repressive regime. The idea that Jews killed

3

Christ was wed to the cry that local Jews were ritual killers of Gentile children. The maddened mobs would move in on a Jewish village and kill men, women, and children in retaliation. Obviously such outrages didn't begin with Hitler. Persecution was a good reason for Jewish people to get out of Russia. The heavily taxed and exploited Russian serfs were at a breaking point, and a revolution was brewing. That was another good reason to get out of Russia.

My father was tuned into what was then the New Left of Czarist Russia, into the ideas of social justice emanating from the Marxists in Germany. Karl Marx had written his Communist Manifesto in 1837. Pre-revolutionary Russia had been infiltrated by socialistic thinking for nearly a century. My father was caught up with the radical ideas.

Joe had invited Harry to his small native town of Ludsk, Poland, and there Harry was introduced to a different social and cultural milieu. There, in 1907, my father married Joe's sister, Raezel. My mother was a shy, simple woman. She came from village values, although she claimed to have worldly views. Nevertheless, she did reflect a village background where there was such a tremendous emphasis on what people think. Getting married was a girl's most important pursuit. Her marriage to a penniless fellow was considered romantic but not very practical by the villagers. But Raezel's parents considered the family unorthodox and were sure their daughter had made a contract with the devil.

My mother's father, Motel, was sombre and orthodox. He was the town negotiator and arbitrator, community "fixer". The townspeople would turn to him for help in their dealings with the authorities. He had helped many young Jewish lads escape the Czar's military draft by having the conscriptee "accidentally" incapacitated for military services. He would be helped to lose a thumb, a toe, to be maimed in some way to disqualify themselves for military service.

Weeks after Harry married Raezel, Joe became restless and went off to Odessa. Soon he wrote his pal that he had a job for himself and Harry in a printing shop. They would both work at creating theatre posters. My father took leave of Mother to seek his fortune in the big town. As weeks turned into months, Raezel wondered when Harry was going to summon her to join him.

Back in Ludsk, my mother's sister, Hanna-Shaendel, began to nag Raezel. It was nonsense to have a husband a thousand miles away. So they packed and surprised Joe and Harry at the print shop. All four took up housekeeping at the back of the print shop and lived there for several months.

During this period, Joe wrote to Abraham Berg in Canada. There was a frantic exchange of letters. Months passed. Finally Berg relented and brought Joe to Winnipeg, followed by his sister, Hanna-Shaendel. They in turn brought out Harry. A year or two later, in 1913, Raezel joined them.

My parents' first residence was a suite above a store on Salter Street near Boyd in the heart of North Winnipeg. Uncle Joe had married by this time. His wife was a red-headed beauty from Odessa, a hairdresser, very feminine and terrifically jealous. Joe had brought her over soon after Raezel arrived. My mother and aunt were very critical of her because she was glamorous, smoked and wore her hair in a modish style.

Joe was so jealous of the attention men paid her that she finally left him and became one of the wealthy women of Los Angeles and the head of a chain of hairdressing salons. Joe remained a bachelor until his death in 1951.

My father changed his name to Parker, and he and my uncle worked in a small printing shop catering to the Jewish community in Winnipeg. My father was a good compositor and linotype operator and set copy in both English and Yiddish. My uncle was a talented layout man, with a good art sense.

My mother's relatives were our only kin in North America. My father was the only boy in a family of four. None of his sisters emigrated from Russia, so my father's family is unknown to me.

To Rose (Raezel) Parker, the Jewish sector, the north end, was Winnipeg. She couldn't speak English. My father couldn't tolerate Rose speaking English badly, so he discouraged her by speaking to her only in Yiddish. My mother spoke hardly any English at the time I was born.

5

CHAPTER **2**

THE EARLY YEARS

I was the first born in Winnipeg in 1918, just two minutes past midnight, a New Year's baby. Mother was in the Miseracordia Hospital, an establishment run by Spanish nuns. At that time there was some feeling that World War I couldn't go on much longer. Surely, it would be a peace year.

The nuns gave thanks to this first birth of the new year and prayed around my mother's bed. This baby, they said, was a symbol of peace and should be named Jesus, after the Prince of Peace.

My mother, not understanding a word, said, in her limited English, "Thank you very much." The nuns, in turn, took this to be assent and wrote "Jesus" on my crib identification card. When my father arrived and saw the name "Jesus", he was very upset. He did not want me to go through life as "Jeezus" Parker. Since I have no middle name, I am somewhat amused how often the "J" gets contributed by correspondents, "Edward J. Parker". Some people put it as "Edward C. Parker". One can talk oneself into some sort of messiah role, but I haven't; although I must have come close to it in my youth, thinking I would save the world.

The year after I was born, Winnipeg suffered a labour strike that paralyzed the entire community. The strike was organized by the OBU, one big union, and it asked every workman to lay down his tools. The print shop where my father worked was also asked to go out on strike. The proprietors, Simken and Wilder, thought that closing the shop would finish their enterprise. Simken suggested that these employees, including my father, all become employers; then they wouldn't have to go out on strike. My father and the two others were offered shares on an earn-out basis, and this took him out of solidarity with the strike. But his sympathy was basically with labour.

My mother's brother, Shloime, also came to Winnipeg prior to World War I. Like so many youngsters, he was a bit of a scamp. He could run well and would race after the horsedrawn streetcars, leaping aboard as they moved along. One day in pursuit of this sport, he slipped and fell under the wheels. His leg was badly injured and skin grafts were needed. Every one of the 10 children in my mother's family gave skin to help. They all subsequently bore marks on their bodies for the rest of their lives. The grafts didn't work, and the leg was amputated. Because of the social attitudes of that time, Shloime was henceforth considered a cripple. The word "kaleke" became an epithet that haunted him.

When Shloime's first wife died, he married her teenage sister, Esther. The family expected it. Esther at the time might have been fifteen or sixteen. Shloime, was thirty-three. To Esther, he was an old man. In addition to that, he was a person with a handicap. Esther took over the care of Chaneena (later called Martin), Shloime's son and her nephew who was seven or eight years old.

Esther was high-spirited as well as high-bosomed and driven by great sexual drives. At the time, she probably couldn't interpret them forthrightly. Her religious and traditional upbringing had taught her that it was sinful to think in these terms. So she lamented

7

her fate from the moment she met and married Shloime. Consequently, he was always the target of vilification. She reviled him constantly, even though many years later she bore him a child, Sydney.

In those days and throughout my childhood, the city of Winnipeg east of the river hardly existed for me. Our house was on the west side of the river, near the river bank. From the age of two, Alfred Avenue was my world. From age six and a half, when I went off to school, it was the centre of my evolving universe. The west side had all the action.

Main Street, the great north-south artery, was one block west of the river. Two streets north was another main artery, Redwood Avenue, boasting a bridge across the river. The bridge had a cement roadway covered in the centre and wooden sidewalks. The Redwood bridge had a centre span that turned to allow the SS *Kenora* to go on its way up the river. The base support of this bridge was shaped like a plow. When ice floes moved north in the spring, the base would break them into smaller sections.

My brother, Morten, and I knew this base. Once we put together uncut logs from our backyard and constructed a raft. It was most unreliable. The logs, tied together with rope, were loosely joined with boards by three inch nails.

The unstable raft held together at first. Paddling with heavy shovels normally used to stoke coal, we were nearly toppled into the river by their weight. The current became swift and we moved quickly downstream. Fortunately, the contraption smashed into the centre base of the Redwood Bridge and my brother and I were able to leap from the raft and scramble onto the icebreaker. There we remained until rescued by a passing boat.

Main Street stretched into the centre of Winnipeg to meet Portage Avenue, which was reputed at the time to be the widest street in the world. It was certainly the coldest, particularly in January and February. Standing at the corner of Portage and Main was probably as cold as Siberia. If your coat was even half open, the winds would turn you into a kite, propelling you into near flight. Child's Restaurant was an oasis of warmth so great and so welcome that you would resolve to have at least two cups of coffee before braving the wintry blasts again.

In December, January, February, and even March you didn't walk outside without promising yourself a warm withdrawal into some apartment block or restaurant about every two or three blocks. You couldn't survive any other way. Jim Gray, writing about the Depression in his book, *The Winter Years*, recalls cold winters in which people moved from one restaurant to the next just to keep from perishing on a long walk home. To me that was not only a Depression experience but an ordinary winter Winnipeg experience.

I remember from the perspective of a Jewish sphere within an inter-ethnic city. Ukrainians and Scots were often our neighbours. But the little north-end Jewish population moved back and forth over 12-16 streets with Selkirk Avenue as the business and cultural centre.

On that street was a synagogue, many businesses, and the Yiddish theatre, the Queen's. Here, New York artists would come. Great stars! They would perform in musicals, comedies and dramas. My father was then the theatre reviewer for the Jewish paper, *The Israelite Press*, and he always commanded four seats about three rows up from the front. Since there were no babysitters in those days, when my parents went to the shows on Friday or Saturday evenings my brother and I were taken along. What a wonderful experience!

When the Queen's Theatre offered "tragedies", we children ran the risk of falling asleep. Usually, however, we were far too fascinated by the stage action. I loved the musical comedies best; corny, exaggerated, romantic, and syrupy. And I was thrilled with the pit orchestra, a threepiece or fourpiece band with fiddler, drummer, trumpet and piano player striking up stirring moods. Everybody was happy, clapping to keep in time and, in mid-winter, to keep warm.

The greatest attraction of the Queen's Theatre was to get Eskimo pies, those ice cream bars coated in chocolate. Imagine children wanting to eat Eskimo pies in February, but we did and thought it a great treat.

The theatre had a roll-up linoleum-type stage curtain. The curtain invariably came down with a clang and the dust flew. Various interesting messages were painted on this curtain. My introduction to advertising really came from reading these notices.

The Queen's Theatre was very important in our lives. It offered shows every Thursday, Friday and Saturday evening, with Sunday benefits and occasionally Saturday matinees. Plays were written in Winnipeg for the company and performed within two weeks of acceptance.

The productions didn't have to pass too many critical standards. My father, on the other hand, was critical. When the repertory companies offered Ibsen or Strindberg, he was appreciative, but at the same time demanding of the artists. The leads were among the Yiddish theatre's celebrities of the day: Jacob Ben Ami, the Adlers, and Maurice Shwartz. Shwartz was one of the great melodramatic actors of the period. These artists also recruited talent from the local community.

Around the age of seven or eight, I developed the specialty of delivering recitations of Yiddish poetry quite theatrically. My father coached me, and at age ten or eleven, I presented myself on stage wearing a white shirt, a bow tie and a full suit. I declaimed about eagles and poverty, people living in ghettoes, and the coming of a new and better day for Jews and mankind. I was exhilarated to stir the emotions of large audiences, but my greatest fear was that I would forget a line. I was booked for many community programs to help raise money for this or that cause, but I was never paid for these appearances.

The Jewish community in Winnipeg, 10,000 in 1920, was a collection of people from Russia, Poland, Germany, England and other countries. They represented political attitudes from left to right on every question – ritual slaughter of cattle, Zionism, economics, municipal politics and world affairs. They divided themselves into two hundred different community groups with memberships as small as 10-20 or as large as 1,000. All very dedicated to their points of view.

So passionate were people about the causes they espoused, that relatives with different views often avoided each other in the street. It was a complex community in which to be raised.

My childhood was spent in a floral hothouse of Jewishness. The Abraham Bergs and other prominent ethnic families felt out of place in English-speaking Winnipeg with its social pecking order based on government, military, and economic groupings. The aristocracy of grain merchants and bankers sponsored dances, theatre and musicals. The north end was not included.

Prayerful Jews properly prepared their Friday evening meal and invited their relatives on occasion to join them. Those who were not so prayerful set up their Friday evening poker games. Then there were all the small "Landsmanshaft" associations, with membership related to the European country of origin, the part of the country and the town. My parents belonged to the Volinier Landsmanshaft, related to the region from which my mother emigrated. Thus Jews created their own community life.

Conservative, religious Jews like the Bergs started orthodox Hebrew schools. Here they would prepare young men, not often women, for religious observance. Young boys would be readied for their Bar-Mitzvahs, their confirmation into manhood. To be accepted into the religious congregation involved knowing some Hebrew. This took place at the Talmud Torah, a three-storey building, the top floor was converted into a synagogue on holidays. It was located on Charles Street, just south of Selkirk Avenue. Behind its heavy doors, boys were drilled in the abc's of Hebrew. Most of the Hebrew teachers were odd types, not economically employable at anything else. I became a student at the Talmud Torah in 1924 when I was six years old. Yiddish teachers were the ones in whose care, loving or otherwise, I was entrusted at 5 p.m. every day but Friday and Saturday. Sunday mornings were also Jewish school time. Going to the Talmud Torah was a tedious experience. Hebrew, a language we didn't understand and for which we had no particular feeling, was learned by rote. Words were written on a blackboard, then sounded, pronounced, and memorized. Hebrew words did float like raisins in Yiddish dough.

We had to wear our caps indoors. This I found amusing. I don't really know the religious rationalization for doing this, although I suspect its origin was related to experience with dust in the desert. Today, it would be said that some honour to God is signified by wearing a hat in synagogue or holy school. In those days, one cap was worn for every purpose. Being boys, we soon crushed the peaks of our caps making ourselves look like drowned waifs.

The disciplined pedagogy mirrored techniques associated with the days of Oliver Twist. We would enter class in line-ups, and a ruler smacked across our knuckles was a rough but effective attention-getter. The one or two years I spent at the Talmud Torah were not very happy ones.

At this time my father wanted the Talmud Torah school to become more liberal, to teach contemporary Yiddish which was more worldly and would involve study of the works of such writers as Sholem Aleichem and I.P. Peretz. He felt that Jewish children of pioneer parents should learn more recent history of Jewish people, their trials in Czarist Russia and in other countries, the immediate experience which formed the basis of Winnipeg Jewry's emigration from the old countries rather than starting from a Bible beginning nearly six thousand years ago and then going forward.

My father's position on education was considered untenable and heretical, and led to fire and brimstone debates. Traditionalists would not tolerate ungodly modernism. The war factions and epithets inside the school were all reported avidly in the columns of the Jewish newspaper, of which my father was a co-owner and contributing editor.

In 1924, at the height of my father's involvement with the Talmud Torah Hebrew school, there was a need to raise substantial building funds. Sam Berg suggested they do it through sponsoring a grand carnival. The Talmud Torah teamed up with the Barnum and Bailey Circus, at the height of its fame at the time. The one sponsored the other, with some part of the circus' proceeds going to the Jewish school.

The circus was preceded by an eight-month money raising campaign that centred around a popularity contest. The most popular of three boy candidates would become king of the carnival, and the most popular of three girl candidates would become queen of the carnival. The boys were in an age group from six to nine, and the girls were in an age group of fourteen to seventeen.

It was really not a matter of coupling the king and queen but of getting youngsters in whom the community could have some pride to give focus to the money raising. Each dollar donated was considered a vote for a potential king. Who would be king? Chubby Slobinsky or me?

My campaign manager was Sam Shore, a candy maker, who by a stroke of luck had stocked his small factory to the rafters with sugar to make candy. When the war came in 1914, and sugar prices sky-rocketed, he became a "millionaire".

Sam dedicated himself to the Eddie Parker campaign. He placed pictures of himself and me in the Jewish newspaper regularly and I became the most publicized kid in Yiddish Winnipeg. But in the end, the Slobinsky family threw in "limitless" personal wealth and their son Norman became king, and I became first prince.

It was quite a pageant. The big coronation was preceded by a great deal of family kafaffle. I was fitted for white satin shorts, a purple cape, a frilly silk shirt, long white socks, and shoes with brass knuckles. Part of the carnival coronation involved participation in a circus parade down Main Street. The crowning ceremonies took place in the Olympic Skating Rink, an indoor hockey palace. Here the Talmud Torah section of the circus parade was placed in a marching sequence. I recall bands and spectators in the rink and being given a special chair near the royal thrones. Emerging out of the stadium came the procession of circus people, followed by a stage coach bearing the king and queen. The king was six or seven years old and his queen about seventeen. She probably thought the pairing incongruous and suffered the age difference between them.

I rode a pony, much to the envy of King Slobinsky who began to sob and demanded a pony ride as well.

At the circus grounds, I was asked to throw goodies to the populace from the royal stand. Imagine my pleasure when I realized I could get into any side show and the main tent without paying. At this circus I saw my first boxing match. When our royal party entered, the boxers stopped and waved at the king and his entourage.

After two or three years, my father severed his connections with the Talmud Torah and gave his support to another Jewish school, the I.L. Peretz school, named after a great Yiddish folk writer. This school was Yiddish speaking, not strong on religion, taught some Hebrew, and was strongly influenced by social democrats and far-left socialists. Ironically, many of the teachers eventually became Liberals and Conservatives. Some of its offspring, Saul Cherniak and Saul Miller, for example, alumni of that school, became NDP cabinet ministers in Manitoba in the seventies.

When I was transferred to the liberal Peretz Schule, I felt more at home. A pragmatic view of life was projected as opposed to the orthodox and unrealistic stance of the Hebrew school. To me the Talmud Torah was involved with concepts of heaven and hell, all intolerable nonsense.

The Peretz Schule propounded the maxim that all people everywhere had worth. The day would come, it hoped, when the resources of the earth supported all people in the world fairly.

While the I.P. Peretz school conducted itself in Yiddish, the Hebrew language was taught as a single, formal subject. One lad behind me once fed me a line unrelated to the text. "All Jewish people ought to light lamps," I translated. The Hebrew text had nothing to do with lighting lamps. My reading was a pretty good indicator that I had not done my homework. I recall writing a correction hundreds of times on the blackboard.

These were busy days for Mickey (Morten) and me – public school, run home at 4 p.m. for milk and cake, practice music for a half-hour, then off to Jewish school from 5 p.m. until 7 p.m., home for supper, and homework until 10 p.m.

At Jewish school, I met many interesting teachers. One of them was the father of Larry Zolf, the CBC commentator. Another, Rappaport, proved to be the most interesting pedagogue I had met to that date. I was 13 at the time. He was a man with a face as craggy as the Rock of Gibraltar. Rappaport demonstrated dramatically what it really means when a teacher loves the children under his care. He wasn't critical of our inadequacies at memorization. He rejoiced in our humour and in the play of our minds.

I was disappointed that my parents didn't have enough confidence to allow him to take me, together with other boys, to the World's Fair in Chicago. This was the fair where the legendary Sally Rand danced, allegedly in the nude, covered only by her fans. Of course, I would have been too young to appreciate that routine.

Rappaport projected a great warmth and, partly because of him, I endorsed socially idealistic sentiments, not only regarding Jewish people, but regarding all mankind.

When I was a youth, it seemed almost incredible that any Jew would be a Conservative or belong to the Conservative party. Such a person would be backing a formation in which he didn't belong. In the 1940s and later, when some Jewish people did begin to work for traditional parties, they gained further acceptance among the establishment.

I remember a Jewish bookstore, the People's Bookstore, on Main Street in the 1920s and '30s. Its shelves of Jewish books, magazines, and records fascinated us. At the back of the store people played chess. The People's Bookstore also produced a few notable corned beef sandwiches, delicious with bottled cokes.

At home, we had a gramophone with a crank-up handle. The Victrola had a position of prominence in our small living room, comparable to that of an icon in a church. My brother and I would take turns winding this gramophone as well as hiding the removable handle from each other, a frustration to our parents. Every record in the house had to be marked "M" for Mickey and "E" for Eddie. We even owned different halves of records. It was always a question of whether Mickey was playing my side or I his.

In the Yiddish Village within the larger city there were three or so Jewish barber shops. You chose one in accordance with your politics. If you were communistically inclined, you would go to the barber on Main Street. If you were Zionistically inclined, you would go to a barber on Selkirk Avenue. This phenomenon of favouring tradesmen and craftsmen according to political belief really fractionalized our community. Patronizing merchants because of their point of view even extended to delicatessen stores.

There was a particularly fine delicatessen, Grosney's, next to the Queen's on Selkirk Avenue, later opposite three movie houses, the Regent, the Colonial, and the Fox on Main Street.

My father gave Mickey and me 25¢ each; 10¢ for a movie, 10¢ for a corned beef sandwich and 5¢ for a coke. Later on we ate with even greater distinction when he put us on a charge account at Grosney's.

It was not until I got into public school that libraries began to matter to me. Before that I thought they were so "severance-inducing" and quiet, that they made me want to get my books and get out. To a kid raised in a noisy ethnic home, the quiet seemed part of a "shush, shush" Anglo-Saxon atmosphere that was restrictive on our high spirits. It took a while to get used to.

I didn't spend much time in synagogues either. Somewhere, at about age 13, I realized that people "bought" seats. If they didn't have tickets they wouldn't be admitted. It seemed incredible to me that anyone would have to buy the right to worship. I didn't contemplate the problem of maintaining a synagogue, keeping a janitor or arranging repairs. It just seemed wrong to me to be stopped at the door because my father wasn't inside or I couldn't show a ticket. This was the community's way of policing itself, obviously on the assumption that people would not otherwise contribute voluntarily their fair share to these institutions.

On one occasion, during the high holidays in the fall, I went for a walk north down Main Street into St. John's Park. The day was glorious and I began to whistle. It occurred to me that I was praying, maybe better than anyone else, because I was so happy. My father compared this with a similar story in Yiddish folklore. It concerned a boy who had no education and was not allowed in the synagogue. In frustration, he walked into the forest, whistling. God heard him, ignoring the prayers of those in the synagogue.

This story confirmed me in my view that one can address oneself directly to an appreciation of life itself, with God or whatever. My view was in harmony with my father's outlook. Thus, from an early age, my life approach did not bring me into any philosophical conflict with my father.

A favourite outing for us children was Winnipeg Beach, a most glamorous spot about 60 miles north of Winnipeg. When we got there for a holiday in the early days, either for a single day picnic, for a week, or for a month, we considered it utopia.

Beyond Winnipeg Beach was an Icelandic village called Gimli. My brother and I travelled from the beach to Gimli a lot, and by the time we were in our teens, we became aware that the lassies in this community were among the most beautiful girls we had ever seen.

During the Depression, the dollar bill was a powerful buck and did a great many things. A haircut was 15¢ or 25¢, large chocolate bars, 5¢. Motion picture prices for adults were 15¢ or 25¢. Maids were paid $4.00 to $6.00 per month, and as poor as we were, we could afford this live-in luxury. Our maid was from the farm and illiterate. Maids were mostly Galician and spoke Slavic which my parents understood.

Our maids were peasants, absorbed in a world of superstition and near voodoo. Not surprisingly, their major preoccupation was young men. They prepared for their Thursday night out with a great ceremony of hair curling and bathing.

One evening, my brother and I became aware that our maid and her friend were preparing strange potions in the cellar. We hurriedly dressed for an expedition outdoors, donning coats, moccasins, sweaters, scarves, and those amazing winter type hats that had ear flaps to tie down.

Once outside, we dashed to the side of the house, knelt down in the snow, and pressed our noses to the basement window. There was always the danger that the frost would prevent our view. We anticipated this by defrosting the pane in advance with warm fingers.

The two girls were involved in some sort of tonsorial ceremony. It involved cutting hair from both the top of the head and the pubic area.

The girls were deeply absorbed. They mixed the cut hair with a liquid and dipped spearmint gum in the concoction. The gum dried was re-wrapped. This, I later guessed, was a love potion, a mesmerizing gift to the boyfriend. It was enough to make one ill. The folk lore was bizarre, primitive and naive.

This episode engraved itself in my memory. It was a marked event in my sex education. It certainly contributed to my evolving wonder about women. What techniques would they adopt in pursuit of a mate?

Although winters in Winnipeg are notable for the cold, my early childhood recollections are of a vital, important season. Winter was an active time – educationally, socially and physically. Before we braced this cold weather, my mother would see that we were well fortified with porridge which she cooked on a gas and wood combination stove in the kitchen.

My mother could not be judged a good cook. She did make good strudel, but her chocolate cake was a disaster – dry and hard and usually only a half inch high.

My mother would prepare for the Sabbath meals on Thursdays and Fridays. It would cook two full days and evenings to supply the soup, meat dishes, and pastry for the weekend and after.

On Fridays, we invariably had chicken, preceded by gefilte fish and chicken soup. The gefilte fish was a treat in itself, a blend of two fishes, a delicacy. It is one of the more successful Jewish foods. A lot of our diet was very heavy, suited to the needs of previous generations of village folk who were closer to the land or who had been porters, draymen, fellows who carried produce on their backs, even if their role was that of middle man. Early families in Winnipeg needed this heavy fueling kind of food.

I don't think we ate many vegetables, out of season they were very expensive and we didn't like them anyway. It's a wonder we didn't get scurvy. We did have potatoes and lots of bread.

We ate bread with bread in fact. We loved my mother's French toast, but she never let us consume it without having additional bread to eat with it.

Chicken was also a staple. Nearly all parts of the chicken were used in Jewish culinary culture, even the neck after the skin had been removed intact. The skin was stuffed with a dressing. Delicious! The starchy filling was made tasty with chicken fat added as part of the mixture. It was a gourmet dish but nearly indigestible.

Apart from wings, breasts, and legs, the webbed feet and legs of the chicken were also a treat. Mickey and I always competed for them. We were drawn to the jelly-like taste.

Mid-European cooking also found good use for chicken livers, and chicken innards yielded unlaid eggs of all sizes, not yet with shells. Put into soups and boiled, they were mild and soft and were very delicious.

Even the cow contributed to our diet. For example, the leg bones, once you got over the image that they were legs and viewed them as bones, could be stewed to yield a jelly known in Russian as "petchah". Mother added garlic, hard boiled eggs and other food stuffs. Served hot, it was a great winter dish.

Mother never worried about our ice box in the winter. We had a back porch, essentially a non-insulated addition to the house. There was a winter door outside the inside door leading to this "summer kitchen". The inside door led from the dining room. Between these two doors, you could place items you wanted refrigerated. In fact, they froze solid. A half hour of this between-door treatment and the hot petchah became hard as rock. Father brought it into the house an hour or two before a poker game and the rock softened into a digestible jelly. Laughter and animated betting accompanied the attacks on the petchah which was eaten with rye bread, relishes and pickles.

Why so much concentration on food? It was important to us culturally, socially and nutritionally. So much time was taken in preparing food that the product mattered a good deal. Even important family meetings were centred around the kitchen or dining table and some form of food.

All of us came home for lunch, and then there were great conversations around the noon meal. In our childhood, we could convey the enthusiasm of our morning's activities to Papa and Mama. Lunch over, my father would put his head down for 20 minutes on the chesterfield in the front room before going back to work. Life was different in those days.

In the summer we spent time with our parents as well. It was pleasant and reassuring to see Papa walk out the back kitchen onto the little porch. He would sit at the top of the steps, his long legs stretched out, and rest his head against the wall of the house. He took the sun and dozed. This was a time for me to come and sit next to him, wait for him to rouse and exchange a few words about what was happening in school, share a joke and revel in his humorous turn of mind.

My mother was a proud, noble woman, with an inner sense of refinement. She read Yiddish papers avidly, particularly the serialized romances and advice to the lovelorn. She would read aloud to us from her Jewish papers. She became riveted if there was a murder scandal being reported.

She took inordinate pride in her children and dressed us similarly, ensuring our clothes were clean and meticulous. My mother's joy in us showed in the way she dressed and fed us. She was anxious I choose the right profession, preferably law.

Her fondest hope was that I would marry the prettiest girl from the wealthiest Jewish family in town. No ordinary girl was worthy of her Eddie or her son Mickey.

Rose Parker was to some extent an inhibitor to my father, in as much as she wanted him home so much of the time. In the early days, my father certainly scallywagged, playing poker throughout the night. Later on when he stayed home, Rose resented the long and late hours he spent writing, but she respected him for it and adjusted to his compulsion to write. She loved to hear her husband speak in public, but she was more concerned with his presentation than with the content of his speech. She was aware of how people behaved, how they lived, but she could not intellectually partner my father and opted out of his discourse to retreat to the kitchen and her chores.

There was also a primitive time when Rose didn't understand my father's moods. She would henpeck him too much, my father's patience would falter and she would run for cover.

Once roused, my father's fury became phenomenal. Out of the door of the dining room mother would dash. At that moment, a plate would smash against the hastily closed door. We children would cower under the dining table. It was a conundrum to me that my father, with all his intellect, could succumb to such an outburst of emotion.

My mother's idea of corporal punishment was little pinches which had no effect and which, as we grew bigger, became laughable to us.

Our way of disciplining her in return, to my shame, was to raise our voices to shouting level. Before I acquired the skill, I was transfixed by my father shouting and my mother running around shutting windows, particularly in the summertime, lest the neighbours hear. My father would finally leave the house in a fury, leaving us shaken by the emotional crises and fearful that our parents meant to separate

When I was shouting, my upset mother would pinch her cheeks, saying, "What will the neighbours think?" She would really bring a bright red colour to her cheeks by pinching them so hard. That was her way of saying, "Shame, shame."

On the other hand, when my mother lost her temper, I could checkmate her outburst by finding a trinket I could destroy, something of little value, a cracked saucer or a cracked teacup.

My mother was a great squirrel, salvaging tidbits of junk to which she would attribute great value. A threat to destroy any such small possession would freeze her on the spot. If I threatened to break something, that would silence her immediately.

On one occasion, when she wouldn't be silenced, I carried my threat through and broke a saucer. She didn't speak to me for a long time.

She loved us, but not demonstratively. She would kiss us in a kind of "I love you, I love you" way, but not the sensual, quiet kiss of sincere warmth and pleasure.

She rejoiced in her husband and children. She took vicarious pride in everything we did and said. It wasn't a permissive pride, but a pride after the event, pride that we were "fine boys" and were achieving things.

We owned our house on Alfred Avenue, Because it was ours, we stayed put, and my fondest memories are associated with that house. We had a small lawn in front, no more than fifteen feet to the sidewalk. Father would sit on the front verandah steps and play the water hose on the grass. It would be very amusing to see a grown man sit for an hour watering grass from a seated position.

Since our front lawn wasn't very big, Father could cover it all without stirring himself from the stair stoop. While he sat, neighbours walked up, leaned across the fence, and chatted about all the local happenings. People truly respected his view and usually his answers were short and pithy, quickly offered and cleverly barbed. He always harpooned the pompous. The self-righteous didn't like his comments very much, but the common people love him for it. It was a trait he carried all his life. He couldn't stand anyone who became important because of one's job or position.

In the winter, warming the house was quite a ceremony. Father would get up around 7:00 or 7:30 a.m. He slept in his long underwear. It was nearly unheard of, at that time and in that season, for anyone to change into pajamas. In the summer sometimes. Working class males slept in their underwear; summer, their briefs.

Father was awakened by a loud alarm clock. He would pull on his socks, shoes, and trousers and go downstairs to stoke the furnace. A hot air system heated our house, but when the furnace went out, it got very cold very quickly.

The fire in our furnace probably went out around five every winter morning. In the coldest months, January and February, the house temperature went down to 10-15 degrees Celsius, sometimes close to zero. Frost coated on the inside and outside of the windows. My brother and I were glad we slept in the same bed. Father woke us at eight, but the house was still cold, and we dressed under the bed-covers. We always placed our clothes close at hand the night before.

Once out of bed, we dashed for the bathroom. Our ablutions must have been something to behold – a quick wetting of our cheeks with about three drops of water. We couldn't bear the idea of dampening our faces in that cold atmosphere, even though we did draw hot water from the tap.

In winter, we dressed in britches, with lots of sweaters underneath heavy coats, a toque pulled down practically over the eyes, and a long wind-around wool scarf, not much face exposed. Then a quick dash down to school. We never walked. It was just too cold.

Our breath through the wool scarves formed icicles. It took a good while before we felt warm and comfortable at our desks. We went to public school, Jewish school, piano lessons, and out to play. The cold never stopped us.

On a winter evening when the furnace was working and we had finished our studies, a favourite place for my brother and me to relax was behind my father's chesterfield chair in the living room. Mickey and I competed for that foot and a half of space between Papa's chair and the hot air vent.

The blast of hot air kept us very warm, our backsides somewhat warmer than the front. This spot had the great advantage of being a private place where we could eavesdrop on my father holding court.

I remember one visitor was Gregory Goborvitsky, "genius" violinist who later organized and for many years conducted the Calgary symphony. Father performed musical duets with him on the violin, and my brother took his first violin lessons from the maestro. My parents were so proud of this association that my brother and his great teacher were photographed by Shapira, the only Jewish photographer in the community at that time.

Shapira was a Winnipeg institution. He was also a specialist in nude photos, but this sideline was hardly suspected by the Jewish community. On occasion he would bring a set of racy glossies to Miller's Bookstore on Main Street to show the Jewish chess club in the backroom delicatessen section of the store. At my tender age, I was denied a view of his product, but I knew it had to be inspiring, judging by the great chortles from the appreciative audience. A local dentist envied Shapira his much better view of womankind. The dentist moaned that he could only say "open your mouth wide," but Shapira could say "take all your clothes off." It was a great occupational advantage. But Shapira was kind hearted. He incorporated the dentist into his act, passing him off as a photographer's assistant.

When I was eight years old, Sam Berg, the son of the prominent Jewish pioneer, Abraham, came to live with us. A bright lawyer in his late twenties he had a weakness for horse racing. His passion for gambling had spurred him to misuse clients' funds and led to his disbarment. Stripped of a legal practice, ruined and bankrupt, Sam Berg was a tragic figure. His future looked bleak and his shame was compounded by his family's early pride in him; Sam was the diamond of the Berg children.

My parents stood loyal to Sam. My mother was afraid he might do something desperate, so she offered him a room in our home.

Sam Berg was one of the most exciting personalities in my childhood experience. I loved him because he was a great hokum artist. He would build up my father's ego by serving as a generous audience for my father's jokes and humour. His entrance into our house was always theatrical, loud and operatic. His greetings were boisterous, merry and good natured. He would address me as "Prince of Wales" because my name was Edward. He drew the parallel with the then heir to the British throne, the former Kind Edward VIII. In later years, he would enter our home calling for the Rhode's scholar, Edward, King of England.

My father undertook the task of restoring him to society and hired him as a journalist for the Jewish-language newspaper. Sam Berg began to retrace his relationship with the Winnipeg Jewish community and eventually launched an English-language Jewish weekly newspaper of his own. My mother helped by finding him a wife.

In the Jewish community, the goal was to find a career that created a good living and involved a skill. The preference was to become a doctor. This represented the most status, and a promising student was encouraged in this direction. Be a doctor first, a lawyer second, and a pharmacist third; this was the sequence of career preferences for Jewish youth. The reasoning was that if you were a merchant and stripped of all your material goods, you had nothing left except your ability to trade. But if you were a doctor, you could immediately sell your services in any new setting.

This emphasis created a tremendous pressure amongst Winnipeg Jews to get one or two of their children into medical school. The Anglo-Canadian establishment protected itself against this demand by setting a quota for Jewish admittance. If you were Jewish and sought entrance into medical college, you had to be more than a good student. You also had to be examined by a committee.

Despite the quota, there was a higher proportion of Jewish young people going through Manitoba's medical college than of any other ethnic group at the time. The result was that the Winnipeg community had many Jewish doctors.

In the Depression, the doctors did not earn very much. Few patients had money to pay them. But there was an awesome respect for them, and I think to that extent they felt compensated.

Most of these doctors were involved in the community, often heading up rival Jewish schools and institutions. They were regarded as intellectuals and you chose one for your family partly because he was a good doctor and partly because he belonged to your social or political orientation.

I never wanted to be a doctor. But I did like music. Our living room had an upright piano. My attempt to play the piano was cut short by my father who later regretted his discouraging remark. "After listening to you play," he told me, "I might say that of your many virtues, you have no ear for music." That killed music education for me. I contented myself with the radio.

The speaker radio with its wonderful cabinet and improved reception was the beginning of all the things that were wonderful – Amos and Andy, Eddie Cantor, Edgar Bergen and Charlie McCarthy, Jack Benny and Fred Allen provided a cornucopia of pleasures.

Our family amusements were simple and usually involved our round dining room table, which was the setting for great family gatherings, food and noisy arguing. We also had many books which my father read and encouraged us to read.

One of my mother's cousins, Bayla Corn, was a grand dame in our family clan. Every Friday evening in her home, the great poker games of the day took place. The Bergs and the Finesilvers would attend. In the winter the children were put to sleep on top of the winter coats on the beds.

At 1 a.m. and again at 3 a.m., we would tug our father's jacket sleeve, urging him to come home, but he wouldn't. The game had just started, he would argue. This game would continue until Sunday night. People came and went. You could go home, wash, change, and come back to play or you could send your wife home with the children early in the morning and stay on yourself. It was comparable to Damon Runyon's continuous floating crap game.

It was also the occasion for the most amazing family therapy. While they played, relatives badgered each other and laughed. They accused each other of faults in family life, bad social standards, poor housekeeping, or lack of literary interests.

My mother, quite naturally, railed against the poker game. To her, my father's absorption in this all-hour, all-weekend gambling was comparable to his previous playing of the violin every evening until three o'clock in the morning. Then, seemingly overnight, he cut out gambling and took up the piano. My mother then took up the game as part of her life pattern. This development became a point of great anguish to me. At 14 years of age, I would come home from Jewish school at 7 p.m. expecting my dinner and my Mother wouldn't be there. There was always food, but Mother might not arrive until 10 p.m.

Mother had another passion. She was a "fixer", a matrimonial social worker and she took great pride in the number of couples she reunited. Her remedies always involved the clan in some way and seemed to be effective.

There were also concerts. Every week great musicians such as Mischa Elman, Jascha Heifetz and Yehudi Menuhin would play in Winnipeg. And there were vital ethnic groups that sponsored folk artists, singers from Iceland, Poland, Germany, and so on. If you wanted to be busy attending most concerts, you could become frantic with commitment.

Father wrote his reviews and editorials while sitting at the dining room table. I don't know how he wrote in those days with us children swarming over his knees. If distractions are an aid to writing, then Father was much assisted by Mickey and me.

Part of our "entertainment" was the Saturday night bath. In Winnipeg, in mid-winter, it was a punishing experience. The ordeal was usually scheduled when we weren't going out and nothing else was happening. Father would stoke the furnace to full blast getting maximum heat upstairs. To help achieve this more quickly, we would shut off the hot air outlets downstairs, forcing the heat load to the second floor. Outlets in some of the upstairs rooms would also be closed to direct the heat into the bathroom.

When we were smaller, up to age 11 or 12, my brother and I bathed together in the tub. Bathing the children was a family affair. Both parents collaborated, scrubbing both boys in the tub. The moment we were out of the bath, we were each quickly encased in a full bed sheet to keep us warm and to help dry us.

We started shivering the moment we got out of the bath. While wrapped in our sheets, we had our toenails trimmed and our hair combed. Large cloths were wrapped around our heads, tied tightly in Arabic style. We pretended we were on an Arctic trek when we dashed across the hallway to our beds.

At the top of Alfred Avenue East, near Main Street, was a little store, a combined dwelling and grocery, Hindin's. It was illegal to buy a drink from a grocer, but Hindin had a practice of opening a trapdoor behind his counter, and patrons would follow him down to the cellar for a drink. The men would leave their children and wives upstairs. When the men ascended, a lot happier, with the scent of herring on their breath, you would hardly know they had been drinking.

Hindin's youngest daughter, Nelly, was most precocious. One early fall when I was eight and she six, our street "gang" organized one of our great orgies in Hindin's backyard. It was a day following wood deliveries. Piled in a heap were freshly cut logs.

In those days, an order of fuel would first involve delivery of a wagon load of five or six-foot length logs. An entrepreneur with a buzz saw mounted on a wagon would then be hired to cut these up. A third party would then chop the by-then foot-length pieces into fire wood.

We improvised an Indian dance, circling around the logs. Up and down we pranced until it became dark. We were determined to top off our reels with a "sex" orgy. Nelly, always an eager candidate for these things, plopped down on one of the logs. I moved spontaneously into the role of medicine man and began the group chant; "Nelly's pants must come down."

So we brought her panties down, revealing her most prominent asset at that age. Wide-eyed, we stared at her pink, round, soft bottom. We screamed, patted and laughed. Now what could we perform with our vulnerable Nelly? A sacrifice! Roll a log on Nelly's bottom. To our surprise and horror, a large splinter penetrated

Nelly's bottom. Nelly uttered a scream of creation itself and the destruction of the universe combined.

It was my bad luck that my father was in Hindin's store at that moment. He was enjoying a taste of herring and a shot of liquor.

My fellow braves had deserted me and, as adults came rushing to Hindin's backyard, I ran forward to meet them, saying, "It's nothing! It's nothing! Everything is all right."

To my relief, Nelly had pulled her panties up and wouldn't say what had happened. For her discretion and valour, she later got the gang's gold star. She was really quite noble.

The ballerina of our street was Norma, but Norma was vivacious. One of our gang's ritual meetings was on the top of a chicken coop in our next door neighbour's yard. One hot summer day, we decided to play "striptease". Our gang climbed onto the top of the chicken coop; apparently within my mother's line of vision from her kitchen window. The chicken coop roof had been baked for some hours by the sun and its tar-covered roof was very hot. As soon as Norma's bare bottom touched the hot tar, she emitted a cry well beyond that of Nelly's intensity.

My mother rushed out and helped Norma off the roof. By this time, the gang were nowhere to be seen. Norma never wanted to see that Eddie Parker or any of the other boys again.

One of the neighbour's garages became our playhouse, the locale where we produced our particular version of Minsky's Burlesque. Here we presented our most ambitious production.

The average price of admission for an Alfred Avenue kiddie's show was 10 nails. Gosh, you could be rich in nails in those days. At that time, I developed almost a monopoly in nails. On occasion, when we assembled a whiz bang show, the price rose to a penny. For such a production there was a master of ceremonies, and I often inherited that role.

In one of my vaudeville routines, I was a father carrying a baby. I pretended I was being wetted by this doll. My audience was convulsed by this appeal to their basic sense of farce. My act was followed by Norma dancing her solo interpretations. The highlight of the concert was a heavyweight boxing match between the street's two lightest weights, my brother and myself. Mickey and I were terribly mismatched. Each was afraid to hurt the other. Once either of us did land a punch, however, the mood would change, and we would flail away at each other. We didn't have proper boxing trunks, so wore bathing suits which normally would be supported by shoulder straps. To make ourselves look more like the real thing, we rolled the tops of our suits down to the waist, tying the shoulder straps in a loose knot to form a belt. Wearing heavy boxing mitts, I landed one telling blow on my brother's midriff. The action immediately made his pants fall. Morten left the boxing scene very quickly, an unhappy loser.

We also played "circus" quite a lot. Mickey fell heir to hapless roles in the circus. One game of chance involved throwing objects at Morten's head poking through a hole. I was the concessionaire, exhorting people to throw tennis balls at him. Someone did throw a hard pitch and knocked him unconscious. My mother's subsequent wrath cured me of engineering show business stunts in which my brother was to be the foil.

I nostalgically remember Noble Court, the six-storey apartment on Alfred Avenue. The basement suites of Noble Court had their window sills at sidewalk level. This proved a great challenge to almost all of the boys on the street. We called ourselves the Shadow Club. Really, we were a bunch of "peeping toms".

One suite was very rewarding. Three girls were its tenants, all between the ages of 17 and 20.

My sidekick, Morris, was very prone to giggle. On one occasion, the most bosomy of the girls was preparing for her ablutions. We had mastered the technique of quietly raising the window while she was in the bathroom and raising the blind a full inch. The view was magnificent.

Morris could not contain himself. He giggled. The girl was startled and everything went crazy.

To my embarrassment and shame, we were caught by the police. I felt like a terrible juvenile delinquent. Here I was, a great achiever at school, a recitationist, the president of my class in grade nine, and my whole career was about to be ruined by this sex scandal.

My father was of course incredulous. He was not really up to this sort of gam. I lived in terror of receiving a Juvenile Court summons, but it did not materialize.

Noble Court was the scene of my first kissing parties, playing post office and spin-the-bottle. We were about 13 or 14.

I didn't make out very well in this field, even as I moved into my later teen years. This was due partly to my unusual conceit as the great story teller, the life of the party. All my friends were on to me. When they gathered at parties, they could chant, "Ed, tell us the story about the werewolf." I'd begin this story about this Indian brave who had died a horrible death, bitten by a vampire. He, in turn, had turned into a wolf and was now himself a vampire. I'd go on and on. Absolute silence. Tremendous tension. The only light emanated from just one candle placed directly in front of me. I stupidly thought this was a great prop and enthusiastically endorsed turning out the electric lights. There were always oohs and ahs and screams, all of which gave me a feeling that I was going over smashingly – a great story teller. When I was through, there were calls of "encore" and "more".

But all those oohs, ahs, and screams were not really related to my story telling at all. There was a great deal of panting and necking going on, and everybody was making out quite well except me. I kept telling my fascinating stories quite oblivious of the hectic activity around me. I was hopeful that there was one little girl listening to me. My story-telling may have been my own lonely siren call to somebody out there in the dark to respond to me because of my talent.

The Red River itself was fascinating. In the winter, a skating rink was made in the centre of the frozen-over Red River, a professional, circular skating rink, a hundred yards in diameter.

The rink was served by a large heated skating shack, and the snack bar featured O'Henry bars. As you entered, you were met by the scent of drying clothes and the noise of people lacing their skates and shuffling around in moccasins. Girls were ordered to one side of the shack, boys to the other.

A marvelous toboggan slide was constructed next to the skating shack. You climbed steps pulling your toboggan up a middle section. The runs were iced passages down which you plunged. A very fast ride, covering a great distance. At the other end a duplicate structure served to project you on a return journey.

Dressing warmly for tobogganing in Winnipeg meant donning three pairs of socks pulled high over the legs of long underwear. If one was shrewd, he'd even wear pajamas under the long underwear. It was bitterly cold on those runs. Leather reinforced britches were mandatory. A heavy coat or windbreaker, toque, scarf, and double pairs of mitts completed the outfit.

Come spring, with the ice break-up, the level of the river rose rapidly and dramatically. Mid-summer saw the river's edge drop seventy or eighty feet from the top of the bank. But in early spring, the rise was threatening, sometimes a mere five feet from the Noble Court apartments at the end of Alfred Avenue.

The river was at its widest in May, two or three miles across and dangerous. In June and July, when the water receded, the banks became lush and high with foliage, a great playground for children building forts and pretending to be Indian braves.

Winnipeg had its young people's courting ground on the west bank of the Red River. This was where our domestics made out a lot of the time.

As a child, I sometimes thought sadly about the love affairs of our "live-in" help. Usually the girl would get pregnant. The guy involved would marry her, or he would not marry her. The worry involved all of us, as though she were a close relative.

Halloween was exciting for us in those pre-teenage days. It was an opportunity for many to dress in costumes of their parents' native lands. You would see Ukrainian, Bavarian, and other costumes plus the improvised masks. People baked and prepared for this day, since neighbourliness was judged by the generosity of the handouts. Often we were invited into a house and urged to perform.

On Alfred Avenue, most of the residents were Jewish. Our immediate next-door neighbours on both sides, however, were Scottish. Our neighbours to the right, the MacLeans, were quiet and kept very much to themselves; they were much respected. Completely private people, they were not involved in the north end community. It was not much of a community for the Anglo-Saxons, save for churches. The MacLeans did enthuse about one subject, their son Gordon, an outstanding pianist who taught me piano for a short period.

Gordon felt enormously encouraged by the uncommon good sense of my musically appreciative and critical father. My father's high judgement of Gordon won the MacLeans to us in a special way. We were always recipients of fruits and flowers from the MacLeans' garden. In turn, my father spent a good many hours socializing with Gordon, discussing the philosophy of music and listening to him play.

Our neighbours to the left were the Kerrs. Mr. Kerr was a street car conductor, a glamorous occupation to us in those days. His son Jimmy and I were playmates, although we both exhibited apprehension about each other's homes that reflected the apprehension of our parents. We were from different cultures.

Mickey and I had some religious superstition, passed on to us by our mother and Aunt Esther. On Selkirk Avenue near the Talmud Torah, there was a dimly lit store devoted to the sale of Christian religious objects. Ornate pictures of Christ as baby, as man, and as God were displayed in the window. The Madonna, the crucifix, and objects of piety were the store's stock-in-trade. As little Jewish kids, we tried not to look at these windows. Fearing for our lives, we ran pell-mell past the store. We then practised little rituals to offset bad spirits, holding our breath or jumping on one foot for a length of sidewalk to avoid a curse befalling us. Fear of another religion seemed deeply inbred.

Being children, however, it was impossible not to hazard a small peek. Then seeing an object like a big bleeding heart, we would turn away from the spectacle in horror. The only way we felt we could be absolved by our god of this sin of transgression was by pretending to spit three times.

Our superstitions were reminiscent of the original problem that existed for our parents in Russia, when ignorance and prejudice reinforced the untrue stories that a Christian child could be sacrificed on a Jewish holy day, its blood drained and drank as part of pagan Hebrew worship. It is horrifying that children could be raised to believe that the Devil was on one side and God on the other.

By the time I was fourteen, my mother realized I was interested in sex. She decided it was time to deliver a lecture on the subject. She called me and said she wanted me to know that "there were girls", rolling her eyes to the left, "and there were girls", rolling her eyes to the right. Yet, my mother's singular sex lecture registered in my memory.

I had a lead in the major dramatic presentation of Machray Public School. At that time in 1932, the *Winnipeg Free Press* stage critic, James McGeachey, came to see our show. His review hailed me as a theatrical find, and my parents were delighted. As a reward, I was allowed to sleep in the following morning. I had a performance that night, and when I came to school, I was a celebrity; everyone crowded round me.

The regional distributing office in Winnipeg reported me to a Hollywood studio and a wire arrived offering me a screen test if I were to get down to Hollywood by a certain date. This was an era when Hollywood film promotion was centred a great deal around talent searches. I don't remember if I wanted to go. But I know my father would have none of it.

Commenting on the screen test offer, he said, "I recognize we have an invitation to take you to Hollywood for an audition, a great compliment, but first let me ask: Do you really want to speak the words that somebody else has written, or would you rather write the words that somebody else speaks?"

He appealed to the right side of my ego.

Grades seven, eight, and nine were significant years. During this period, I became aware of group feeling, group support and peer pressure. I felt that I as an individual had no validity. Unfortunately, the in-groups were related to sports. I wasn't good at sports, but I found a role for myself by acquiring a megaphone and cheering on my friends at the inter-school games. My schoolboy psychology worked. My chosen friends were certainly in need of fans who would be their supporters and boosters. Thus I became part of the entourage that contributed to the status and good feeling of the school athletic heroes. In my heart I felt I had some worth beyond that of a camp follower, but I had no way to demonstrate my sense of distinction.

As class elections approached for grade nine, I learned first-hand how political lobbying works. The incident involved the selection of class president. Harry Fainstein, a nice young boy and a very good football player, had been president of our class in grades seven and eight. He wanted another term.

I chose to see a danger that he might not be elected and here uncharitably created a problem in order to solve it. In our class of 43 pupils, 20 were boys and 23 were girls. What would happen if the girls nominated a girl for class president and united behind her? She would then have 23 votes and we poor males would have a girl as chief of state. Unthinkable!

The captain of our football team, Reuben Cristall, was a class leader. Everyone curried favour with him. Reuben did not aspire to be class president, but I persuaded him that he should be concerned about a girl becoming class president.

To that end, he agreed to my strategy to make sure that only one of the boys in the class was nominated and thus not split our vote in the election. We would have a preliminary and private run-off between the boys. Whoever became the candidate, all the boys would unite behind him. We marked our ballots in terms of preference – first, second and third. Somehow my name was added to the ballot.

When all the votes had been transferred, who was the candidate for the class – me!

Everybody was ashen. How did Ed Parker end up in first place?

Suffice to say, the strategy had worked, and I became president of the class. Consequently, I created all sorts of jobs both for girls and boys and had many deputies in charge of this and that. We even had a printed school paper, *The Pupil's Pal*.

My business acumen led me to believe that if I were to take this paper around to one or two commercial establishments, I might sell some ads. This proved to be true. My first sale gave me a dollar. It was Quentin's Dry Cleaners. The College Theatre gave me some passes, plus a dollar. I could now afford ditto materials. For weeks I had gone around looking in store windows at duplicating machines, while other youngsters were looking at bicycles. Duplicators were my passion. My greatest dream was to own a ditto machine.

What great joy and excitement it was to see one's own material rolling off a duplicator. When it progressed from one hand-printed issue to one typed and duplicated in numbers, *The Pupil's Pal* became a potent propaganda organ in our school. We could now produce not only the 43 copies needed for our own class, but endless other copies to serve all the grade eight classes in the school. We dared a subscription price, 2¢. We sold a hundred copies with $2.00 in advertising; we were awfully close in revenue to being able to afford commercial printing. Now the advantage of having a printer as one's father came to the fore. My father's partner, Frank Simkin, readily agreed to print our eight-page paper for $1.00 a page.

Short financed, we sallied out to sell more advertising. We succeeded. Simkin boosted our price to $16.00 an issue when we began to show a profit. In the coldest weather, –20 degrees Celsius, off we went to Genzer's music store or Lasker's book store or Holt Renfrew to sell advertising.

Lasker, an erudite, articulate pixie, spoofed with us, asked if we were reading any books and found me less than an avid reader. He called me a doer and activist, but he worked on my conscience and asked me to report back on any book I would read in a week. In the end, he gave us an advertisement, making the time spent profitable.

The biggest success was when we sold an ad to Holt Renfrew. We couldn't sell Eatons and Hudson's Bay. They were beyond our reach. But Holt Renfrew, an upper register establishment store where Jewish people rarely went to shop, was quite a feather in my cap. Holt Renfrew featured fashion life drawings in their ads, thus giving our publication quite a tone.

As a "press baron," I became widely known throughout the school, to the principal, teachers, and students in different grades. Power! I didn't know quite how to use it, but I liked the recognition, a great compensation for not being an athlete and not getting on the sports teams. By way of a turn-around, I could now "give" publicity to the athletes, both girls and boys. As a consequence, my attention was coveted by those who wanted to be sports editors and writers. I had all the makings of a patronage type politician. *The Pupil's Pal* allowed me to reward those who had helped elect me president of the class. It also generated some money in the way of commissions. It kept eight to ten of my classmates wholly involved with me forming the beginnings of a "machine" which would the following year move into high school politics.

When my cousin Avril Berman moved to the north end, he became a disturbing factor in my life in many ways. He was certainly resentful of me when I became president of the grade nine class. But he became the advertising manager of the school paper and was a pretty good salesman.

Things were going fairly smoothly until a political crisis engulfed me. There was an inherent contradiction in the job of being class president. You represented both the pupils and the teacher – a conflict of interest on some occasions. The class president was monitor of the class when the teacher was out. He was supposed to maintain class quiet and to put the names of pupils who talked on the blackboard. Avril Berman talked away and his name appeared very often on the board.

I tried to protect Reuben, whom I regarded as my political boss. But he flaunted his privileged state and became an offending talker. One morning, I put Reuben's name on the board and Reuben saw red. That afternoon after school, he and three other boys jumped me, tumbled me, washed my face with snow and bloodied my nose.

Near supper time, Reuben sent a message that he wanted to see me "on the waterfront". When I appeared, a tribunal was assembled – Reuben, Avril and two other boys. Reuben said that I obviously wasn't appreciative of the role of president, that I failed to speak up for the students against the teacher, that I did not represent student protest, that I was really something of a stooge for the teacher, and that I would have to resign tomorrow. They planned to unite behind Avril Berman.

I came to school the next day and Reuben nominated Avril Berman. To my astonishment, a girl nominated me and I was elected by a united girls' vote. They were appreciative of all the jobs I had given them.

Then I went to Reuben and said, "I'm president, but I don't think I can make it without your support, and I would like you to be business manager of the paper."

Reuben had never been thought of as anything but a guy who could kick a football. He was so flattered by the prospect of becoming business manager of the school paper that he became my friend again and my tenure as president of the class was secured.

I learned that if you create a plan for a program of activities and involve many people in that plan, they will sustain you in office, because without you the plan might not go through. In other words, they need you to guarantee them their jobs. I came to understand machine politics. This lesson stayed with me all my life.

To finish my public school experience, I was chosen as the grade nine valedictorian.

* * *

In grade ten at St. John's High School I again became president of my class, much to Avril's chagrin. Then I won a seat on the student council.

My years at St. John's were rich and exciting, not the least for having an inspired teacher, Ada Turner. The school drama director and my class teacher for both grades ten and eleven, she specialized in English literature. A magnificent reader, Ada Turner's voice had a mesmerizing quality.

Intelligence and interpretation were her assets. When she read poetry, I became aware of how moving great literature was. I was journalistically inclined because of my father, but I hadn't developed any special feeling for language. It was Ada Turner who most inspired me to create literature.

I was thrilled to be part of a group of boys invited to her home on several occasions. She served us cookies and lemonade, read poetry, told ghost stories, and introduced us to the subject of spiritualism. We loved her and were tremendously moved by her acceptance.

I soon moved into the management of the school year book. I became managing editor and appointed Reuben Cristall as business manager and Harry Fainstein as advertising manager.

I put together a monthly high school newspaper called the *St. John's Times*. There was already an existing newspaper in the school run by the son of one of my father's partners, Manny Wilder, together with his friend, Maurice Lucow. My associates and I joined forces with Wilder and Lucow during the summer. My job was that of managing editor. I offered to solicit advertising for the paper and thus assure a properly financed printing job.

When we had our copy in type, Wilder demoted me to advertising manager and upgraded himself to editor-in-chief. I told him that if I didn't become editor, I would take all the advertising away and collapse the paper. Thus I became managing editor, Maurice Lucow literary editor, and Wilder associate editor.

I captured the propaganda medium of the high school in my junior year and became a potent political force in the school. Activity leaders, wishing to have their activities covered in the paper, rendered favours. The paper also was a great excuse to meet girls. The *St. John Times* ran a gossip column called "We Snoop to Conquer". It was a poor pun, but it helped sell the paper – 5¢ a copy, a high price at the time and we made a profit.

In competitive bitterness, Avril Berman circulate a rumour that I had used the profits of the paper to buy myself a suit. I wasn't beyond thinking our paper was a private enterprise and that I was entitled to this reward. The charge created tension.

My reputation as a student leader was of great concern to me. I was setting the stage to become a candidate for the much coveted Governor General's medal. This award was given to the best all around student for achievement in academics, citizenship and sports.

I was laying the basis for this resolution by joining as many extra curricular activities as I could and taking over most executive offices; forming a drama club, leading a debating team, writing the high school paper, getting into the prestigious yearbook staff as business manager, serving on the student council and singing in the choir. I was also attending the I.P. Peretz Jewish School, taking part in Yiddish theatre and being an active member of my peer group. I felt no need to be buttressed by anybody. I was "Mr. Talent", I was "Sammy Davis Jr." of my day. My mother told me so and I felt invincible. I was "Mr. Everything", a good speaker, a good actor, an able organizer and a great card at parties. I didn't go to parties merely to enjoy them; I had to make them the greatest event that had ever happened.

My feeling of invincibility was abruptly checked, however, by my father's hand. At fifteen, I had cast my brother in a school play. I was director. Morten played a comic role but forgot to bring the most important prop in the play, thus ruining the action. In my anger, I reviewed all his shortcomings and accused him of being chronically late for school, of consorting with bums and of being irresponsible. I carried on this harangue one night, to the point where I was actually heel-following my father around, harassing Dad with, "Aren't you going to do something? Aren't you going to hit him?"

My father did let fly a slap, not at Mickey, but at me. Its ferocity made me reel to the door.

Here I was, president of my class, champion debater, president of the drama society getting a whack from my father. At the time, I believed sanity and justice had gone topsy-turvy. The righteous was being punished. My mother, of course, immediately rushed to my defence.

Within 48 hours, however, I realized my father's judgement was right. I was becoming a tormentor of my brother, setting standards for him and demanding that he serve them. It wasn't that my brother didn't need upbraiding, but that I was the wrong person to do it. Although my concern was, in the main, to help Morten, unwittingly I was contributing to his resentment.

Grade eleven was one of the happiest years of my life. I again became class president and a member of the student council. I was very disappointed that I didn't get nominated for school president. The great compensation was that I became editor-in-chief of the yearbook, a great distinction in that period. It was my aim to put more elements into this yearbook than had ever been put in before – including two covers rather than one. I raised a lot of advertising support for the yearbook and had it printed in my father's plant.

Still conscious of the Governor General's medal, I was determined to gain some points in athletics.

I was very weak in sports. In my grade eleven year I had become proficient enough to run the one-mile event in inter-class meets. I finished third out of a field of ten and had thereby won a point. I had made a successful attempt at being an athlete. To further my athletic image, I organized the cheerleaders into choreographed routines, forming pyramids and patterns.

As teenagers, we had a wonderful social life. We never dated any one girl. About nine or ten boys would arrange Saturday night house parties and invite nine or ten girls. Also, girls' class would invite an entire boys' class.

These class socials were very important events. Sometimes we had toboggan parties, and private homes offered refreshments, hotdogs, and cokes. Moccasin dances followed.

Formal school dances offered dance arrangement cards. You negotiated whom you would dance with, for the first, second, and third dance, and so forth, knowing that the last dance was to be the girl whom you would take home and probably get to kiss.

The girls who worked on the high school yearbook intrigued me. I and my boyfriends regarded the girls who shared our extracurricular activity interests as "friends". But, when it came to sexual explorations, these were often not with girls in our own school or neighbourhood but with "foreigners" from another high school. During summer holidays, I and my gang would meet pretty non-Jewish girls at Winnipeg Beach. We would go to their homes in the fall for necking sessions, since we didn't live in their district, we were not accountable to their parents.

In the Winnipeg Jewish community, when I called on a "nice" girl, her parents would say, "Oh, so you're Harry Parker's son." I immediately had an identity and a responsibility. From the outset it was assumed that I would want eventually to marry their daughter. Do you like my daughter? When are you two going to get married?

Tremendous anxiety not to get ourselves compromised characterized the skittish behaviour of my male peer group.

As early as grade nine, we had pricked our fingers and made blood oaths. We would not do three horrible things: smoke, drink, and have sexual intercourse, certainly not until we were 21. Above all, we would be very careful not to get ourselves compromised by women. Nothing was to stand in the way of our achieving political prominence in the country. One of us might even become prime minister.

Harry Fainstein and I were singled out by Ada Turner for special invitations at the end of grade 11, our final year in high school. He and I, the contenders for the Governor General's medal, were to spend a weekend with Miss Turner and her adopted son Harold at their summer home on an island near Kenora, Lake of the Woods.

For children of north-end Winnipeg, Lake of the Woods was something beyond our economic horizon. Kenora was only 125 miles away, 55 miles further than our finances would allow our parents to travel. Our budget only permitted journeys of about 60 or 70 miles, to Winnipeg Beach. We were brought by car to Ada Turner's island, met by Harold, and taken by motor boat to the Turner island. What a glorious experience!

We talked, ran and swam. I had my first surfboard experience and my last. Harold operated the motor boat. I had enough nerve to stay on for about 10 minutes, then panic overcame me and I was in the water.

The weekend was memorable, marred only by one of those traumatic adolescent things. In the excitement and the pleasure of the holiday, I had a wet dream. To my horror, I woke to find that I had soiled the linen. Feelings of humility and degradation engulfed me. I would be found out by the teacher whom I revered. At about five in the morning, I took the sheet to the lake and began scrubbing it. Now the whole sheet was wet. I didn't want to destroy the sheet, so I hid it.

For the rest of the day, I was miserable, a commentary on innocence. The fact that I might function in any less than a god-like way for Ada Turner was beyond my thinking.

My sense of drama was highly aroused that day, and events were firmly engraved in my memory. A deer darted onto the road and our car hit and killed it. This first experience at killing anything was a dramatic moment. None of my family ever used guns or even fishing rods. That dead deer made killing abhorrent to me.

* * *

Chosen as the grade eleven valedictorian, I was nearly certain I would receive the Governor General's medal.

In mid-summer before starting university, I learned that Harry Fainstein had been awarded the gold medal and I was runner-up. Harry, whom I had beaten for the presidency in grade nine, to whom for three years I had given all the number two jobs in the debating teams and in acting leads, was number one in the athletic field. There was little consolation in being runner-up.

My brother and I were seemingly unaffected by the Depression. But I sensed our parents tension in their negotiation with the butcher and baker when they came to collect their bills on Sunday mornings. While the printing shop had tremendous problems, the partners were still working and making a living.

During my teenage years, I worked at the printing plant for part of my summers. *The Israelite Press* was a significant environment of interest throughout my entire youth. When I was about five years old, the newspapers coming off the press and the scent of newsprint excited me. The big press mesmerized me as the large sheets came off smooth, and the folding machine cross-folded them neatly.

When I was 13 years old, I would sneak into my father's plant on a Sunday, put together some type, and try out a project on a platen press. However, I didn't always put the type back in the right compartment and didn't wash the type properly. On the following day, the compositors would complain to my father. He would pretend to be very disturbed that I was causing trouble. Privately, he was pleased that I was showing an interest in printing and the graphic arts process.

The Israelite Press, known also as Universal Printers, boasted a bank of six linotypes. My father's machine enjoyed a commanding position, first violin in a symphony orchestra. It seemed that all the linotypes followed his lead.

In the middle of the Depression, the plant began to publish its Jewish newspaper five times a week. It was incredible that in a small city, an ethnic paper could actually survive coming out every day. However, it was doomed to lose money, which it did.

Other factors had caused the plant to suffer financially. The underlying one, of course, was the Great Depression. Advertisers couldn't pay their bills in cash, so they would pay the printing plant in goods from their stores.

The Israelite Press began to owe money, and my father had to work 12-14 hours a day at the linotype to bail out the company. I would often visit the plant in the evening and see my father hard at work, the cigarette smoke curling up along the side of his nose.

The Press at one point owed more money to the paper company, its creditor, than its total value as a company could realize in a sale. The paper company could have taken the plant over at will, but there was no advantage in owning a Jewish newspaper that had gone bankrupt and was holding equipment that couldn't be sold.

Instead, the paper company introduced a tall Anglo-Saxon comptroller to work in the plant on a day-to-day basis as supervisor. He had little to do but walk around the plant. Bored and alien, he might say to each partner, "You ought to work harder," as his contribution to managerial direction. Of course, the partners needed no prodding to work hard.

He was often puzzled by my father's particular style of working. My father not only set type on the linotype, but he also composed his editorial and feature articles directly onto the machine. He had a virtuoso skill, effecting great economies on production.

Many talented people, singers, actors, politicians, would visit him at work on his linotype. Famous Yiddish actors like Jacob Ben Ami, Maurice Schwartz, Molly Picon and other celebrities met with him at his work station. Father would draw up an extra chair, open a coke, take out his marshmallow cookies and they would talk for half an hour.

Following the visit of one such celebrity, the comptroller came out and said, "Mr. Parker, you can't afford to give your time away like this, remember you are trying to work your way out of debt."

A man rarely given to temper outbursts, except at home with my mother, my father picked this tall man up by the seat of his pants and the collar of his coat and threw him out of the second-storey window. The man could have been injured as there was a sidewalk below, but it was a rainy day and fortunately he landed in the mud. He picked himself up and left.

My mother could foresee a great court case with my father up on an assault charge. My father's precipitous and violent action created a dilemma for the shop, but no charges were laid, the comptroller never returned and the paper company sent no one in his place. Gradually, over the years, the plant was able to bail itself out of debt.

The summer when I was sixteen years old, I volunteered to help promote the circulation of its newspaper. I traded rather brazenly on being a personality in the community and the son of one of the paper's partners and made a deal with Frank Simkin. If I could increase circulation by a hundred readers, a lot in that depression period, I would be allowed to write an English language column, a first for the Yiddish language paper.

I was aspiring to an editorial role in my father's newspaper. Simkin said, "Go ahead, sell subscriptions, or sell advertising."

I went from door to door introducing myself as the son of Harry Parker. My father was a well known and beloved figure in the community, and the Jewish women welcomed me with great ceremony into their homes. I was well spoken and well groomed. I was the "Eddie Parker" whose picture had been published countless times in his father's paper, a local celebrity, someone who had been seen on the community stage.

Offered tea and cake, I was often asked to recite a brief poem in Yiddish during my short visit. Then I would say that I was disappointed that she was not subscribing to my father's paper. Often, the women explained that there wasn't enough money and I would reply, "I don't want you to subscribe, but I do want you to have the paper for three months free. Meanwhile, would you help me fill out a questionnaire?"

I then elicited suggestions regarding improvements for the newspaper. "Would you enjoy having one or two serializations of romantic novels?" The women would say, "Yes." "Would you enjoy having more pictures in the paper?" "Yes."

They said yes to most of my offers, and I said, "Please watch our paper and many of your ideas will be implemented." This was highly complimentary.

I came back to Mr. Simkin with two hundred new subscribers, people who had agreed to take the paper on a complimentary basis, which is quite different from registering subscriptions.

After the three-month trial period half my contacts had subscribed, establishing me as somewhat of a hero in my father's printing plant.

My grandfather,
Eedel Parker.
(Ch. Schwartz,
Photographer)

My mother Raezel (Rose is the Anglo-
Saxon derivative) was a shy little
person who basked in the light of a
vivacious, extroverted sister, Hannah
Schaedel. (Shapira's Studio,
Winnipeg)

Father, Harry Parker, shortly after
immigrating to Winnipeg and finding
employment at the Israelite Press.

I arrived in 1918, to the delight of Mom and Dad.

Some baby! (Burns Studio, Winnipeg)

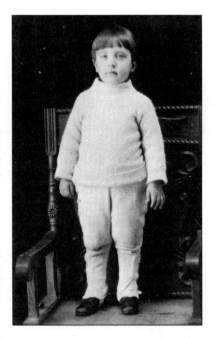

HEBREW FREE SCHOOLS

CARNIVAL CAMPAIGN

EDDIE PARKER
Candidate for
King of Carnival

June 10th, 1924.

Dear Friend:

The preparatory work for this wonderful Carnival Campaign is just completed and will mark it as unique and different to any of the past years.

That you may know the interesting details, etc., a Committee will take pleasure in calling on you and explaining the plans, the aims, the objects and hopes which if achieved will make every Jew proud of Winnipeg and the West.

Between now and August 13th and 14th, great excitement will prevail, great interest is being aroused in the choosing of Eddie Parker as "King of the Carnival."

Six year old Eddie was nominated by a large committee and is himself busy mastering his rocking-horse and soldiers ready for the event, but—

He must be elected by votes which are from the Bonds entered in his name. We respectfully ask that every Bond you buy, every Bond your friends buy, you mark for Eddie Parker, and so make his election sure.

Join the army of Friends who are surrounding his Banner and boost, vote and work for EDDIE PARKER as "King of the Carnival."

THE COMMITTEE.

Photographer Shapira saw a lot of me during my child-hood.

King of the Carnival campaign handout

Now that's more like it! Shapira's Studio, Winnipeg

(Above) Brother Morten and me, with mother and family friend, Sam Markson.

My favourite Uncle, Joe Perlmutter. (Otto Linke Studio, Milwaukee)

Mom and Dad at their Alfred Avenue East home. Circa 1940.

Our house near the Red River on Alfred Avenue was the centre of my evolving universe. (This 1993 photograph courtesy of Harry Gutkin)

Machray Public School was a good 17 minutes walking distance from home and a half hour when dawdling. (Provincial Archives of Manitoba)

*I was in Grade 10 in the years 1934 and 1935 at St.
John's High School and became President of my class. (Provincial Archives of Manitoba JM 2931)*

*Anything but a 'jock', I still managed a place on the soccer
team. That's me second from right in the front row.*

(Above) Fourth from the right, first row, in the St. John's Technical School Boy's Choir, 1935.

(Left) This three-storey building on Charles St., just south of Selkirk Avenue was converted into a synagogue, the Talmud Torah. (Jewish Historical Society of Western Canada JM 639)

Peretz School graduation photo – circa 1932. Left: Mr. Rappaport, Teacher. Right: J. Zipper, Principal. That's me centre front. (Trojan's Studio, Winnipeg)

The Israelite Press building at 165 Selkirk Avenue. (Jewish Historical Society of Western Canada JM 3499)

(Right) The Queen's Theatre was very important in our lives, presenting on stage the leading Jewish performers of their era. Circa 1920 (Jewish Historical Society of Western Canada JM 2346)

Shapira's Studio on Selkirk Avenue was a Winnipeg institution. The photographer bribed children with chocolates to keep still while he fussed with focus and flash material. (Jewish Historical Society of Western Canada JM2819)

(Left) Abraham Berg, his mother and sisters, Winnipeg. Circa 1912. (Jewish Historical Society of Western Canada JM 2773)

(Below) A group of Jewish authors, circa 1940. Front row, left to right: Cantor Benjamin Brownstone, Yechezkill Brownstone, Harry Parker. Back row, left to right: J. Zipper, Falik Zolf, Morris Pullan, Max Miller, Harry Gale. (Jewish Historical Society of Western Canada JM 485)

CHAPTER 3

COLLEGE –
THE MID THIRTIES

The events of 1935 affected me deeply. Many things were happening in my family, in Winnipeg, in the world and within myself. It was both an enchanting and a disturbing year. That summer, at Winnipeg Beach, I decided to register at United College on the University of Manitoba campus.

Winnipeg Beach was utopia. It had a long sandy beach where we practised running track-distances. I often went to the jutting pier. That's where the girls were. Despite the danger of splinters off the wooden planks, I would lie back and try to look the sun-tanned hero. Under challenge, I would dive off the pier at the deep end. I wasn't a very good swimmer, but I tried things to impress anybody. On Sundays, we had bonfires in the evening, and musicians played sing-along songs.

Winnipeg Beach boasted a pavilion with a huge dance hall. Admission to a dance was five cents. Boys and girls were seated on bleachers around the dance floor. Parents watched as we went up to the girls and asked them to dance.

Winnipeg Beach was sort of a miniature Coney Island, like the CNE in Toronto, but on a peanut scale; a roller coaster, ponies, games of chance. The boardwalk was glamorous despite the swarming fish flies. We were drawn to the beach like fish flies to a bright light. Many social and romantic relationships were established there.

Molly Rogers, a friend and talented stage actress, two years my senior, was a member of the tennis club. I considered her a star personality so I also became a member. I became fairly proficient at tennis, playing many sets with Molly. I became part of her group and met a lot of young people. It was in this setting that I first heard about the university world.

Molly Rogers was then in her second undergraduate year at United College, called Wesley until 1938. She talked of the appeal of that campus. Molly was the only Jewish student at United at the time and had become very prominent through her work in dramatics, the best actress the college had developed in years. She found herself very much at home at United and urged me and my friends to be independent, to eschew the public university and to attend this church college.

Among my classmates, I was the main campaigner for the university. The great feat was to talk my gang of eight boys into going to United College. I felt that with our superior organizational ability and drive, we would make out very well there.

The money that I had contributed to my university fees had been earned as commissions selling advertising for the school yearbook and the school paper and some from my job as a shoe salesman.

I worked with about six other young males on the floor in a Selkirk Avenue shoe store on Saturdays. We were paid the enormous sum of $1.00 to work from 10:00 a.m. to 10:00 p.m., and received bonuses of 10¢, 25¢ and 50¢ for selling older-model shoes. I was encouraged to impress the pretty cashier by proving myself as a hotshot salesman. All she had to do was to smile every time I brought another pair of shoes to wrap up at the counter. She would say, "Oh, you're great." That was enough to make me wind up and sell more shoes.

Before going to university, I was able to bring together a group of friends with whom I had acted in high school plays. We formed the "As You Like Us" Drama Club, abbreviated to AYLU.

On Sunday nights, some 28 teenage boys and girls would meet at my father's printing plant to play read and play act. We would turn out the lights in the outer office and the cast of a radio play would pretend they were broadcasting, speaking the lines from an adjacent lighted office. This primitive illustration fascinated everyone.

Eventually, we got some of the big-time amateur actors from the Little Theatre downtown to help us and our Sunday Theatre workshops became very well known throughout the city.

I was a reasonably good propagandist. I managed to have some item regarding AYLU printed in the daily press, and it came to the attention of a theatre group which had been formulated by left-wing young people. They were going to put on an anti-war play, "Bury the Dead," written by Irving Shaw. At that time, Shaw was even more distinguished as one of the most exciting of the radical playwrights of New York.

This "theatre of action" group had too few of its own principal members to round out the entire cast. We, in AYLU, had no political attitudes as a group. I personally had a left-wing attitude, but AYLU itself had no political formation. AYLU just wanted to get parts for its actors.

In the end, almost all the AYLU members got into the play, landing most of the major leads. We came close to assuming majority control of that theatre. We talked over the possibilities with the theatre of action founders and formed the Winnipeg New Theatre.

The Winnipeg New Theatre attracted Molly Rogers and many others of her talent level. For many years it continued as the major theatre grouping in Winnipeg.

When I had elected to go to church college rather than to the provincial university proper, my father thought it a great idea. "You are in tune with me," he said. "You never learn much going with people with whom you already share bequeathed concepts. But you always learn a great deal from people who have concepts entirely different than your own. You will have some good debates."

Between 1933 and 1936, Hitlerism had penetrated our newspapers. As Canadian high-school students, fully aware that Nazism had achieved total destruction of all political opposition in Germany, we had noted and assessed the annexation of Alsace-Lorraine, the take-over in Austria. The plan for the total extermination of the Jewish people was already in motion, and Hitler's Mein Kampf predicted world conquest.

My father was enormously involved in the events of the day and was caught up in the war against Nazism. He would sustain his morale with his ability to interpret day-to-day events. He had a creative mind and I always found his intellectual rapport rewarding.

In Canada, people were as divided on the Nazi issue as they were in Germany. An alderman in Winnipeg's City Hall, Alderman Penner, a German-Canadian, was an anti-Fascist. We were never confused that if one was German, it would follow that he would be pro-Hitler.

There were Canadians at the time who did believe in an authoritarian structure, a dictator at the top, a society which would militantly preserve law and order, making sure that all opposing groups were labeled enemies of the state.

In Canada we had a German Bund, a counterpart of the party in Germany. Its largest following was in Saskatchewan. Members wore brown shirts and sported Swastikas on their sleeves. In Quebec, Saskatchewan, and Manitoba, street meetings and rallies were called against the Jews.

On one occasion, the Kosher meat butchers of Winnipeg plotted to smite the homegrown Nazis. They brought clubs to a public meeting and cracked some heads. In court they were emotionally defended; the mood of the day helped to get them off.

The social temper of our time was highlighted by the rise of Fascism and Nazism. Hitler was waxing ominously in Germany, and in Spain a democratically elected government was embroiled in a civil war. Right-wing revolutionary forces under Franco were openly supported by Hitler and Mussolini and military aid against the democratic government of Spain.

Communist young people and anti-Fascists throughout the world volunteered to support the Government of Spain, while the free world agonized about staying "neutral".

Officially, the western nations were neutral. At the time neutrality meant you were sympathetic to one party but didn't help it. You were actually not neutral; by not helping, you were allowing an opponent to win. This tenacious argument served as the basis of many debates at high school and university.

Winnipeg had set the stage for an inter-ethnic experience. The volatile cauldron of egalitarian ideas led us, as young people, to explore the concept of a universal society in which we should value each other as individuals. The universal society for us at that time was epitomized by Canada as a whole. Moving freely in Canadian society to us meant marrying whomever we chose and whoever reciprocated our feeling, regardless of ethnic background. My brother would eventually marry an Icelandic girl, my cousin Martin an English girl, my cousin Syd a Welsh girl, and my cousin Manly Shore a Ukrainian girl. To us Canada represented the ideal social structure in which we could go through the public schools and not be discriminated against.

Even at the university, my brother and I were only dimly aware of the establishment forms. There were Anglo-Saxon fraternities, but Jewish kids and other nationalities formed compensating fraternities. I had no fraternity experience. Instead, I was enormously involved in university life as a whole in the greater fraternity of campus living, true community living. We met like-minded people, members of the opposite sex, kids from different ethnic backgrounds who shared a common idealism about Canada.

This was the time of the Great Depression, "the dirty 30s". While Canadian society itself had failed in terms of providing a viable economy for the people, we students lived an active undergraduate life, busy discovering each other.

In conjuring up a better society, we visualized one in which every human being would be included. In miniature, the university was that better society. Attending college was a sure step by which we could move towards a larger national identity.

Poverty did not stop the truly desiring student from getting into university. A student could audit a course without being found out or bootleg lectures and not pay fees.

Of course, poverty obliged many other young people to opt out of school, many had to go to work earlier than they might have and most of them gave up thoughts of higher education. Those who didn't find work opted for other ways to make a living; the poolrooms and crime.

At that time the poolroom was synonymous with crime club. It was an aimless and dangerous existence for any young person. Yet, when World War II came, college kids and poolroom kids joined up.

For the idealists, the fight was against Fascism and about defending Canada's freedom. For others, the war created jobs and that in itself became attractive. Army pay, uniforms, and some glamour – what an improvement on aimless destitution.

The summer immediately prior to my going to university, my father underwent surgery to have a tumour removed. For years he had suffered a growth developing between his nose and eye.

My father would sit at the linotype, head cocked, smoking a cigarette to the lip level, the cigarette smoke running up to his eye, past his eye duct, making his eye tear. Over the years, this irritant ultimately closed the tear duct and a growth began. It was treated in Winnipeg, but not as a malignant tumour.

In 1936, when it became a conspicuous growth, my mother accompanied him to the Mayo Clinic in Rochester, Wisconsin. The tumour had been diagnosed as cancer. My father survived a critical, delicate operation and came out of surgery virtually unmarked.

Although quite shaken by this experience, he returned to his job and community life as a popular humorist and speaker. Throughout all my university years, I was concerned about my father. My mother, brother, and I saw Dad go back to the Mayo Clinic and eventually have his right eye removed. He wore a white patch with great stoic dignity.

During those years, my mother became very close and dear to him. This was the point where their love and marriage, I think, really found its greatest meaning. He sharpened his humour and kept going to work.

Gradually, after his eye operation, my father began to lose the sight of his other eye. He was reduced to working with a magnifying glass, but stubbornly he would not give up working at the linotype machine.

The saddest moment came some years later, on an afternoon I was visiting him at the plant. He suddenly stopped working. He couldn't see. He asked me to read the copy to him while he continued setting on the machine. That lasted for one hour. He went home and refused to go back.

Later, I helped him rationalize that he should go back to work as a sort of consultant foreman and supervisor. To this extent, the plant played its part extremely well. It provided him with a salary in his sick years.

* * *

That fall of 1935, laden with a sense of awe and excitement, I began my freshman year at United College. The Depression had created a great deal of disillusionment in our society and the professors reflected it. Many of them were ex-clergymen, others practising ministers. At United, professors reflected the entire spectrum of radical thinking; Social Democratic, Trotskyite, Marxist, Christian Co-operative, and Anti-Fascist. At the University of Manitoba, on the other hand, in a mass of Liberal-Radicals, a pro-fascist group centred around the German department and included a brilliant but doctrinaire history professor, Fieldhouse.

I brought my high-school "buddies" with me: Harold Karr, Harry Fainstein, and Reuben Cristall. We, the group of four, were the first "team" of Jewish kids from Winnipeg's north end to direct itself to higher education through the conduit of United Church College. Dressed in newly purchased suits, garments which were to last throughout college, white shirts, appropriate ties, well shined shoes, scrubbed and combed, we were typical freshmen. My off-the-rack suit was reddish brown and flecked with blue. As freshmen, the novelty of wearing black undergraduate gowns gave us a feeling of kinship with Oxford and Cambridge.

We thought of ourselves as the more aggressive half of the self-proclaimed inner circle of geniuses, the "Flashes", a St. John's High School boyhood grouping of ten lads with pride in scholastics, athletics, student government and the arts. All of us, through me, had been deeply committed to executive tasks at high school, class councils, student publications and theatrical ventures. I had served the group as main cheerleader and program instigator.

That first morning at United, we had arranged to meet in front of the college gate. The Flashes were entering a strange new environment, the castle-like building on Portage Avenue. Every physical aspect of the college interior made its impression that first morning: the massive front doors, the few steps up to the main lobby, the few steps down to the basement lockers, tuck shop and corridors to the harem-like quarters of the co-eds common rooms, the sub-basement passageway made exotic with perfume through which the girls in residence wound their way to Sparling hall.

As the weeks rolled by, the group of four relaxed, met classmates and stopped moving as a wary guard. Soon we were even making dates with co-eds. For all of us this was the first time we were out of our social, ethnic ghetto.

We were apprehensive about anti-semitism. We might experience prejudice, be refused. Our parents had prepared us for rejection. It happened sometimes in the most surprising ways. Jean Partridge, the darlingest of girls and one of the calendar model, Vargas-type co-eds took me aside in the tuck shop one morning, a month after registration. She seemed visibly unhappy, distressed. She had accepted a date with Harry, without doubt the most eligible, romantic draw of our group. Her small-town parents were rigid with anxiety when she told them the name of her first date for the first major college formal. The name Fainstein meant a Jew.

Impossible! Their protected daughter's first big social date could not go so awry. She was to call it off and asked my advice on how to do it without hurting Harry's feelings? I was no great help.

In our first-year class elections, my buddies planned to get me into the executive. I couldn't make the class presidency, but I did become social convener, a good way to begin. My job was to organize parties for the first year.

Fresh initiation in the fall of 1935 was, in the main, wholesome and fun. First came a Friday night wiener and marshmallow roast on the bank of the Assiniboine River. Seated in a circle around a huge bonfire, some 100 freshmen mingled with an equal number of college-wise sophomores singing songs, learning cheers, and being convivial.

There was a special initiation ceremony in the second week for the males in first year. Wearing beanies, we were lined up in front of a classroom on the second floor and brought into a darkened chamber, one by one. We were then blind-folded and told to repeat an oath of allegiance to our alma mater. We were then told that we were obliged to swallow the eye of a cat. In actuality, the item placed in the palm of my hand was a skinless, peeled grape. To swallow it was an impossibility. I nearly fainted. Finally, forgiven the disobedience, I was pronounced initiated. I exited gratefully, later to be told the secret of the freshman trial by torture in a subsequent year.

The climax of welcoming activities was the wildest night of the year, the Freshman parade down Portage Avenue. Led by enthusiastic seniors, freshmen in the vanguard, backed up by the rest of the current student body, a straggly line of shouting, full-of-beans college kids stopped traffic, marched down the centre of the street, and gloried in attracting attention. It was a once-a-year disruption of Winnipeg's night life and, since damage was nominal (the odd theatre door taken off its hinges), the mayhem was generally tolerated by the public.

Into the Capitol theatre we would stream, spend five minutes shouting our college yells, and then leave to invade the Lyceum and Metropolitan movie houses in turn. The final stop was the celebrated night club, the Cave on Donald Avenue. Here we lost a few who, finding the free admission too attractive to ignore, stayed and danced to Howard Green's 12-piece orchestra.

United College had a storybook atmosphere. In the basement the locker room was the site of learned discussions, speculation on the number of virgins in first, second, third and fourth years. Questionnaires on such vital concerns were drafted and circulated. Students engineered games and stunts in an attempt to startle professors. The college main floor featured the library and auditorium. The second floor had access to the chapel balcony. The third floor comprised seminar rooms and small alcoves where one could find one's favourite professor and join him at tea. Our involvement with the teachers had a great deal of influence on our social attitudes and lent charm to our existence.

Early that fall I joined the staff of the university newspaper, *The Manitoban*, as a very eager-beaver reporter. It wasn't long before I became assistant news editor, a position of distinction on a daily campus newspaper.

My career in journalism began with the advice of Earle Beattie, a friend I had met in the early thirties. At that time he was known as E.J.B., associate editor of the *Winnipeg Free Press'* young people's section. When we met, to my surprise, he was only a year or so older than me. He was most complimentary in his published review of my editing of the St. John's yearbook and I, in turn, invited him to join our high school As You Like Us Drama Club. As our friendship ripened, Earle contributed guest columns in English to my father's Yiddish-language newspaper.

Earl had dropped out of high school to become a copy boy at the *Free Press*, and I had persuaded him to attend United College. He was so enthusiastic, he had persuaded the Dean to allow him to pick up admission credits in the United Collegiate and to register in the undergraduate bachelor of arts course.

Earle had been earning some $60 a month as correspondent for the *Free Press*, a princely sum at the time. By way of reciprocity, he persuaded me to seek the post of college correspondent for the *Winnipeg Tribune* daily newspaper, and Bill Osler, the brusque, Clark Gable-type city editor, accepted my offer.

My *Tribune* editor was a former minister, Rev. Edgar Whitehouse. He was also the newspaper's church editor. He thought it would be most interesting to send a Jewish lad to cover Christian churches. I found myself on Sundays getting a lot of soul uplift from such diverse groups as the Holy Rollers and Father Divine's Mission, as well as the Anglican, United and Catholic churches.

In time I was able to pick out churches and ministers who impressed me. It took me a while to realize that every calling, medicine, education, law or technology, attracts drones as well as bright bees, and you can't always judge the calling by the man.

It took only three or four weeks before I came to the attention of the "desk" and of Bill Osler, city editor. Osler had a penchant for trimming his mustache fearlessly with his editorial shears while seated at his desk. He commanded respect. Bill Osler was "Sir" to me. "Yes Sir!" I moved on the double when he called out "Parker."

One of my church stories caught Osler's attention. He commanded me to his desk. Would I like the odd extra assignment covering a musical event, going to court as relief for the police reporter, attending a large social event for the women's editor, attending part of a long night session of school board and city council, helping out with Varsity sport coverage? I would get space rates, of course.

It seemed marvellous to me. Osler had presented me with a journalism course and instant faculty. I could hardly believe my good fortune. And I had been forewarned that the *Tribune* was anti-semitic! What I wasn't sure of was the enthusiasm of the reporters and editors to whom I had been assigned. Most important, said Osler, was that I find light relief features about college life. This would be my specialty and would sustain me on a continuing basis. I was to ask for the photo assistance of Harry Rowed when required.

At the end of each month, to get paid, I had to clip out my articles which had been published in the *Tribune*, paste the cuttings on long sheets of paper and submit the whole as an invoice. I would measure the length of my output and the *Tribune* would pay me 20¢ an inch.

I became so enthusiastic that I gathered news about everything at United College and the "desk" used a great deal of it.

Before long I was averaging $30 to $40 per month. My returns were exhilarating, viewed in terms of what that kind of money meant to a student during the Depression. I became known as an "ace" space reporter on the *Winnipeg Tribune*. Since I was also working on *The Manitoban*, I had the opportunity to rework its news for the *Tribune*. I quickly recognized that if I kept my ear to the ground, I could eventually land one or two scoops.

I canvassed everybody for assignments. The women's page editor agreed to take copy about school dances. A bonanza for me! I would write down the names of those who attended college dances and the entire list would be published. The society pages were hungry for copy. Name gathering took place at the door or backroom of concert and dance halls. If I dated a girl, she was expected to be co-operative in helping me gather names. Not much of a fun date, but that didn't discourage me or them. On the other hand, I had many dances to attend. Stimulated after an event, I would bound back to the paper at 1:30 a.m. and type frantically to meet the early edition deadline.

I loved to hang around the *Winnipeg Tribune* office. Here I could use a typewriter and be in the company of real newspapermen. I had a nose for news and got many stories. About some, the city editor had serious doubts, wondering whether the events had really happened; some of my features I had actually helped stage.

For example, being in a United Church college, the student theologues were very good foils for me. I decided I needed a story about theologues, so I put a note on the centre hall bulletin board. The announcement deplored drinking at college dances, professing outrage. The note went on to say how depraved and horrible the practice was, how our society was stupid. The note suggested that "we" theologues meet at 4 p.m. and decide whether we should take baseball bats to the dances to smash any flask we might see protruding from someone's hip pocket.

When I came to the room at 4:05 p.m., it was full. I sat at the back of the room. There were about 30 or 40 theologues present and a number of other undergraduates. No one, of course, was running the meeting, but people do rush in to fill vacuums, as I learned, and the group decided to speak out on the issue at chapel services.

In the case of the drinking-at-dances issue, I went back to my paper and wrote the story about the theologues. The theologues were a favourite story source for me, providing me with quite a series of items. Finally, two or three of these candidates for holy orders apprehended me in the college corridor one day and said they were going to blacken my eyes. I suggested that they hit my left one because I was more photogenic from that angle and that it would make a great picture for the *Winnipeg Tribune*. This stopped them dead.

Other colourful stories occurred to me. I would get girls to carry books on their heads to illustrate a point made in a psychology class. Professor Cragg had said that girls were pretty dumb and would be better off carrying books on top of their heads than trying to get the contents inside their heads. So I posed a line of comely co-eds standing with books on their heads. It became a front-page newspaper spread in the *Tribune*. On another occasion, the same group of co-eds covered their heads and veiled themselves with cloth, ostensibly to forsake the dating of boys for a month. One of the girls was Gudrun Bjerring, later to marry my brother, Morten. She was then on her way to becoming campus queen.

Most students welcomed the opportunity to pose for the comic situations I invented. I had lots of news features. My college campus stories were considered good, front-page, light-reading relief. My copy, in the main, was published as submitted, and Beattie's editor pushed him to compete. Earle spent a great deal of time declaring that I wasn't finding news, but staging it. True, but it worked.

I did however, have a nemesis in the *Tribune* hierarchy. For many months I had sailed along thinking all the *Tribune* editors thought well of me. Not so. Irascible managing editor Fred O'Malley considered me pushy, and humiliated me in front of staff one evening. He ordered me out of the newsroom on a federal election night. He resented that I was just hanging around looking for involvement. "You're in the way," he barked.

O'Malley was cross-eyed and he always looked at degrees left or right of his target. I found this perplexing and infuriated him further when I took his comments to be addressed to someone else.

Most of the editors at the city desk level perceived me as a "smart-ass" college kid. Many of the desk men hadn't gone to college, a direct result of the Depression. As my copy chiefs, they took pleasure in pricking my editorial pride. On occasion, they would catch me spelling the same name two different ways in the same story. The fact was, I often employed my brother to help me with the copy output. He would come along and help me type lists of names taken at the dances. Often we duplicated. City editor Bill Osler once bellowed, "Who in hell told you you can write, Parker?"

I learned my craft the hard way, the traditional way by being shouted at and insulted. But I was appreciated; my copy received a high rate of acceptance. My stories appeared on the society pages, in the sports pages, anywhere I could generate university coverage.

Being Jewish was a concern which faded into near oblivion as my college career proceeded. Early in my first year, I had received my first invitation to a Christian home from John Crowe, one of four Crowe boys to attend United. I had yet to be a guest in anyone's home for dinner, outside of relatives, and this was a Sunday feast. Originally a farm family, the Crowes were accustomed to a table laden with food. It was Thanksgiving. My gentle, diffident, European mother had instructed me to watch and emulate others in handling cutlery, in helping myself at the table and in being respectful during any prayers. My being Jewish was the highlight of the dinner conversation. I knew far less about the Bible, Talmud, and such matters as did Crowe senior. The experience of that induction into a Christian family ways stayed with me throughout the years.

* * *

In my second year at university I became news editor of the campus daily, *The Manitoban*, and gained a seat on our class council as co-convenor of social events.

I had elected to major in history and economics. Harry Fainstein had moved to Los Angeles to pursue a law degree at U.C.L.A. and changed his name to Fain and Reuben Cristall had switched to a pharmacy course.

Universal Printers had tendered to print the student newspaper. Since it was my father's plant, I couldn't do much to promote it. On the other hand, I was enormously alert to story angles.

I had noted that *The Manitoban* was being printed in a Norwegian-language non-union plant. I had spotted pre-teen children washing floors there. I agitated my United College colleagues, both the art students and the theologues, to protest against this Dickensian horror. The issue was trade-unionism and the university community. It was unthinkable that in Winnipeg, the site of the 1919 general strike, in a depression, a non-union shop could be allowed to print the university paper.

I conspired to call the entire *Manitoban* staff out on strike. At United College there were lots of radicals, including professors, who zealously supported me. My own role was ambiguous. I was a member of the strike action and also a writer for the *Winnipeg Tribune*. There was nothing like staging your own news events.

Then, one night at *The Manitoban*, at a given signal, we laid down our editorial tools and gathered up all copy. I had unfortunately tipped the *Winnipeg Tribune*, and a photographer appeared. Since I was photographed, I had become part of the news, and I couldn't get paid for writing the news.

As a result of my obvious involvement in the strike, an evening student council meeting was called. The president, "Mac" Robinson, was very shrewd and didn't allow me to get the floor. I thought

61

of him as Mr. Establishment. He was a fourth-year law student, a very cool guy. He demolished my character and taught me several lessons about conflict of interest. One, he exposed the fact that I was one of the people that organized the strike. Two, I wasn't without ulterior motive; I had wanted to make money through the *Winnipeg Tribune* by writing the story of the strike. And three, I wanted my father's printing plant to get the job.

I was publicly humiliated by his attack and quit *The Manitoban*.

Now I had more time for dating. As students, no one took anyone for granted socially. We tried to impress our partners with our social graces. In the depth of the Depression we wore tuxedos to formal occasions. Since most of our dances were formal occasions, I purchased a tuxedo for $18.00.

A date meant you bought a corsage and borrowed the family car. An evening proceeded with some style. Rarely were a couple alone in a car. Normally, two other couples joined you and there was a high level of excitement and laughter as one girl inevitably sat on her beau's lap. After a dance, it was off to a restaurant for cokes, chips, and milkshakes. Goodnight kisses at the door were the climax of a great date.

In those days, a sense of furtiveness dominated in boy-girl relationships. If you aspired to a long necking session with anyone, it had to be unknown to your college confreres or you were subjected to the most painful ribaldry. Group knowledge of your romantic interest would oblige you to continue dating the same girl for a period beyond your sustained interest, a circumstance few wanted in those days.

During the summer, I followed in Molly Rogers' wake as a promoter of theatre. She and other students of that day had organized a quasi-professional group, the Varsity Players. The company toured with plays in repertory. Our locale was Lake of the Woods in northwestern Ontario, a scenic lake-dotted region boasting awesome pine trees and rock formations. Here on a beautiful shoreline we had the use of a cottage as our base and rehearsal centre. We toured holiday resorts, finding great acceptance and popularity. We had a big banner attached to our truck announcing the arrival of the Varsity Players. I became infatuated with one of the girls in the company, Edith, the daughter of a Senator. We exhibited tremendous shyness with each other, despite the fact that we were all actors. I managed an awkward kiss once and when it happened, body chemistry boiled in both of us. We experienced feelings of love for each other which disappeared with the next play in which she played my mother so convincingly that my mood changed. Edith was outstanding as a tough matriarch. At the end of the summer, we brought the plays back to the university and performed them for summer school students. Theatrical activity was a great way to feel vital, to relate to people in holiday resorts and towns and to get to know our backwoods.

In those days, circa 1936-1940, we were wrapped up in play readings. Hardly a week went by when we didn't meet in somebody's home and read plays as part of our social entertainment. We would get four or five copies of a play, assign parts to all and read. Then came coffee and cakes. Social play-reading was an essential part of our university and community experience in the pre-television period. Radio gave us exposure to plays, but we didn't feel as involved as we did in our own live play rehearsals, whether on stage or in the classroom.

I continued to feel part of my ethnic community even when I had plunged fully into university life. At the same time I really didn't want to revert to the Jewish community for my personal commitment to humanity. I was really drawing away from parochialism.

In my third year of university, the editor-in-chief felt I was a good enough newspaper man to forgive me all of my previous strike-making tactics and appointed me managing editor. Being managing editor made you a very powerful man on *The Manitoban*, in line of succession to the position of editor-in-chief.

By this time, I had built up my *Winnipeg Tribune* coverage to a point where I was getting anywhere from $80.00 to $100.00 a month. Salaries on the *Tribune* at that time were $15.00 to $20.00 a week. I was making more money producing space coverage than the reporters on regular payroll.

* * *

Arthur Phelps stood out clearly among my teachers. He was a great humanist, intensely interested in young people. Whatever the job meant to him by way of income, it meant more to him by way of joy in teaching. Twinkle-eyed, bright and provocative, he was a slim, elfin figure. He used his black academic gown as a prop, throwing it over his head on occasion for effect, declaring that good poetry could be heard even when muffled by cloaks. He made us sit up and take notice. Phelp would read poetry in mock atrocious voices so that we would be scandalized to hear beautiful poetry so crudely handled. He would ask if we could still see the beauty in the poem. Then he would read works meaningfully, using his beautiful, melodious, resonant voice.

One of my greatest compliments as an undergraduate was to be invited to Professor Phelp's home. His charming home was in the southeastern part of the city, a forbidden land of Tudor-style gates. It had a fireplace, an item associated with Winnipeg aristocracy. During those few evenings at Phelps, tea, cakes and toasted marshmallows were simulations to me of undergraduate life at Oxford and Cambridge.

Professor Phelps' delightful wife joined us often in discussions of literature. She was warm, motherly, intelligent, and engaged us in talk of poets and ideas, rejoicing with her husband in our reactions. Life couldn't be sweeter.

Phelps saved me from getting expelled. As a student reporter, I wasn't above engineering events to promote news stories. One instructor, outraged that United College was getting in the newspaper every day with stories featuring pranks, proposed to the faculty council that they expel Ed Parker.

Phelp delayed the drastic action, offering to talk to me first. My argument was that it was good for the college to be in the news. People would know we were alive. They would become aware of our existence. Phelps suggested that I speak to the venerable Dr. Riddell, the college president.

White bearded and white haired, Riddell was an impressive figure. Jewish students were a novelty to him. I met Dr. Riddell under tense circumstances. My plea was that he appreciate that I was helping United College by getting publicity into the press. If I had a more orderly way of collecting news, I could avoid rumour. I suggested that the college give me an office and typewriter, rather than kick me out.

I was amazed by his positive response.

"We are a small college," he said. "Where could we find you an office?"

'Under the stairwell in the basement," I suggested.

Within a week, the college carpenters had built a pantry-like press office with wire mesh for windows which became a press office for me and my *Free Press* competitor, Earle Beattie.

There was a certain naiveté in some of my United College teachers. Many thought that if you were Jewish, your feelings ought to be carefully respected in Christian matters. While the three or four of us who were Jewish were expected to go to chapel for a ten minute midmorning service, no one would insist. Our Christian teachers were anxious to make us feel comfortable and appreciated in this tradition. One of my distinguished teachers, Watson Kirkconnel, my Latin professor, would send me Christmas cards, but he would mark out "Happy Christmas", as though he thought I might not be observing that holiday. To me it seemed a reflection of high gentleness. Kirkconnel was a man of considerable colour and humour. It was a joy learning Latin from a teacher who would popularize Julius Caesar's battles in the idiom of Chicago gangster talk. Julius Caesar became Little Caesar, his chariots bulletproof cars and his lancers machine gunners. His candour about erotic poetry helped me appreciate that the Romans were great eulogizers of breasts, hips and yielding ladies. Because of my aroused interest in these matters, I didn't do so badly in Latin.

There was something custom-made about my education, a rich variety of subjects, intense involvement with my professors, an activist role as a liberal, social insight into world affairs and a great search for individuality. My free spirit wouldn't allow me to join a political party of the left, although my heart was with the disadvantaged.

Being a reporter proved an extremely good entrée into campus life. If I were going to cover some event, I could always ask a girl to go along with me, not as a date, but as a friend.

It was extraordinarily flattering to me when my dates would come back to the newspaper and wait for me to finish writing my stories. My work sometimes kept us up to 2:30 a.m. Since no streetcars ran at that hour and we had no taxi money, we would walk four or five miles to get home.

After some late shifts at the *Tribune*, I would often just roll up on the top of a reporter's desk, pull my navy coat over myself and sleep, having first informed the night desk to be sure to wake me before managing editor O'Malley arrived. My great fear was to be caught sleeping on my desk.

* * *

In my fourth year at United College, I missed getting the editor-in-chief position on *The Manitoban* and my brother became managing editor. I learned that it wasn't how good you were but with whom you could ingratiate yourself that was often the decisive factor in appointments.

Morten, eighteen months younger, had succeeded me in many of the activities in which I had been prominent. At public school and high school, he followed me by a year, becoming president of his class each year as I had. He picked up almost all my extracurricular positions as I vacated them. In one field in high school, however, he surpassed me. He became school president.

I did, however, become the president of the class of '39. My class was about to elect the same lad who had been our president for three years. On being nominated, he demurred, saying, "Well, I don't know. I've had this post for three years." I was up on my feet in a flash saying that when a man doesn't want to run he ought not to be pressed in to it. Then I sat down.

The poor guy couldn't say he wanted the job at this point and no one would press him on it. Nominations were thrown wide open.

Since I had been the last man on my feet, several voices called out "Ed Parker". In a flash, I became president of the United College's Men's Club in the graduating year, the first Jewish lad to lead a graduating year at a United Church college.

My best friend at college was Douglas Fraser. Tall, intellectual, bespectacled, seemingly reserved, he had a pose of culture, a Canadian patrician who surprisingly could be provoked to physically plunge himself into a broohaha if it were scheduled as a campus lark. Being asthmatic, he often paid the price for his physical exertion, and I frequently stood at his side trying to wedge him free from wrestling engagements.

In our last year, we braced ourselves for the annual invasion of our campus by some 200 youths from the Broadway campus of the University of Manitoba. Doug rallied me as president of college men to put up a good defence. I was strong on strategy, but discretionary on the use of brawn. The invaders were on the stairway, nearly on the second floor of our building. Step by step we forced our adversaries down the steps, out the door and off the campus.

It was a great victory. I credit Douglas Fraser with brilliant and selfless generalship. There was slight damage to the stairwell and several colleagues had their shirts ripped down the back. Surprisingly, the most revered college objects, the large, framed, class montages of graduating classes, were not shaken from the walls.

Fraser and I attended a national students' conference in Montreal that year. We aired questions of equal language rights for the French-speaking Canadians in provinces outside of Quebec. Coming from the ethnic melting pot of Winnipeg, we couldn't buy "bilingualism". English was the common denominator language. If a second language were to be learned, it might as well be a second language of one's own choice.

We believed that all students born in Canada had equal rights. No one should have a privilege different than anyone else's simply because of favoured ethnic descent. I acknowledged that the French were here first, historically. But, so what? English was our reality. A sensation-arousing motion surfaced on the convention floor that French be taught on an equal status with English in all provinces in Canada. An amendment that all ethnic groups be viewed as cultural equals in Canada, and someone to second it, was needed. Fraser rose from a dormitory sickroom and seconded my motion of amendment. The resolution, as amended, passed to the effect that every ethnic language be recognized, defeating the French-Canadian gambit.

On a personal level, I was in a state of suppressed anxiety concerning my father's health during my college years. As my father's tear-duct cancer advanced, he needed morphine to ease the pain he mutely endured. My mother wasn't up to giving him his injections. Although I was normally squeamish, I performed this ministration with good spirit because of my great love for my father. I later developed a sense of guilt, fearing that I was shortening his life by giving him too much morphine out of compassion to relieve his pain.

At about 1:30 a.m., he would rouse me gently, saying, "I am sorry to wake you at this hour. Could you give me a needle?" My reward however, was truly gratifying. He would say, "I feel free of pain. Would you like to spend an hour with me and talk."

He might start off by asking, "What do you think were the particular qualities that Jesus, Spinoza, Freud, Karl Marx, and Einstein had in common?" His contention was that one thing they had in common was their ability to be innovators, to reject the conventional ideology of their day and to become nonconformist philosophers.

In those early morning hours, my father was teaching me. Since I had studied philosophy at university, I was able to reciprocate with a rather cliché discussion of famous philosophers.

Bill Lawson, when I was in my third year and on his college council as drama president, was intuitive enough to engage me on the subject of my anxiety and helped me balance my life.

Amid the serious themes, there was time for levity, for contemplating dating bureaus, the number of freshmen who could cram into a telephone booth, and how to evade police detection and play an illegal pinball machine. Ever on the lookout for a story, I couldn't inveigle anyone to pose next to a pinball machine to help illustrate a feature. Finally, photographer Harry Rowed persuaded me to raid the college dramatic society locker and make myself up as a hobo, disguised by a large mustache. The resulting photo was published on the front page of the *Tribune*, only Harry and the editors had my mustache removed and the picture retouched so that I became easily recognizable.

After acquiring my Bachelor of Arts in the spring of 1939, I enrolled in law school, in effect to qualify as editor of the university newspaper. My brother and I applied for the editor-in-chief position on *The Manitoban*. As head of the men's club at United College, I had been able to influence the entire male undergraduate vote in the campus-wide election of the president of the University of Manitoba student council. I had thrown my machine support behind Rod Hunter, a former senior of United College.

The first time I had applied for the post of editor, I had wanted to achieve appointment purely on merit. But the second time around, I made a deal. I would back Rod if he would support me in becoming editor-in-chief of the University of Manitoba paper. This Rod did, and I thereby won the appointment in the spring of 1940.

I had mixed feelings about my appointment. Morten, whom I hired as my associate editor, was a good loser, but I felt he had cause to deeply resent my success.

* * *

During that summer I articled myself to a lawyer, but my heart was not in law. I really wanted to major in newspaper work. That fall, I hardly attended classes at law school and, at mid-term, I transferred into an honours history course. Here again, I barely attended. Instead I devoted myself to turning out the campus journal, increasing its frequency of appearance from twice to three times a week.

The editorial page was dominated by my name in unashamedly large type in the masthead. I was not learned in the virtue of understatement at this stage. I was able to effect great changes in *The Manitoban*, changing its organization, format, and content, and physically moving it out of its cellar offices into a special building. We took over a floor of the student activities building, setting up an interesting desk arrangement. I almost lived there. Highly stimulated by the opportunity to produce lead editorials at will, I set out to influence my campus.

Being editor of *The Manitoban* proved a most effective education in practical journalism for me. One of the great privileges in working on *The Manitoban* was that I was free to experiment with layouts. Our budget permitted us to use colour and, on occasion, even to put scented inks into the paper.

In the course of my tenure, I developed a warm relationship with the president of the university, Sidney E. Smith, later to become president of the University of Toronto and, for a brief time, Minister of External Affairs for Canada. Smith put me up to a few gambits, telling me that if I were careless enough to attract criticism, he would disassociate himself from my activities.

In was 1940, the year of the "phony war", when pamphlets, not bombs, were being dropped on Germany. The prevailing Allied Powers mentality was to let the Russians fight the Germans. "We will propagandize them with pamphlets, make them see how Hitler is misguiding them." It was a strange period: Neville Chamberlain and appeasement had proven disastrous, but Winston Churchill and the militant attitude against Nazism had yet to assert themselves.

Sidney Smith was sure that the army, navy and air force would take over some of the student buildings in the name of defence. He put me up to writing several editorials, sounding an alert, arguing that, if universities were subordinated to military needs, we would lose the very values of our society. The military was supposed to principally defend the business community. A small uproar took place in support of the military. Smith did not denounce me but just rode out the storm, and I survived as editor. It was on this occasion that I learned that Smith was a consummate politician. He had to be. On another occasion, he even denied support for a position on academic freedom which he had articulated to me. I was to take whatever beating on his behalf came my way. My reward was that, on other issues more meaningful to me, he did support me. This was an early insight for me into the fact that politics are played everywhere. My editorship itself had come through a political deal. Consequently, sustaining myself as editor-in-chief in collusion with the university president was the product of political rapport and empathy between us. It certainly stripped away any sophomoric illusion that one deals in terms of openly argued principle; instead, you deal by implied arrangements. I may put you up to something today, but I won't support you in the open politically tomorrow.

I almost got axed, however, when one of my literary editors published a tasteless version of Chaucer's *Canterbury Tales*, updating the stories to involve modern-day clerics. Had I seen the article before publication, I would have vetoed it. Church men wrote denouncing an editor of Jewish background showing such intolerance. The article also offended my father, and I made profuse apologies. The local archbishop wrote and criticized me for this breach of editorial control. In the end, I suspended the responsible editor.

It was also a period in which I co-authored and promoted a musical comedy. When Earle Beattie, Sam Seetner and I wrote our musical comedy, "You Can't Beat Fun", in 1939, we saw the main university function as one of developing leaders. The world, we judged, was in such a mess. The idea to create the musical comedy originated at the Y.M.C.A. swimming pool. On one of the rare occasions when I did take time for a swim, I was accosted in the water by Sam "Sleeves" Seetner. Earle and I called him "Sleeves" because his jacket sleeves came down to his knuckles. He played piano brilliantly and, when he readied his hands for the keyboard, back would go the sleeves, at last revealing his shirt cuff.

That fateful day "Sleeves" approached me with flattery. I, as he attested, was a powerful man on campus. As editor-in-chief of the university paper and a member of the student council, I could espouse his cause and help him produce an original musical comedy. I couldn't entertain the prospect of such an involvement too enthusiastically. At the moment, I was not attracted to musical comedy as a form of creative expression. My self-protective reflex was to cast about for someone who could help me out. I selected my sidekick Earle Beattie.

Earle was intrigued and we divided the tasks. I would conceive the plot, Earle would write the dialogue and lyrics and Sam would compose the music. The result was a compelling work, "You Can't Beat Fun". At first our project was not taken seriously by the campus community. We auditioned our book and music before the drama society committee. Suddenly, explosive enthusiasm reigned and the society voted us their entire year's budget. We auditioned our work again for the Glee Club executive and the prestigious campus organization fell before us, broke with tradition, and elected to forego its annual "Giblet and Sultan" presentation in favour of producing our show jointly with the dramatic society.

The end product was quite a sensation. The curtain rose on an eerie celestial set, a glowing globe of the world, half sunk into the stage. Around the globe's rim hovered black-gowned, mortar-board-wearing professors. These bearded sages sang the overture, a symphonic piece, beginning with the catchy lyrics "The world's gone screwy; The world's gone mad, We had no leaders, and that's too bad". Great feats of percussion and blaring brass accompanied the off-stage thunder and lightning. Leadership could still be found on one spot on the globe – Kenmore College!

The next scene spotlit a father and his two daughters, one a Betty Boop character and the other a scientific and serious Joan. The spotlight switched to introduce a not-too-serious Johnny and his ra-ra father, and a third light focused on a serious Dick with his practical-minded dad. After several gags about university life, each candidate exhibited a different point of view; one seeing the campus as a place for fun, another for girls, another for study, and so forth. The four then met in an enlarged spotlit circle in centre stage, singing "Me for Varsity". Gold curtains behind them then opened to reveal a Gilbert and Sullivan version of a classic campus. On stage came the university president, declaring in song "The university is a true democracy." Proclaiming himself a liberal educator, he had responded to student demands that he reshape the curriculum to reflect current values. Each of the four students elected to major in one subject; one being love, the other, rhythm, the third, a variation of both called "hotcha", and the fourth, a home economics course. As the president explained, "Men must eat, and that is a fact." Johnny, the smart one had joined the home economics course, "cause that is where the girls are." Subsequent scenes demonstrated the essence of these courses.

The second act developed romantic complications between the four principals, and these confusions carried the story through scenes at a student council meeting, a great college ball, and the academic corridors. Scrim curtains fells behind the ball scene to introduce one of the hit songs, "Since dear little Flora has got an angora, I weep for the state of my clothes."

The show played to capacity audiences for two weeks in our major civic auditorium. Each night there were cries of "Author, Author." The creators, Beattie, Seetner, and myself, dressed in tuxedos, came on stage in response to cast and audience applause and took our bows. It was pure euphoria! We were highly elated by our theatrical success. Rave reviews, one in Variety, brought us invitations from campuses in the United States.

I did scout the campus at the University of North Dakota for such an engagement, but the project was unmanageable. Of course, what helped put the show over in the first place was the fact that I commanded a newspaper and could publicize and promote support.

* * *

The *Winnipeg Tribune* had a tradition of annually inviting the editor of *The Manitoban* and his staff to be guest editors and reporters on a regular edition of its paper. The *Manitoban* staffers were paired with their *Tribune* counterparts. I was coupled with the publisher McCurdy and I seized the opportunity to present him with an idea on how he might expand his circulation. McCurdy was intrigued and asked me to write him about it. The most heady development for me that day was to be invited for lunch with McCurdy at the Fort Garry Hotel, where he said, "Get in touch with me when you have finished your course."

My editorials came to the attention of the editors of both metropolitan daily newspapers in Winnipeg and I was hopeful that my editorials might help land me a full-time job on one or the other. I had been seduced by the glamour of bylines. Even though the *Winnipeg Tribune* bylines were more to protect their editors than to honour me, I was delighted to see my name in print. Being recognized as a writer made me something of a celebrity in the city and I revelled in the role.

Long before editorial staff work became my own experience, I was exposed to the newsroom atmosphere through my father. In the 1930s, newspapers played a heartbeat role in community life. There was a great deal of excitement and tension on election nights, when hundreds of people would gather in front of the Israelite press and the Winnipeg Tribune to read the bulletins being posted.

Newspaper-sized bulletins were quickly created by poster artists to announce the running results, and the crowds would cheer. My brother and I filled the special role of messenger boy on these nights, running with the latest returns being telephoned from the polling booths to the poster-makers, then taking the bulletins outside for posting.

At this time the only people who were attractive to me were not those who had prospered and become smug, but rather those who were poor and who centred their lives around the Communist-oriented Arbeter Ring School. They would invite me as a young editorialist to talk to them. I was hungry enough for this recognition and enjoyed these people while recognizing a spiritual difference between them and myself. The Marxists felt that I wasn't subject to discipline and wouldn't follow their political views as group policy. They were right. I looked critically at cadre communists and saw them as unoriginal thinkers. If Moscow decreed something bad, they all parroted that it was bad. If Moscow told them something was good, they exhibited a tremendous faith. I believed theirs was a faith based on papal infallibility. I perceived their objectives as commendable, but not necessarily achievable by virtuous individual or group behaviour.

Cadre Communists felt that I was not very reliable as an ally and left me in the ill-defined status of a friend. To Winnipeg Marxists I was a bit of an enigma, but an interesting guy. They, of course, had a valued fear of being picked up by the RCMP. One or two family friends, Communists, were grateful when I would sometimes give them a lift in my car. They would suggest that I pick them up at an imprecise location, two blocks south of Portage on the west side, that sort of thing. I wouldn't know where they were going and would drop them off somewhere near, but never at their destination.

CHAPTER 4

SOJOURN INTO JOURNALISM

In the spring of 1940, my postgraduate year, the stage and screen editor of the *Winnipeg Tribune* died suddenly. I aspired to fill the vacancy, an audacious ambition for a neophyte not as yet on the fulltime staff of the *Winnipeg Tribune*. Nevertheless I had come to the attention of the publisher both for my work on his paper and on *The Manitoban*. I had gained some notoriety prior to the 1939 federal election from my campus editorial, "We'll vote Liberal but we won't like it." I wrote to the publisher, McCurdy, and asked to be considered for the job of entertainment critic.

McCurdy like me and recommended I meet Moscarella, the business manager. I was hired at $25.00 a week by Macdonald, the advertising manager. I was being paid to write advertising copy, but as a bonus I was also given two entertainment pages to edit write. This section was to be free of the managing editor's direct supervision.

I couldn't be happier. Suddenly I found myself writing advertising campaigns during the day and covering shows at night. I could take girlfriends to shows and bring them back with me to the editorial room. While they waited, seated at a nearby desk, I pounded out my reviews from midnight to 2 a.m. I soon became known as the movie man. My desk was next to the aisle on the advertising floor, not on the editorial floor. This I regretted at first because I missed the peculiar bustle around the city desk. On the other hand, I was greeted daily by the newspaper's executives whose offices were on that floor.

As a writer among ad-sales people, I enjoyed a special status and considerable respect. I was directly responsible for the type and photo layout of the entertainment pages. I got to know the linotype operators who set my copy and the foreman who made up my pages. In those days, an editor had access to the composing room. I was naturally drawn to the printers because of my background in my father's plant, and I persuaded them to feature my personal column in a most startling and attention-arresting way. My column was titled "From the Back Row". I chose the title from my father's belief that performers do not really acquit themselves of their responsibility to an audience unless they satisfy the man in the back row. As a critic, I saw myself as that man in the back row.

My composing room allies set my editorial copy most prominently in double-column width with alternate paragraphing in boldface/ or indented type for maximum effect. They then placed the effort smack in the middle of the page. No other writer on the paper was so featured. The first day the column appeared, managing editor O'Malley was livid. He said he hated my guts and accused me of brazen self-aggrandizement. Fortunately for me, there was such rivalry between the business executives and the news editors, that the advertising manager who was nominally my boss backed me up. "You do what you want," he directed. "These are our pages."

I did very well as a reviewer and soon developed a following. Of some personal satisfaction over the years was the fact that I had covered the Winnipeg Ballet in its early stages and had encouraged its growth. Regrettably, my "inspired" writings on behalf of the arts was not the activity for which I was to get credit or a raise on the *Winnipeg Tribune*. Being a writer, according to ad manager MacDonald, was of little importance. There were a lot of writers. It wasn't a significant occupation. But helping to sell more advertising would bring me fame and financial rewards. Building up the ad lineage of the classified advertising section would win me "brownie points".

Ian Macdonald, tall, brusque, and well-groomed, bristled with self-importance. When we first met, he was cordial, but hurried. Seated near the corridor to his office, I could testify that he invariably arrived late at ten and left at four. But he expected a long day from everybody else. It would impress him most, he said, if in addition to my other duties, I would "guff up" copy that would help "beef up" the personal ad column of the *Winnipeg Tribune*. This task was to make writing scenarios for advertising an "in-house" sensation and an outlet for my creative fiction.

"Dear blue eyes, we have been lovers for five years, always happy, celebrating birthdays and anniversaries together and having weekly meetings at the Green Briar Inn. Last night you said nasty things and I walked out on you. Today I am contrite. Please come back to the Green Briar Inn tomorrow night at 8 o'clock. I will be wearing a yellow daffodil to indicate "all is well." Please wear a rose to say you forgive." Signed, Pinky. The following day, an ad signed Blue Eyes declared, "Pinky, what makes you think I will go to the Green Briar Inn at the hour you suggest. If you really love me, meet me at the Green Briar Inn at 7 o'clock." And so the daily serialization continued.

Obviously, every ad was construed to have several references to the Green Briar Inn. These scripts occupied 84 lines of advertising space instead of the usual two or three line ads. Billings zoomed. The ads attracted a readership and almost became editorial issues, and the Green Briar Inn paid for the exposure. I wrote similar scenarios for teacup readers, carpet cleaners, whomever.

"Uland," went one, "I read your teacup at the Dixie Diner. There was one piece of good news I should have told you then. I felt that you wouldn't believe me, but now I think that it would be in your best interest to know. Come see me." Signed, Madame Zamboola.

The entire personal ad column had originally been averaging around six inches to length. It now burgeoned into three or four full length newspaper columns, and again, O'Malley was furious with me. I was seemingly converting the classifieds into editorial interest columns. Because of the poignant reader interest in the ads, people in increasing numbers were buying the *Tribune* ostensibly to keep up with the amusing personals. O'Malley was apologetic and grudgingly declared me the best writer at the *Tribune*.

The height of my success came that first year with a dream assignment for a cub reporter. Frank Morris, the drama critic of the *Winnipeg Free Press*, and I were to cover the world premiere of a Hollywood motion picture to be staged in Regina, Saskatchewan. It was an unusual event in Western Canadian experience. The movie was "Northwest Mounted Police" starring Gary Cooper and Madeleine Carroll. Morris and I shared a room at the Hotel Saskatchewan, were wined and dined by Hollywood press agent George Fraser and introduced and photographed with Madeleine Carroll.

On movie premiere day, the two Winnipeg newspapermen were ensconced in a chauffeur-driven limousine and included in the triumphant motorcade through the city. Smiling without let-up and waving to the crowds, I had a taste of what it was like to be on display for any length of time. I couldn't relax my facial muscles for more than an hour on my return to our hotel. On the third day, Morris and I were given the privilege of returning to Winnipeg in the special train chartered for the occasion.

The *Tribune* did me proud. O'Malley unbent a little and featured an front-page photograph of Miss Carroll and myself engaged in animated conversation. That picture did more to make me a local celebrity than my nine months of steady writing.

A premiere celebration of the film for Winnipeg was staged at the Capitol theatre and I was urged to invite a half dozen of my editors. I included Fred O'Malley who, together with a large party of executives from both papers, stood nervously in the wings awaiting Miss Carroll's arrival.

The actress was radiant despite wearing a black dress. She was in mourning for her lover, a French resistance fighter. The style of the gown made up for its sombre colour. It was cut particularly low, embarrassingly so for those standing next to her and encompassed in her radiance. Few of us could look at Madeleine Carroll straightforwardly without being abashed and discomfited.

But not so for Fred O'Malley. His crossed-eye affliction had become his asset. He could peer penetratingly down Madeleine's accommodating neckline. To an observer, O'Malley seemed to have his gaze somewhere else. O'Malley, face only slightly reddened, sated himself in scrutinizing the celebrated bosom.

The next morning, back at my desk at the *Tribune*, I learned that I had scored a triumph with O'Malley. He had praised me to my boss, Ian Macdonald, and had recommended that I be considered for a $2 a week raise at salary adjustment time. It was a rare acknowledgement of my existence. To my surprise, he confided that he was leaving the *Tribune* in a few months. He was to become manager of the Canadian Daily Newspaper Association, based in Toronto. He wanted to maximize *Tribune* advertising and leave on a high note of personal achievement.

MacDonald told me that I would only expect a raise of a dollar or two every six months and that there was little future for writers in Winnipeg. "Go east, young man," he counselled. He would help me if I first proved myself as an advertising copy writer. He would reward all who helped. I was to pass the word along among the advertising personnel. Word circulated quickly.

Roland Estall, a UK-born Canadian, impeccable in dress and manners, was the one advertising salesman to whom I warmed. Along with layout artist Gordon Bennett, he had dreamt up a campaign to encourage husbands to take their wives out to dinner at least once a week. I would write the messages, Gordon would draw the cartoons and Roland would round up the restaurants to "hook" on to the main message. Sponsor names and addresses would appear in sub-boxes to the main message like freight cars attached to the display "locomotive". The campaign of three-quarter-page advertisements ran for ten weeks.

Macdonald was ecstatic. He dubbed the campaign as the principle of "hooker" advertising and for weeks Bennett and I prepared campaigns for vacation trips, new car models and a variety of special services. The *Tribune* advertising lineage showed a week to week increase.

Estall, intrigued with the unorthodoxy of my copy writing, asked me to help him develop a fresh approach for a different kind of restaurant client. Pepper, a Hollywood caterer was to open a major "foodeteria" on the south-west corner of Main near Portage Avenue.

Estall sold Pepper on the idea of a co-operative full page advertisement to be underwritten by his major suppliers and restaurant renovators. The advertisement was similar to a regular news page of the paper under a banner line proclaiming Pepper's arrival. On this novel ad's successful appearance, Estall and I received commendation from Macdonald before an assembled sales staff.

Shortly thereafter, Eddie Zorn of Famous Players phoned the *Tribune*. Zorn wanted me to attend a special press conference for Norma Shearer, glamorous, Canadian-born, MGM movie star. She was to launch the latest Canada Savings Bond Drive of May 1941. Zorn wanted assurances of publicity in the Winnipeg press.

If the *Tribune* would pay my return railway pass to Montreal, Zorn would pick up my hotel and other expenses at the Mount Royal Hotel for a day. Here was an opportunity to enlist Ian Macdonald's promised reward for my past efforts. His influence would help. Macdonald curt-nodded his assent, quickly got on the phone with O'Malley and Moscarella, and the deal was arranged.

The Mount Royal Hotel was at the peak of its residential splendour, a wonderful experience for this westerner. I was rushed in and out of a photo session with the star. Introductions were so rapid that I hardly knew that the experience had happened. Shearer, her arms laden with dozens of long-stemmed roses, insisted on standing on my left, the better to display her legendary, perfect profile. I was flustered and embarrassed. All I could manage was, "You're my favourite movie star, Miss Shearer," and then I grinned for the camera. I felt very juvenile, a sort of Andy Hardy clone.

Regrettably, I had gleaned little story material on Shearer to mail back to the *Tribune*, so I concentrated on covering the launch itself. The glossy eight-by-ten photos of Shearer and myself were flattering of the star, but hardly galvanizing of myself. Still, they were evidence that I had been in the presence of a film goddess.

Mingling like a country bumpkin among the sophisticated eastern press people, I was drawn to a rotund, cherubic gentleman, Morgan Powell of the *Montreal Star*. Powell and I politely but animatedly disagreed on almost everything – quality of recent blockbusters, talents of different actors and purposes of film as an art form. Intrigued, Powell invited me to visit him and to continue our discussion in his newspaper office that afternoon. I took him at his word.

Powell had not returned from lunch when I arrived. I was then asked if I would like to see someone else. "Yes," I improvised, "the managing editor."

A.J. West, almost a caricature Britisher, was the true commander of the editorial and news battalions. Slim, diminutive, bristling, he hardly looked up as I entered. He then leaned back in his chair and fixed me with a steely gaze. I effused about his paper and claimed that the *Montreal Star* was highly regarded by my *Tribune* seniors. Continuing, I explained my presence in Montreal and expressed a private desire to be shown through his printing plant. My father, I explained was a compositor and linotype operator and I had developed an inordinate love of printer's ink. My interest in his paper's production facilities took West by surprise. The *Star's* up-to-date printing plant was his pride and joy and boasted the latest innovations in typesetting techniques. I was quickly introduced to and then immediately guided by the plant foreman through the top floor "shop" and the basement pressroom.

On my return to West's office he was keen to hear what I thought of his operation. It was, I opined, exemplary.

West couldn't be more pleased. Abruptly he popped the question; "Would I like to work for the *Montreal Star?*"

Would I!

Was I bilingual? I had won an inter-high-school French essay prize in Winnipeg, I boasted.

Concerned that West have no doubt about my enthusiasm, I said that I would jump at the chance.

"Fine," said West. "Start Monday morning. We are shorthanded."

This was Friday. I demurred. I would have to give notice to the *Tribune.* "Well then, in two weeks, latest," West declared. "You are hired for $35.00 a week." A handshake and the interview was finished.

Outside, walking down St. James Street, I was overcome with confusion, dizzy with elation. I was only making $25.00 a week at the *Tribune.* I didn't consider the extra costs of living away from home. The *Montreal Star* was big time to me. I wired my resignation from Montreal to Moscarella. I knew in my gut that I was handling the situation badly.

Back at the *Tribune* on Monday morning, the strain was everywhere as I approached my desk. "See Moscarella," Bardal bawled.

Moscarella was furious with me. He snarled that if it was more money I wanted, I could have asked them first. "I think you went there on false pretenses," he charged. "You meant to get another job. I think you ought to give us back the price of your railway ticket."

It was the first time I had quit a job. I had botched my handling of the situation, and I felt as if I had behaved in an unethical manner. Although I knew that job-hopping was the prevailing practice, I hadn't given the *Tribune* the chance to retain me.

Within a day or two I was carried away with the fact that I was going to Montreal and a great new experience. My mother was much troubled, and my father was saddened but wished me well. Both were very proud of me and my next step forward. Mickey was at that time trying to represent my father's share-interest in the *Israelite Press* by learning the trade, serving as a printer's devil and hating it. He had taken four years of university, had one subject to clear, and was doing this apprenticeship in the summertime. I had persuaded him to learn the trade, thinking that we might inherit a major role in the future of the *Israelite Press*.

* * *

My morning magnet was St. James Street, the nation's financial vortex, site of the *Montreal Star*, centre of newspaperdom in Canada. The *Star* building was old and venerable. The elevator, a turn of the century relic, was a cage affair operated by a character called "Pop". The third-floor newsroom had a traditional layout with senior editors in offices facing the street and copy-handling editors seated in a semicircle around an editor. The clerical staff occupied a small area separated from the editorial work area. The city editor had an assignment desk to himself, set flush against a wall.

A series of experiences took place while I was learning to live by myself. Alone in my room, I tended my clothes. I was armed with a sewing needle. My mother had insisted that this was as important a tool as a typewriter, and I darned my socks with abandon, mixing wool and thread, any colour as long as the effect was hidden below the heel. The product was a complete mosaic. I also turned my shirt collars.

I didn't want to turn a girl's head by seeing her more than once or twice a week. Most evenings my routine was to eat something en route to my room, have a brief snooze and then, about eight p.m., dress and cruise the streets. I soon tired of this. Reduced to boredom at times, I took up the hobby of soap sculpturing. Oddly enough, it proved an expensive pastime for me, a bar of soap costing 5¢ at the time. I carefully carved human heads and occasionally sent one of my better pieces home to my mother, automatically my greatest admirer.

Of my $35-a-week salary, I sent $20 back to my parents. My net per week was barely enough to see me through. Lonely, in a strange city, I welcomed my city editor sending me out to cover service club meetings during lunch hours or in the evenings. That meant a free meal. I soon knew the standard menus of all the hotels. I was almost an authority on roast lamb. The service club beat was a great help to my lean pocket book. Of course, this coverage was in addition to my regular assignments.

One day I was sent out with a photographer to a Montreal suburb where I was to witness the municipal council ceremonially burning their now paid-up mortgage document. When the event was over, to my astonishment, the Reeve poked $25 in bills in my hand. It was the first time in my newspaper experience that I had been given a bribe. I turned to my photographer associate. "I have to give this back," I insisted, "because it's wrong." His reply was sharp. "If you do, we will kill you. All of us have to make some money on the side to live." But the $25 was very much on my conscience and finally I went to tell West about it the next day. He had a far-away, sad look as I talked. He obviously didn't want to hear about it. He spoke rather about my need to master the French language and to become a competent bilingual reporter.

I was learning the hard way that petty handouts were a way of life in Montreal. In Winnipeg, such press corruption was absolutely unthinkable. In the west, despite its lowest-in-Canada wages, we were indeed motivated by idealism, high ethics and love of journalism. The reporter who had the city hall beat in Montreal probably made more money than the managing editor. This explained why senior desk editors coveted *Star* reporters' beats.

Montreal was a whole new cultural experience for me in my first weeks at the *Star*. It was assumed that I understood spoken French. I was given the lonely duty on the all-night desk. One evening, a frantic caller seemed to be reporting a murder, and I garbled all the information. It had turned out to be a fire. The morning desk caught the error in my memo, and my bilingual gig was up. I really couldn't cope with French, and I was back on day duty as photo editor.

Captioning pictures was duck soup to me. I had a theatrical sense and I would look at a photo imaginatively, visualizing what had been happening when the picture was being taken. My captions became commentaries. My photo lines got longer and longer, supplanting, often, the original news stories. The desk ran my copy with minimal editing. The *Star* was an almost sloppily edited paper. It was a journal in which the newspaper's emphasis on a bilingual staff meant that the French-Canadian reporters wrote poorly in English and correspondingly the English reporters wrote equally badly in French, invariably misspelling French names and places.

West thought my captions were editorializing and in one instance he perceived that I was assuming collapse of the non-aggression treaty of 1940 between the Soviet Union and Nazi Germany. He admonished me for bias.

These two ideologically opposite forces, the Soviet Union and Germany, had combined in an arms-length agreement to divide Poland between them and to bring their armies to face each other at that middle. I didn't view this as much of an alliance. To me it was a handshake between adversaries designed to keep each other from throwing the other off balance at the moment. My strong conviction was that these two forces had to clash.

A week later, late June 1941, Hitler attacked the Soviet Union. Within days, Churchill reared and proclaimed Russia our ally, and the *Star* received letters praising its editors for their perspicuity.

I was viewed as an instant pundit, since I had been predicting such a development in daily newsroom scuttlebutt. By some fluke of assumption, I was declared the paper's Russian expert. It now seemed that the *Star* might send me to Moscow as a correspondent.

My personal orientation was not critical of Moscow at the time, and I certainly wanted to be a war correspondent. Managing editor A.J. West authorized me to write to the Soviet Ambassador, Omansky, in Washington.

As I was preparing to do this, a most interesting incident happened. At the time, Canada didn't recognize the Soviet Union. The

Editing the United College newspaper, The Manitoban, *1940*

(Left) The mysterious stranger poses at an illegal pinball machine. When the photo was published on the front page of the Winnipeg Tribune *with the fake moustache removed, a certain Parker was the butt of many jokes.*

The United College Dramatics Club. Brother Morten is at the far left, front row.

Wesley Mens Club Executive.

(Left) The official program for "You Can't Beat Fun" co-authored by Samuel Seetner, composer, Earle Beattie, book and lyrics, and myself, story line and production. Monty Hall, later of Hollywood game show fame, was one of the leads.

(Below) Earle Beattie, Sam Seetner, and myself at United College. Working on our 1939 musical comedy, "You Can't Beat Fun".

Certificate of Merit 1939-40

A YEAR OF MANITOBAN

IT SEEMED almost an impossible task, realizing three issues of The Manitoban each week for more than five months, but it has been done. One man obviously, could never do this alone. It took the combined efforts of every individual on the paper to wean "Canada's Other Great Newspaper" away from its palsied, characterless career as a semi-weekly late in news, dilute in features, and doubtful in its sports page literacy. Slowly but surely, The Manitoban has stretched its decaying limbs, taken on new life, limbered up, and become rejuvenated. Today, local dailies as well as the broadcasting stations look to The Manitoban columns for their university news—unable to outscoop it. The sports page editors, young as they are in comparison with those of former years, have adopted a sincerer approach to their task and have rivalled their professional contemporaries in neatness of style. The features section finally evolved itself into a weekly supplement bent on regaining the prestige and standard of its predecessor in 1931. The editorial page has been blessed with correspondents grinding every type of axe and contributing to the vitality of its discussions. Brimming with journalistic health in every one of its departments as it goes into its twenty-sixth year. The Manitoban is destined to realize its proper maturity within

the very near future. Thanks for this must be extended right down to the lowliest cub reporter scavenging news for the date book editor.

The first U.M.S.U. activity to commence the year and the last to finish. The Manitoban has enjoyed a chequered existence during its first year as a thrice weekly. Moving into the new U.M.S.U. Administration Buildings, its staff

EDWARD PARKER — editor-in-chief, who has expressed his appreciation of staff co-operation during the past year, in story and cutlines, on this page.

set to carpentering and won for themselves an inspiring office atmosphere. Then in the rush of the routine "three-a-week," special issues were prepared: Freshmen Issue, Souvenir Jubilee Issue, Christmas Issue, special Sub-Committee Issues—the most popular, of course, being that of the Co-eds Association, and Color Night Issue. Even after regular production ceases with the annual Literary Supplement this Friday, three more specials will have to be prepared. Experiment was not lacking in the various departments of the paper. For the first time in its history The Manitoban availed itself of background color cuts. It also drew more attention to its editorial material by placing it for the first time on page three. All in all, a year of much activity, in which the members of the Varsity fourth estate supplemented their experience on the paper proper with that offered at Press Club meetings and a "one day class in journalism" at The Tribune.

Today the editor takes occasion to gloat and to feel guilty in so doing, for he realizes how much his associates such as Van Sommerfeld, Sid Sheps and Mort Parker have minimized the threatened impossibility of his thrice weekly task. It is to them and to their sub-associates that he wishes to express his heartfelt thanks and appreciation.

—E.P.

NEWS EDITORS
(Top to bottom)

WALTER S. DEWAR — whose bility to invent a feature news ngle has helped to brighten many ront pages.

DOUGLAS BREWER — a fine organizer of reporters and a good udge of news stories.

VINCENT MacDONALD — a patient and tireless editor with an xtraordinary liking for scoops.

MORTEN PARKER — who did some fine pinch-hitting for the editor on many occasions and undertook the difficult task of proofreading at 5 a.m. on Mondays.

VAN SOMMERFELD — managing editor who bore his heavy responsibilities excellently and was a source of great help to the editor.

BRADFORD HENDERSON—who has laid the groundwork for a fine weekly feature section of The Manitoban which might expand with the increasing contributions from the campus.

SPORTS EDITORS
(Top to bottom)

HARVEY DRYDEN — an energetic sports editor with a flair for digging out human interest angle in athletic contests.

GREN ALLEN — the man responsible for most of the excellent page lay outs on page four. A fin writer.

NORM THOMSON — a hard working editor who is fast developing into one of the best sports commentators The Manitoban has ever boasted.

FROM THE MANAGING EDITOR

I should like to take this opportunity of thanking all members of the Manitoban staff who, during the past year have been so helpful and co-operative in the gigantic task of turning out a thrice-weekly news paper. To our news editors I should like particularly to express my thanks for the clockwork regularity with which they have been able to turn out a news page of truly readable interest.

To the sports editor I extend my sincerest appreciation for their fine work. To our feature editor I extend my congratulations. As for our business staff, we are still on sufficiently good terms with them as to be able to borrow money.

Lastly, to the man who made this all possible, our Editor-in-Chief, Ed. Parker.

Thanks again!

—S.F.S.

SIDNEY G. SHEPS — efficient usiness manager who has been ermed the "Rock o' Gibralter" as tribute to his abili'y to overcome l financial storms.

JOHN PANKIW — art editor of The Manitoban whose satirical cartoons and feature draw ngs have approached professional excellence.

FRANK KUCERA — ace photographer who has helped the paper achieve the reputation of the most profusely illustrated campus newspaper in Canada.

AUBREY HALTER:—wide-awake advertising manager whose temper was always swset when page editors protested his increasing en croachments on their space.

The Manitoban *Certificate of Merit 1939-40. Brother Morten followed me as Editor-in-Chief*

The proud University Grad. (The
Crux Studios, Winnipeg)

Morten and Mother.

At United College I found myself a person of some interest to others, the anomaly
of being Jewish and yet an individual completely integrated with others in a
church college. When I elected to go to a church college rather than the provincial
university proper, my father thought it a great idea. "You are in tune with me,"
he said. "You never learn much going with people with whom you already share
bequeathed concepts."

My brother Morten figured importantly in both my life and in my recollections of family experience. My parents welcomed his arrival with as much enthusiasm as when I had arrived eighteen months earlier.

Left to right: Morten, Matt and June Saunders, myself.

The occasion was the World Premiere of "The North West Mounted Police" movie. The tables are turned as Lyn Oberman, Preston Foster and Robert Preston interview yours truly, then Stage and Screen Editor for the Winnipeg Tribune.

Interviewing Madeleine Carroll, star of the "North West Mounted Police" film. The noted actress was dressed in black mourning the death of her lover, a French resistance fighter.

Interviewing Colonel Frank Knox, Secretary of the United States Navy, on my first day on the job for the Montreal Daily Star. *June 16, 1940.*

(Above) The "horseshoe" in the pressroom of the Montreal Daily Star *newspaper. I'm seated, second from the left. 1941.*

(Left) The glamorous Canadian-born MGM movie star, Norma Shearer, launched a Canada Savings Bond drive in Montreal, May 1941. Ms. Shearer, her arms laden with dozens of longstemmed roses, insisted on standing on my left, the better to display her legendary profile.

Russians had no embassy in Ottawa and there were no diplomatic exchanges. With the sudden turn of events, the Russians sent their first delegation to the U.S. and Canada. It was a military mission to arrange support for the war against Germany. The Moscow delegation arrived one July morning and registered at the Mount Royal Hotel. The *Star's* hotel reporter couldn't get through to them. It became a job for the *Star's* Russian expert, namely me. In plain fact, I did not speak Russian. I had picked up a few words from the Ukrainian maids employed in our house when we were children. I could say "butter" and "bread", a few words of this sort. Obviously, a crisis was building for me. Our news desk put a call through to the hotel and asked me to go on the phone and speak Russian.

Since it was such a novelty to have Soviet Russians in Canada, several desk men and reporters hung around to hear how my effort would go. The hotel switchboard answered the phone. I asked for General Galikov, thinking the operator would say he was not taking any calls. Instead, she put the call through and I heard, "Da."

"General Galikov?"

"Da," he replied.

I knew enough words to say I would like an interview, "Ya chotchu interview."

The one-word reply was, "Nyet." Obviously, "No."

Meanwhile, my colleagues were cajoling me.

"Go ahead, talk more Russian."

My future as a foreign correspondent depended upon this moment. The only remaining Russian I could muster were the words "Ya lublu," "I love you," not precisely what I wanted to communicate. Out of pure desperation, I blurted in Yiddish, "Comrade Galikov, you can speak Yiddish perhaps?"

Back in Yiddish came the reply, "How is it that a Jew should be working on a reactionary newspaper?"

"Aren't some Jews reactionaries too?" I countered.

He laughed.

"So," he said, "what can I do for you?"

"I would like to have an interview."

"I can't give you an interview," he explained. "We have no official embassy here and I would not be permitted to protest in the event I was misquoted."

"I won't quote you," I offered, "Just talk to me in good faith."

"Well, come up then," he conceded.

I visited him in his suite. A chunky short fellow, Galikov was later to become a hero at the battle of Stalingrad. I had an interview which I wasn't able to attribute to him, but the content became the basis of articles and editorials.

I related this story to the editor of the *Israelite Press*, who, delighted, wrote a feature about a Winnipeg son who had found a practical use of his knowledge of Yiddish, a justification for long years of Yiddish school learning.

"If you learn Yiddish," my father once counselled, "you will have a great advantage." There was, he said, an old saying, "If you scratch a Russian, you will find a Jew." I had indeed scratched a Russian and found a Jewish general. But I didn't get to Russia and the question didn't come up again.

On one occasion, I covered an important labour meeting and found the main speaker, a British lord, completely incomprehensible. Stuck, I imagined what I would have said in his place and attributed those thoughts to him. As a result, this nobleman called my editor and, to my surprise, instead of complaining, proclaimed that I was the best reporter ever to cover his complicated views.

Managing editor West and the city editor seemed to sustain an ongoing vendetta. They would scream insults at each other across the editorial room. The blasphemy and obscenity was so great that the news desk editor would quickly arrange to give us reporters assignment to get us out of the room. On one occasion, I was told to go and check how many cars in the city bore American licence plates. Of course, in my case, as an eager-beaver cub, I took orders quite literally and wrote such a story. It never ran.

West, a shrewd manager, had heard that some of his staff were considering the formation of a branch of the Newspaper Guild, a U.S.-based trade union for journalists. Aiming to nip in the bud my indoctrination into such an evil organization, West summoned me into his sanctum one morning, sounded me out on trade unionism, found me ambivalent and warned me to guard myself against dangerous affiliations.

I was particularly careful not to mention that I had organized with others and led a student strike at the University of Manitoba to protest having the campus paper printed in a non-union shop. My father, I said, was co-owner of an ethnic printing shop in Winnipeg. This information pleased West. I did not add that Harry Parker was also a long standing member of the International Typographical Union.

West, avuncular, praised my devotion to work, my taut writing style and my good news sense in reportage. As an acknowledgement of my talent, he had decided to elevate me to a desk job. I would still be sent out on special assignments from time to time. This posting, he explained, made me part of management, and that would prevent me from joining any potential trade union.

* * *

Since I loved the legitimate stage, I made a point of going to Her Majesty's Theatre every opening night. Live theatre! Although I was not doing stage and screen reviews in Montreal, I made myself known to the theatre manager as a friendly *Star* reporter and a former stage and screen editor in Winnipeg. The manager introduced me backstage to some of the stars and cast members. I was soon adopted as an insider.

Every night after the show, around eleven p.m., I would rendezvous with the casts of the shows, people like Fay Wray, Anna Sten, Mary Boland, Montey Wooley, Conrad Neagle, Aubrey Smith, Paul Lucas and Elisa Landis. I got to know them well. In turn, they persuaded the theatre management to hire me as their press agent. Here, in Montreal, one could moonlight with a second job. It wasn't quite ethical to be a press agent and a reporter at the same time, but the *Star* allowed me some leeway in getting publicity blurbs into the paper.

At this time, I asked my friend Irving Zweig, whom I had met at the national student conference I had attended the previous year, who he thought was the most beautiful débutante in town. He said, without doubt, Sybil Cohen, a Vivien Leigh type. "But she is beyond you, rich family, real snob." I was undaunted and wrote her a fan letter on *Montreal Star* stationery, explaining that I was from Winnipeg, a newspaperman eager to meet people, and that she was commended as a leading Montreal beauty and personality. Could I meet her? I allowed some days to pass and then I phoned. She was flattered and invited me over to her Westmount house to meet her family. I wore my best suit, designed by Joey Tessler, Winnipeg's 'swinging' tailor. The garment marked me as a brash Westerner.

Tessler, a sports and humour writer, emerged in 1940 as a tailor to the indiscriminate. He had visited me when I was ill in Winnipeg and showed me some cloth that he claimed was amazing. He could punch a pencil through it and the threads wouldn't rip. He demonstrated its invulnerability for me and I, in fever at the time, was impressed. It was the kind of cloth you could turn into awnings. Since I was prostrate, he measured me horizontally while I was lying in bed. The result was a blazing double-breasted garment, big lapels, a Bonnie & Clyde type of suit. Amazingly, it was a good fit. When I appeared before Sybil Cohen in this suit, she barely stifled a guffaw. What a rube from western Canada I must have seemed! I also had acquired a terrible conversational affectation at the time. When she introduced me to her boyfriend, I kept calling him "guy," which really annoyed him. It proved pretty good one-up-manship, since he behaved very haughtily with me. Sybil was intrigued with my connection with the theatre and quickly accepted my invitation that she become a press agent assistant to me.

I was rather shy with Sybil, probably because she struck me as a bit of a cool patrician. She kept talking about New York as the ultimate mecca, and all I could talk about was Winnipeg and what a great town it really was. The last thing she wanted was to date someone who yearned to return to Winnipeg and had this wild taste in suits. I did, during the course of our acquaintance, manage to get into more conventional clothes.

During this time in Montreal, through Irving Zweig, I met a comely Finnish-Canadian girl, blonde and willowy Anna Lisa Paju. Beautiful, unaffected, disarming, I could have fallen in love with her, but at this stage I had the mental reserve that if I were to become a somebody in the future, I could have no entanglements so early in my career. Time spent with Anna Lisa meant dreamy romance, long walks and hours of conversation seated on the strange iron stairways built outside of buildings in Montreal. I didn't get to meet her parents and guessed that Anna Lisa had some reservation in this regard.

Anna Lisa had been my special girl in Montreal. We climbed Mount Royal on summer evenings and listened to open-air symphony concerts. I was, in my own eyes, a dashing figure, a big city reporter with assignments to go to a variety of glamorous events, from Chinese festivals to military jamborees. I could wine and dine while working.

Anna Lisa loved Chinatown, but was put off by the adjoining red light district. Later, on my own, in my assured role as reporter and voyeur, I had to find out what Montreal's red light district was all about, at least from the outside.

Going by the houses and being summoned, winked at and called chéri was vicarious excitement. Women would bare their bosoms as they sat at open windows. This was almost more tension than an imaginative 23-year-old could take.

Back at the paper, West had displayed a liking for my work and made me his protégé. He probably knew that I was moonlighting as a theatrical press agent, but winked at the practice. This moonlighting meant another $10 a week, a handsome sum in the summer of 1941, and I was in my element. Most importantly, I had developed relationships with theatre people.

One actress, Ann Marshall, became a lifetime friend. She was very beautiful. Again my romantic illusions soared. We walked the streets at midnight and I lived up to a self-evoked image of personal gallantry. Shy about holding hands or kissing, I rejoiced in merely sitting with her on street curbs until the early hours. Ours was basically Hollywood emulated innocence which had its own appeal to our erotic senses.

My biggest stage-star crush was Anna Sten, a Russian-Ukrainian actress who had become a Hollywood star. She entertained me in her hotel rooms, fed me caviar and regaled me with stories of past grandeur. I would talk a mile a minute and, as a consequence, we never did embrace. In a strange reversal of preconceived sex roles, it was I who was afraid of being seduced. Anna emoted about how she, as a woman, needed the involvement of a man always, needed the right kind of sexual stimulation, needed the company of a charming guy. She was really giving me the business. I was flattered but scared. To me, this star contact was unreal. I wasn't ready emotionally for it. I was content with a pleasurable platonic relationship while she was there. I played the role of a dedicated, bright-eyed press agent to the hilt.

In Montreal I introduced myself to the Sala brothers, Eric and Emeric, leaders in the Bahai movement, a religious community to which I was referred by a newspaper associate in Winnipeg. I became their house guest and was invited to their farm estate, where they owned cottages and stables. Weekends were great there. We swam, talked and organized the world. The Salas, as Bahais, were openly in favour of a one-world concept, but they frustrated me when they eschewed any political approach for advancing towards this ideal.

One day, I was introduced to horseback riding on a Spanish steed, "Romeo". I was encouraged to lead him into the St. Lawrence River for a swim sans-saddle. What I didn't know was that a horse, when it swims, keeps its head out of the water and its bottom submerged. I thought he would float horizontally. To my surprise and dismay, I found myself going down like a submarine as he stopped wading and began swimming. In panic, I scrambled onto the horse's head, but he threw me off. I was a half mile from shore and I began to swim frantically. Knowing I was a weak swimmer, I began to shout to my comrades to help me. They seemed more concerned about the horse. Someone shouted, "Stand up. It's shallow." I did. I was only waist high and felt the perfect fool.

I furthered a business idea with Eric that evolved out of my experience as a movie editor on the *Winnipeg Tribune*. My mind was oriented to starting newspapers and promoting circulation and advertising. I had learned that movie pages commanded the greatest reader interest in dailies in contrast to other sections of a newspaper. Something as high as 60 percent or 70 percent of a paper's subscribers glance at the entertainment section. I thought it would be wonderful if I gathered all the press material that Hollywood issued to editors – serializations, still photos, contests, and so on – and set up a throw-away shopping paper that was high in reader interest and had great appeal to advertisers.

Emeric thought it a very good idea and advanced me $500 towards furthering the project. Later that fall, I was to test the concept in Winnipeg, with my brother as associate editor. Lonesome for my family, I had been receiving poignant letters from my father. I increasingly became preoccupied with the thought that perhaps he didn't have too much longer to live. I had been away from my family for four to five months.

In mid November, I told managing editor West that I wanted to visit my seriously ill father, and I was given leave to go back to Winnipeg for a short period. He gave me two-weeks advance pay and assured me that my job would be kept open for my return. I had no intention of returning to the *Montreal Star* while my father was still alive. I meant to promote my "audience" newspaper and to stay in Winnipeg.

On my return home in the late fall of 1941, my father was enormously happy to see me. He was not to die at this point. I wrote to A.J. West to inform him that I would not be returning while my father was alive. He wrote saying that he felt my duty was to stay with my father and that I should consider returning to the *Star* at a later date. After six weeks of pay, I thanked him profusely and formally resigned.

From a very early age, I had aspired to become either a lawyer or a journalist, but part of my ego remained tied up with the *Israelite Press*. My hope was that some day I would be its chief editor. Apart from the immediate threat of losing my father, sadness also came with the realization that his partners would survive him, and the dream of the Parker boys owning a newspaper as opposed to working for one was lost.

I visited Eddie Zorn, the general manager of the Famous Players chain in Western Canada and sold him on the idea of an audience-oriented throw-away paper. He agreed to buy $50 worth of advertising a week, enough to cover the cost of printing 25,000 eight-page tabloids. We had to match the Zorn contribution with additional advertising to achieve $100 a week to meet our expenses. My brother and I were the principals of this little company, *The Winnipeg Audience*. We wrote to all the key movie production people in Hollywood and in return, received a tremendous amount of editorial material, glossy photos of the stars, news stories, feature serializations, scene pictures and press books. Our enterprise was exciting and glamorous. We found an office next to Mr. Zorn in the Capital Theatre building and felt very close to the action. The Parker brothers were in show business, acting out a Mickey Rooney-type, glamour-kid script.

Regrettably, our paper, *The Winnipeg Audience,* didn't satisfy the original formula, which was maximum reader interest, maximum circulation, lowest advertising cost. Had it been circulated to every house in the greater Winnipeg area, it would have had assured advertising appeal and impact. We just didn't have enough financing.

My brother and I tossed coins to see who would sell advertising on any particular day and who would prepare copy. Both of us preferred to write. Neither one of us reacted well to the rejections which came with selling but we did manage to promote a basic amount of advertising to keep the paper afloat.

We were also fortunate to find a young girl who yearned to become a newspaperwoman and offered to work for nothing. Hardly a skilled secretary, she was, however, diligent and anxious to please. She had a very persistent habit, however, of excusing herself to go to a sink at the back of our office and wash her hands incessantly, nearly every twenty minutes. We guessed, as amateur Freudians, that this compulsion apparently had something to do with suppressed sexual desires. Her presence in the office gave us the look of big timers, with a blowzy secretary and a broken down typewriter.

In and out of our office came all sorts of Damon Runyon-type characters, the people who hung around show business areas in Winnipeg. One of the fringe benefits of our enterprise was that we could go to the distributors' small screening rooms to preview films. We were among six or seven people privileged to have a first look at a forthcoming attraction. Since I had enjoyed such a privilege when I was the movie editor of the *Tribune*, now, as my own publisher, I sensed a new and more intimate status with Winnipeg's movie business people and was invited to their parties and behind-scene events.

Show business fans sought us out, but we were too naive to take advantage of the succession of young pretty usherettes who came to visit. Puritans of sorts, we were mindful of our peer-group structure: "Don't get involved with any girls or your career will be stopped dead."

One of Winnipeg's most successful theatre managers was Henry Morton, proprietor of the prestigious Garrick Theatre. While he gave us token advertising, he said he would be much more interested in our services as press agents to promote attendance at his movie house. An opportunity soon arose to test our ingenuity. A particularly inept movie was coming to town, not a sleeper, but a stinker, "The Shanghai Gesture" starring Victor Mature and Gene Tierney. This turkey had to be one of the world's worst pictures. Morton said he would give us $5 for our weekly advertising and another $50 for stunt promotion.

We were being paid to use our wits. A solution occurred to me from my experience in promoting classified advertising for the *Montreal Star*. I recommended business personal ads plugging "The Shanghai Gesture." The come-on ad ran something like this: "Do you have the sultry appeal of a Gene Tierney, does your voice register with the magic impact of a Victor Mature? If you feel you have a theatrical talent, you can have it auditioned and tested in the Garrick Theatre's 'promote your voice' contest. Please dial this number and say the following, 'I am the most alluring woman in the world. Men have thrown themselves at my feet since I was fourteen. It has meant nothing to me to push men aside after I have used them ruthlessly.'" This script had little to do with the actual movie, but it aroused interest. Men would be invited to say seductively, "I am irresistible to women," and so on.

Within hours of these ads appearing in the press, every phone at the Garrick Theatre was tied up. Overnight we had to get a battery of six phones set up in our own office away from the theatre to handle the incoming calls. Children would phone, declaring "To know me is to die happy." Hundreds of people tried to get through. It became a local craze. This sort of stunt hadn't been attempted before.

People in fact came to the movie to see if they were indeed as good as Gene Tierney or Victor Mature. There were lineups for three or four days for a movie that was failing everywhere else on the continent. By the fourth day, unfortunately, the public had caught on that "The Shanghai Gesture" was a clinker and attendance collapsed, but I had had a further taste of press agenting and I was heady with the experience.

That winter of 1941 I was preoccupied mainly with the publishing of *The Winnipeg Audience*. I also undertook to produce a protest play, "Awake and Sing" by Clifford Odets, a story of Jewish family life during the Depression. To make the acting more realistic, I collaborated with a Yiddish writer in adapting and translating the English spoken by the old folks in the play into the language they would have normally used, Yiddish. The scenes would play more naturally. The production was an artistic success and received great press reviews, but it was a box office disaster. After all, you had to be bilingual to understand it.

In spring 1942, my father was once more taken to the hospital. He had been in a coma for some days, but in the ambulance he struggled to raise himself, asking, "Where am I?" In the hospital, when he was approaching his death and fighting to maintain consciousness, it seemed ironic to me that Sam Berg and Sam Shore should be near his bed discussing him as though he had already died.

I went back to work, and then, that afternoon, my brother met me as I walked towards him on Main Street and said, "Dad's dead." I experienced an irrepressible feeling of relief mixed with guilt. I knew the pain my father had endured and I knew the hopelessness of his surviving his illness. I remembered my father's admonition to me, "When I stop living, stop grieving and start to think of my life as a unity, a whole and in retrospect. Start rejoicing in the part which you think was remarkable." But his departure found me with conflicting emotions, my grief welling up and my father stifling it, exhorting me to rejoice in the life he had lived and in his remembered admirable qualities.

Most importantly he wanted to be remembered as a man who had loved and respected his sons. My brother and I continued to respect our father's intellect as much greater than our own. He had always challenged our statements, but, on the other hand, he respected the fact that we held our own viewpoints. Our father really listened to us. Nothing brings out an awareness of another person more than the fact that he is listening to you. During our school years, he had encouraged us to think out loud in his presence so he could help us build our argument for school debates.

Back at our home, Aunt Esther was frenetically soaping up mirrors to prevent them from reflecting images. My mother sat stunned and silent. Hundreds of people came to the funeral. It was a funeral that couldn't have a religious base, because this wasn't the way Harry Parker had wanted it.

My father's funeral bier had an honour guard throughout an entire day. I hadn't seen this before. My father had held few public offices in his life, none of importance. But he had made himself heard on occasion from the floor of public meetings and community platforms, had written humorous and satirical skits and verses, and was much beloved in a Mark Twain or Sholem Aleichem way.

The funeral hearse didn't proceed to the cemetery directly, but made the rounds of Jewish institutions with which he identified. The procession made stops at the *Israelite Press*, the conservative Talmud Torah, the social democratic I.P. Peretz school and the Marxist-oriented Sholem Aleichem school. The casket was borne by hand and his portrait was prominently displayed in each locale. When we finally arrived at the cemetery, we, his family, couldn't get close to the grave because of the crowds, but we recognized the folk tribute. A particular compliment to me was to see many of my university associates in the crowd. My respect for my father had become widely known at the university.

May 6 became a dramatic date for me. My father had died on May 6. In 1945, May 6 was the date when Hitler assumedly killed himself. That date signalled the end of the war. On May 6, 1958 my daughter Ara was born.

The weeks of May went by. Our tabloid paper was failing, hardly meeting its printing bill. We had to shut it down before it created insurmountable difficulties. We had been disappointed in the advertising salesmen we had attracted. Crack people who had promised to come off their jobs on the *Winnipeg Tribune* to help us, didn't when the crunch came.

In June of 1942, I renewed my correspondence with A.J. West at the *Montreal Star*. I couldn't see myself going back on staff at the *Winnipeg Tribune* after publishing a rival, if modest, publication. I would dearly have willed at that time that my father's firm offer me an editorial role, but David Simkin, the son of my father's partner, was not anxious to have either Parker boy come into his enterprise. We were journalist-publisher types and a threat.

Bitterness towards the *Israelite Press* came following my father's death when management negotiated for the purchase of his stock from my mother. She had 3,000 shares and 30 percent of the entire capitalization of the company. Despite the 1941 economic turnaround and despite the fact that I was educated in economics, the company lawyer persuaded me to counsel my mother to sell our father's shares. If she didn't, he predicted, she would lose out entirely.

He was of the belief that the remaining shareholders would avoid declaring dividends, and the stock would be worthless in my mother's hands. He foresaw Simkin et al. withdrawing net earnings through bonuses to themselves. As I learned later in life, a company aspiring to grow would not deplete its treasury through salary withdrawals.

The $3,000 offered to my mother seemed the world to us then, but of course it really wasn't much. The arrangement was to pay my mother $50 a month without interest. Ten years later, the printing end of the *Israelite Press*, Universal Printers, was sold for $1,600,000. Had the Parkers held on to their stock, we would have had about half a million dollars worth of equity!

After the sale, my brother resolved to stay in Winnipeg and go back to university. His girlfriend, Gudrun Bjerring, had a lover's pact with him. She would take a job in Ottawa and he would follow her at some later date. It was flattering to Morten and complimentary to all of us in the family that Gudrun felt so drawn to Morten. She had been elected Freshman Queen in her first year. In her graduating year, she became Lady Otick of United College and president of all women at the University of Manitoba.

My brother furthered a romantic relationship with her in a gentle unobtrusive way. He would meet her for walks after school and talks between classes. Gudrun would see him between five and seven some evenings and then she would go off on her many other dates. Gudrun's social engagements were mostly with boys of the establishment, the sons of wealthy grain exchangers and brokers. She was the belle of United College and the University of Manitoba.

To my mother, a romance with a non-Jewish girl was not appealing. But she had often said to us that, if it were Princess Elizabeth who wanted to marry one of her sons, then she would overcome her objections to intermarriage.

My father had thought very highly of Gudrun. Perhaps the fact that Morten was part of a newspaper family influenced her to seek a job as a reporter. On graduation, she went to work for the *Winnipeg Free Press*. Here again, she was most popular and most successful. One of the people she interviewed was John Grierson, then National Film Board Commissioner. Grierson, a Scotsman, had shaped the film bureau of the federal government into a dynamic and exciting film agency. He was the father of the National Film Board of Canada.

A witty and rapid-thinking man, Grierson was impressed with Gudrun and had offered her a job in Ottawa. Gudrun had agreed. She had expected Morten to continue to write short stories and poems and to send them to her. When he defaulted, she would suspend corresponding with him as a sanction. She became Morten's taskmaster, urging him to reach certain objectives. Her role with Morten was not unlike the one I had played. As a result, Morten wrote two or three magnificent short stories; one of them won the top prize at the University of Manitoba in 1941, the Chancellor's prize for the best writing of the year. As editor-in-chief and front-page columnist for *The Manitoban* in 1942, he wrote some very perceptive features.

As for me, I decided to go back to Montreal and take my chances on getting a job. I had a non-committal letter from A.J. West saying that, if I came, we could talk about employment possibilities. I would stop over in Ottawa for a few days en route.

CHAPTER **5**

OTTAWA –
THE WAR YEARS

Ottawa was an exciting, frenetic city in wartime. I took a room at the YMCA. My roommate was a handsome navy officer, Donald MacDonald, later to become provincial leader of the NDP in Ontario in the 1950s and 1960s. We became good friends on short acquaintance.

One of my first destinations in Ottawa was to visit Gudrun. Obviously, Morten was topic one on our talk agenda. She then told me that a college friend of ours, Doug Best, who had attempted a career with the *Winnipeg Free Press*, was now doing all the hiring and firing for one of the biggest departments in wartime Ottawa, the Department of Munitions and Supply. She suggested I see him, which I did.

The scene was out of Hollywood, Doug Best surrounded by two or three secretaries and long line-ups of job seekers forming outside his offices. Best enjoyed the idea of spending a moment with Ed Parker, a fellow graduate of United College, editor-in-chief of *The Manitoban* and a campus wheel. He particularly relished the situation of my coming to him for a job and this proved a very fortunate development for me.

There was a vacancy in the publicity department of the Department of Munitions and Supply. He directed me to see Gordon Garbutt, then publicity director and second-in-command of the branch. In those days, if the personnel department sent someone, you hired him. Garbutt, a small-town, conservative-type newspaperman, was suspicious of college graduates. He had worked his way from copy boy through the editorial jobs to managing editor of a small-city newspaper. Fortunately, I impressed him as, at least, polite, and he introduced me to his boss, Rielle Thompson, an Irish Canadian proud of his French first name. Thompson had made remarkable efforts to master the French language. A tall thin man, he was a grand extrovert and quick to laugh.

"If you can write good letters, you're on," he declared. "I don't care if you can write anything else."

He regarded effective letter writing as the most telling of skills. My own respect for creative letter writing was certainly stimulated by Rielle Thompson. He set me the challenge of writing a letter of acknowledgement to a correspondent. My draft must have pleased him. Within a day or two I was hired as a publicity officer in the Department of Munitions and Supply, a burgeoning denizen of government under one of the most aggressive and interesting ministers in Canadian history, the Hon. Clarence Decatur Howe.

I rushed to my room at the YMCA to share the great news with my roommate Donald MacDonald. MacDonald was extraordinarily complimentary and impressed. It was then that he confided his own ambitions.

"I envy you working for C.D. Howe," he explained. "Howe is one of the great men of government. I envy such people more than anything. I want to run for parliament." Then he speculated out loud, "If I were to run for the federal parliament, for a Quebec constituency, I would present myself as a Liberal. It's the only way to get elected in that province. In Ontario, I would run as a CCFer, out of conviction."

102

He later became leader of the Ontario New Democratice Party and opposition leader in the House in the fifties and sixties.

My first morning at work, I required a front-desk courier to guide me through the rabbit warren that constituted that all-important centre for Canadian munitions and supply planning, direction, and management. Director Gordon Garbutt greeted me cordially and took me on tour of the offices. The office to which I was assigned was to be shared in the first months with our bilingual translator.

Months later, I shared an office with our first woman associate, Phyllis Poland, a young but seasoned newspaperwoman from Montreal, with whose husband I had worked as a reporter on the *Montreal Star.* Phyllis converted me to a full-status pro-feminist. She also proved my greatest supporter when I ventured quite often to concoct daring stunts to gain favourable publicity notice for our industrial achievements to boost labour morale and to serve other such worthy wartime objectives.

I was assigned the job of roving reporter, and my schedule included a different division to visit each day, from guns, tanks, ships, planes to raw material and controls, that sort of thing. In the course of the months, I found myself not only writing news releases, photo lines and articles, but also speeches and text for the department's annual book, *The Industrial Front,* a summary of regulations and achievements.

Now employed in Ottawa, I moved out of the "Y" to a room down the street in a ramshackle rooming house. The place made me feel queasy about its cleanliness. I slept on top of the covers rather than under them. I was afraid of bed-bug infections – a well-founded anxiety. The general stench in the place was so bad at times that, on one occasion, I bought fresh grapes, the kind you use to make wine, and hung clusters on the curtain rods and on the bed frame. My place soon had the scent of a vineyard.

My early rooming circumstances provided material for stories which I wrote for the amusement of new acquaintances. When I was lonely, I wrote.

In Ottawa, Irving Zweig, my Montreal friend, was my great private audience and booster for my creative writing. Big, burly Irving, on his arrival in Ottawa, had no place to stay. I invited him to share my modest room. He was going to work for the National Research Council.

All I had was a single bed. In those days, we were hardly aware of such a phenomenon as homosexuality. The idea of two grown men sleeping in one bed was as natural to us as first-generation Canadians as it would be to two immigrant Greeks or Poles in similar circumstances. Irving, however, was so huge that we couldn't both be on our backs at the same time. By arrangement, one would sleep on his side when the other was on his back or on his stomach. We learned to alternate on the slightest movement. Zweig at times would fall off the bed and take me with him. Before he fell asleep, Irving would find everything very funny, including my counter-attacking the house odours with the scent of grapes.

A young lady in that house caught my eye. Rather shy and of Slavic origin, she gave confusing signals. We would talk about becoming lovers and she hinted that she would leave her door open at certain times so that I might visit. I hardly knew how to act, but her proposal fed my sexual fantasies rather well at the time.

In my early weeks in Ottawa, my problem was to meet people socially. Walks along the Rideau canal, mainly by myself, were a major recreational activity most evenings. I resorted to the gambit I had employed in Montreal, asking who the most popular Jewish girls were and then writing to them on my office stationery. The girls I did meet this way, however, were prim and small-town Ottawa. As in Winnipeg, when I called at their homes, I was sized up immediately by the family as a potential prospect for marriage.

Within my first month, I met girls in the office I could date and take to movies, but my behaviour was quite diffident. My new-found associates at work introduced me to the wonders of a streetcar ride to Hull and an evening spent drinking coke and eating sandwiches at the Standish Hall located across the river in high-living vibrant Quebec. The establishment was exciting and glamorous, noisy with the shouts of Canadian military personnel and visitors from throughout Canada. I was also intrigued to hear patrons speaking a mix of English and French. But I was lonely and homesick in those early weeks, a universal condition which helped me empathize with other temporary civil servants.

Eager for social involvement and leisure time activity, I searched the Ottawa newspapers daily for news of amateur theatricals. I was rewarded almost immediately. The Ottawa Little Theatre was holding open auditions for its fall production of "My Sister Eileen."'

My reasoning led me to believe that Ottawa's notorious shortage of males during wartime would find my acting talents in demand. The leads were indeed for women, an obviously astute selection of play material. Nevertheless, there were many bit parts for men. I was given two roles, a street drunk and a fully uniformed Brazilian sailor.

My involvement with this play's production committed me to surrender most of my free evenings for some six weeks, a most fortuitous development. I met and enjoyed the company of talented actors, including Leith MacDonald, who was delightful in the lead role, Amelia Hall, later to become one of the valued players at the Stratford Festival, and Marjorie Margolies, one of Ottawa's most popular actresses. My circle of friends was widening. It was through Leith that I met Lorne Greene. Subsequently I was instrumental in recommending him to be the narrator of our department documentaries. Greene already was celebrated as the CBC "Voice of Doom" on the nightly national news, the most important radio broadcast of the day.

I first became aware of homosexuality in Ottawa. In my reportorial rounds for the Department of Munitions and Supplies, I routinely checked for stories with the heads of various divisions responsible for the production of a range of items from guns, ships and planes to contraceptives. One such assistant director, Stewart, thought I was particularly amusing. A very friendly fellow, he invited me to his apartment for a drink and then artfully turned all conversation towards the virtue of affection of one man for another. This alerted me to his strange pre-occupation, but I didn't then understand him. I played it so dumb, he decided not to make a play for me and backed off. He was in every way a gracious gentleman. Subsequently, we became platonic friends, and I accepted him as a person, apart from his sexual preferences. I also appreciated his restraint and social discretion.

Stewart seemed masculine in every other way, but his early talk was a useful alert. Sometime later he introduced me to a friend of his, then working on the *Ottawa Journal*. We were sitting next to each other at a table in the cafeteria at the Château Laurier. Suddenly, I was startled by his placing his hand on my knee and squeezing. My instinct was to punch him. I rose as though triggered and left. This incident was very disconcerting. I was later to learn more about the depth and prevalence of homosexual activity in Ottawa. Out of context with any experience I had had previously, this was one of my early surprises in life.

The Ottawa Little Theatre gave me my first taste of identification in a new community, and very shortly my aggressive, competitive, social spirit was aroused. I was soon organizing a drama club for those who were not getting enough acting exposure at the Ottawa Little Theatre.

At that time, above a restaurant called Bowles, a small recreation hall was run by a venerable but modest society called the Ottawa Civil Service Recreation Association. It then had 200 or 300 paying members. I was to play an important role in bringing this organization to life, but at this point, my interest in it was peripheral. Irving Zweig introduced me to the society's Friday-night dances. The stenographers and clerks of the civil service would come to socialize. There were subdued lights and soft music, with much dancing and a considerable number of wall flowers. It was wartime. On any one social evening, there could be 150 girls there coveting dances with 30 men, a strange experience. Oddly, I was more intrigued with the amplifier system than the young maidens. This basic broadcasting set-up was something I could use in simulating radio program productions. The recreational society was only too glad to let me form a drama club that would meet on Sundays. I gathered twenty people together, including my friend Stewart, who brought some of his friends, all "straight" I thought, and we "broadcast" radio plays. Scripts were typed by volunteers. Sunday evenings became a great social event for me.

* * *

Irving Zweig and I, by this time, had moved out of our original rooming house and found a room in the apartment of an elderly Jewish couple. I was enormously amused by my landlady's speech eccentricities. She had a speech pattern whereby she repeated either the first or middle word of each sentence, in a flourish at the end, "So you are comfortable, so." "Why don't you come home early, early why?" She was so amusing that I wrote several short stories about her. These stories beguiled friend Irving so greatly that he took to duplicating my scripts and reading them to his girlfriends, as seduction ploys on his dates. Irving would invite them to make themselves comfortable on his bed and offer to read them Ed Parker's stories. This was a good excuse, I'm sure. I was falling into my teenage pattern of providing stories as background for other people's love-making.

Irving and I found the Château Laurier cafeteria a marvellous place to meet people from other departments. One Saturday afternoon, an arresting-looking, handsome woman, probably fifteen years my senior, joined in our conversation. A native Ottawan, her name was Ann Cohen. Ann swept Irving and me into her entourage and took us to her home to meet her husband. Her home became a meeting place for young people like myself, writers like Len Peterson and Gordon Burwash and their girlfriends. The hit record at that time was "Oklahoma", and we must have played and danced to it every which way.

The Cohens would drive my friends and me to beaches and fried-chicken restaurants in the Laurentians. Ann encouraged me and built my self-esteem, and I found myself a personality in Ottawa, among other talented people. At the Cohen soirées introduction followed introduction, and through the many bright people working in the publicity offices of different departments, a potentially dynamic group of social activists coalesced.

At work I was the wild idea man on the munitions and supply staff. My brainstorms seemed always a bit risky for my cautious superiors. Nevertheless, they listened to me whenever an idea was needed for staging a publicity stunt. For example, to commemorate the production of our first Lancaster bomber, I suggested that this first bomber should be launched at a big press rally at Malton, Ontario, and then flown directly overseas, bomb Berlin, and return, hopefully unscathed. My proposal was duly judged as wild, but was nevertheless sent to the minister, C.D. Howe. To everyone's astonishment, he approved it.

I didn't contemplate the macabre possibility of the crew being shot down in their sortie over Germany. I hadn't even realized that Lancaster bombers couldn't fly such a distance without refueling. The plane had to proceed from Toronto to Montreal to Gander. In actual fact, it wasn't the plane from Malton that did bomb Berlin, but we did transfer the original National Film Board crew to the one that did. The result was a film called "Target Berlin", for which I was co-writer with Jeff Hurley. In this way, I developed a close liaison with the National Film Board and particularly with Hurley. The latter sang my praises to John Grierson and urged him to hire me.

Through my developing involvement with the film board, I was able to influence my munitions and supply department to sponsor the budget for a film about our country's industrial effectiveness during the war. The resulting documentary, "Smoke and Steel", was widely exhibited in Canada and among our Allies. Grierson wasn't particularly happy that I was collaborating in the writing of the film in my capacity as a munitions department publicist. He preferred having his own people produce the film scripts. He took great pains to see that the film board was not viewed as a servant of any other department. To correct the situation, he tried the ploy of offering me a job.

It was tempting, but Rielle Thompson intervened quite crossly. He felt I was being pirated away from him. Job hopping in the civil service wasn't ethical. I, too, had mixed feelings about the offer and divided loyalties. I couldn't face the idea of taking advantage of my own opportunity and leaving a short-handed department which had been particularly good to me. Thompson, in his affection for me, invited me to his home for Christmas dinner and leaned heavily on the theme of loyalty and of his aversion to interdepartmental staff stealing in wartime Ottawa.

I stalled for time, suggesting by way of compensatory activity, that I organize monster afternoon and evening movie screenings at the Capitol theatre for all M and S employees. We would feature NFB documentaries, including "Smoke and Steel". Both Grierson and Thompson were pleased with this suggestion and the Hon. C.D. Howe promised to address the crowd at each performance. John Grierson offered to introduce Howe.

To ensure capacity attendances, I had printed and distributed about 10 percent more tickets than there were seats in the Capitol theatre. Thompson went into a panic and threatened to have my head if an overflow crowd were left outside the movie house. But it all worked out fine. The house was indeed packed, standing room only, but everyone was accommodated. I was hero for a day.

At that time, my brother's fiancée, Gudrun, was very anxious to have Morten come to Ottawa. She showed Grierson some of Morten's writings and identified him as Ed Parker's brother. Grierson knew me favourably by now. I also knew Ralph Foster, then the head of graphics for the National Film Board. With Ralph, I talked up Morten's abilities. As a consequence of Gudrun's and my intercessions, Morten was offered a job in the graphics department.

In the interest of their own careers, Morten and Gudrun became increasingly apprehensive that I, too, might join the film board. A family compact group would have been too cozy, they felt, and would attract criticism and opposition. My role with my brother in the past was that of an elder sibling and Gudrun became instinctively protective on Morten's behalf. She wanted Morten to prosper in his own right and felt that I might overshadow him. She certainly seemed more defensive and anxious whenever I talked about the possibility of my working for the NFB.

Later in life, when he became a movie director with the National Film Board, one of Morten's most successful documentaries was a film called "The Weekly Newspaper". Morten's reverence for our father was reflected in the themes of many of his films – fighting cancer, building trade unions, helping underprivileged countries and advancing human rights.

My liaison with the film board was only one of many preoccupations. I was soon caught up in other things. The munitions and supply department itself was a most exciting place. War related industrial achievement stories were in the making.

One stirring event I instigated was a visit by five Chinese generals to accept the 500,000th Bren gun produced at the Inglis plant in Toronto. Our department organized quite a press junket in honour of the event.

Through Ann Cohen, Irving and I met a rather elegant, middle-aged bachelor, Myer Lipson. A retired millionaire in his 40s, he was planning to spend his winters in Florida. He had a very impressive apartment and offered it to us rent-free if we agreed to pay the maintenance costs of $100 a month. We were earning $50 a week each and could swing it, although $100 a month was a high rent at the time. Eventually, we recruited two additional chaps and the four of us cavorted in our "millionaire's" pad. We invited Ann Cohen and her group of assorted friends regularly, and Ottawa became home and a happy social area for me.

The Somerset Street apartment was something like a set for a stage comedy. It had two beds, plus a couch which came apart in two sections. We called the latter contraption "the rack" and tossed quarters to see who would sleep on it.

Entertaining a girl privately with three other men in an apartment was a complex situation. Each of us was supposed to knock on the apartment door before entering, thus giving inmates time to compose themselves. Irving made the most expansive use of the apartment. He would turn the radio on softly, invite his girl companion to kick off her shoes, and then entertain her by reading my unpublished stories. This was his "sure-fire" seduction technique. If I returned unexpectedly and knocked before entering, he would desperately whisper at the door, "Walk around the corner." I walked around the corner quite a lot in those days.

* * *

One of the most poignant assignments given me at munitions and supply involved interviewing returning Dieppe veterans. The department had sent me to Montreal to meet the first group of survivors of Canada's tragic raid on the coast of occupied France. This military action in late 1942 was a negative propaganda exercise, designed to demonstrate that a second front and an Allied attack on Hitler from the west was impractical. Most of the journalists in Canada were very cynical of this fiasco. The action, it was widely believed, was planned so that it would fail. Many Canadians lost their lives as the troops came against insurmountable fire and were withdrawn. When I met these returning soldiers in Montreal, they were openly anguished and embittered. They dunned, among other things, their equipment, like the Sten gun. Some said the best equipment was the Lee Enfield rifle, a one-shot-at-a-time weapon from World War I. They claimed they had better results with it than with any of their automatic weapons.

Among these survivors, to my surprise, I encountered my former city editor of the *Winnipeg Tribune*, Bill Osler, who had become a major. He had been severely wounded. Stone drunk, he nevertheless recognized me. I had a flush of guilt, not being in uniform as he was, but he didn't treat me with any deprecation. There was great sadness. He told me that he was never going to be a newspaperman again. He was going to retire to a farm in Alberta. I was much affected by the interview.

Accompanying me on this assignment was another PR man, an explosives publicist. When we arrived in Montreal the night before our Dieppe project, he said, "Let's go for the girls." To his surprise, he found me diffident. He thought me quite a prude. The next day he saw this shy, unassertive guy Parker turn into a journalistic dynamo, interviewing dozens of Dieppe veterans. I was very energized and I dug out some tremendous stories about weapons, both the faulty and the effective. I offered my stories to the *Montreal Star* and they ran my copy on the front page.

In our publicity section, we had few opportunities to meet with the already legendary C.D. Howe. When we did, we saw a man of quick decisions and great temper, but a man of action. Our modest publicity division consisted of five men and one woman. I didn't find the tremendous work load onerous and found periods of lull when I could attempt some creative writing. Writing five and six publicity stories a day was normal. Our productivity could have equated a branch of thirty or forty people.

The steno girls who flittered around pleasantly coveted me, the only bachelor on staff, as a romantic catch, but I didn't catch on to the courting signals of women. On one occasion, I was invited by one of our ladies to a weekend at her summer home. Thompson's secretary came. In the middle of the night, she was awakened by lightning and came to my bed for comforting. I actually consoled her without daring to make love to her. She broke into tears. I thought she was just frightened, but obviously she was frustrated and angry. Men were at such a premium in wartime that one was offered various sexual opportunities. But every flirtation seemed to suggest a compromising situation. It could be dangerous in our work, somebody could hold some sort of blackmail against us. We weren't without anxiety about wartime spies. This possibility was of course highly dramatized in our work, but, as publicity officers, we were in possession of security material.

The Ottawa scene was an unreal world. Far from the fighting front, my colleagues and I were nevertheless caught up with the excitement related to the war news. The fun part, embassy cocktail parties and press conferences for world leaders such as Franklin Roosevelt, De Gaulle or Princess Juliana of the Netherlands, gave us a sense of being privileged.

My work with the Department of Munitions and Supplies proved a rewarding professional experience. Although I had a very high opinion of myself, I was also taught some humility. Director Gordon Garbutt didn't accept my copy as anything close to perfect. He was tough on me on occasion and he explained his craft and taught me the ropes. He would always press me to defend my work, to make a case for my editorial approach. On the other hand, Rielle Thompson liked my journalistic flair. As for the rest of the staff, I was on the whole reasonably popular with them, although considered in the main a kid. When I had received the job offer with the National Film Board, I instantly became more valued in my publicity department. The staff collectively made a pitch for me to stay.

* * *

I was residing in a rented room on a street next to the prime minister's home. We were practically neighbours. Mackenzie King would walk his dog on Sunday mornings on Rideau Street. I would pass with a "Good morning, Mr. King." He would smile and say, "Good morning," in response.

It was a ceremonial thing we did for weeks. I wouldn't accost him or start conversation with him, although I felt that he wouldn't have been adverse to a chat. But I was too shy and I respected his privacy. It was interesting that all pedestrians left him alone on his walks. Mackenzie King was a figure who commanded respect and awe in me. I had written my famous University of Manitoba editorial in 1940, "We will vote Liberal but we won't like it," inspired by King's parliamentary experience. As a student, I had concerned myself about Mackenzie King all though the Depression. Here was a Prime Minister who had survived in office for over 20 years, interrupted by only one period out of power, between 1930 and 1935.

King had been roundly booed by Canadian troops in the United

Kingdom when he inspected them during a visit. Shocked by the discourtesy and very much concerned about his own image, he sent the word out to key people in public relations work, "Think about what Mackenzie King could do that would provide him with a more imaginative image, a common touch."

At the time, King George VI of England was greatly publicized and applauded for having limited himself to five or six inches of water for his bath, thus demonstrating that the King was conserving water and making sacrifices during wartime.

I addressed myself to this approach in a publicity meeting with the prime minister. It wasn't that I wanted Mackenzie King to take a bath in five or six inches of water. We hardly had to conserve this resource in Canada. I did, however, think that it would be in his favour if he were to don overalls and do "token" work for an afternoon in the Ottawa Car and Foundry plant, turning out some of the nuts and bolts. King didn't entertain the idea very long, dismissing it with a glower. I crept into the woodwork and could feel my superiors saying "Never let Ed Parker close enough to King to make any suggestion like that again."

It was not difficult to meet people in high office in Ottawa on a casual basis. A favourite meeting place was the Château Laurier cafeteria where royalty mixed with commoners. The atmosphere was exciting and stimulating, the food marvellous. It was there that I met David Lewis, then secretary of the CCF destined to become national leader of the New Democratic Party in the late sixties and early seventies. Through Ann Cohen I met some of the greats of the CCF – Tommy Douglas, later to become Premier of Saskatchewan, and Clare Gillis, MP from Glace Bay, Nova Scotia. As a civil servant, however, I guided myself circumspectly, relating to people of all parties in the context of my work as a government publicity officer. I fraternized with the publicity officers of the Wartime Prices and Trade Board, of the Wartime Information Board and of the National Film Board. Many were newspaper men whom I had met at the *Winnipeg Tribune* or the *Montreal Star.*

So far removed from the bombings in Europe, our lives in Ottawa were truly a world apart. The German armies moved eastward until they were finally defeated at Stalingrad. That was the turning point in community emotion. Ottawa in spring and summer meant pleasure, having walks along the Rideau Canal, dancing in the parks, canoe trips, rides in Ann Cohen's car, fried chicken in little restaurants in the suburbs. If we had been more objective, we could well have developed strong guilt feelings about our involvement. It was wartime, and yet here I was, 23 years old, having a remarkably happy time, going to soirées at Standish Hall, Sunday movies in Hull, and recreational club parties on Friday evenings.

The Hon. C.D. Howe, Minister of Munitions and Supply, was concerned about the availability of recreational outlets for the thousands of temporary civil servants in Ottawa. Our publicity department was encouraged to be sympathetic to the needs of civil servants. Much as it served my fantasies, I couldn't take it upon myself to personally bring happiness to 20,000 single young women. However, as a consequence of my involvement in the drama club, I was invited to join the board of directors of the Civil Service Recreation Association.

The Ottawa Civil Service Recreation Association (OCSRA) in 1942 was a modest organization with only 500 members. It provided a program of bowling on Sundays and dancing on Fridays. There was a great need in Ottawa for mass recreation, but the organization was too limited to meet the demand.

I raised the question with my boss Rielle Thompson about the possibility of my helping the Ottawa recreation association more directly by way of publicity. Since we were promoting labour morale everywhere else in Canada, why not labour morale in Ottawa. Thompson confirmed the need and mentioned that Prime Minister Mackenzie King had received far too many letters from concerned parents asking the government to do something for the young people in Ottawa. The temporary civil servants were obviously not happily engaged during their leisure hours. Thompson suggested I develop photo stories on recreational programming in Ottawa, featuring the work of the Civil Service Recreational Association.

This was a publicity bonanza. I had a budget of $1,000 to spend on photos. Working with the National Film Board, I arranged glossy-style coverage of the recreation activities. There was only one problem – there wasn't much to report.

The board of directors of the OCSRA invited me to propose a plan to promote and enlarge their association. I startled them when I came up with a recommendation that we build a large membership in the thousands. We would try to interest the Minister of Finance, the Hon. Mr. Ilsley, in arranging a 25¢ per month payroll deduction per member.

Ilsley agreed, subject to the provision that we get a minimum of 5,000 members. Although the target figure stunned the committee, it didn't disturb me very much; I was too young and brash to think small. I had $1,000 of publicity money to use and the OCSRA voted me more. By this time, I was running the publicity committee. I recruited Morten, Gudrun and other members of the National Film Board, in fact, anyone I knew in the radio and information bureaus as well. Our publicity committee grew to about eighteen people, larger than that of the original recreation association board and we planned a campaign to register members en masse. I inveigled the NFB to take photos without charge. Most importantly, I recommended a corporate name change, and the OCSRA became RA.

I was busy simulating activities. For example, I would recruit beautiful girls and handsome guys to come to the Château Laurier Hotel swimming pool. There I would direct them to have a merry time, splashing away, setting up by implication an RA activity. Other civil servants were shown boxing, painting and attempting ballet. In this way, I had a variety of activities dramatized from arts and crafts to music and drama, from coin collecting to fencing. These photos became the main ingredient of a tabloid newspaper.

Bill Cranston, later a senior consultant to the province of Ontario,

116

owned a printing plant and offered to publish and distribute the tabloid at no cost in return for the privilege of selling the advertising. Our first issue carried the banner headline, "Recreation for 10,000." We listed and offered every recreational activity imaginable. My assumption was that people would check more interests than they could possibly indulge. It was a smorgasbord table, with the invitation to fill your plate beyond capacity. The first newspaper spoke of free movies, concerts and other mass entertainment. All this would be worth much more than the annual $3 membership fee. Free movies on Sunday at least once a month would themselves be worth 50¢ times twelve, twice the value of a year's membership fee. Members couldn't lose. The campaign offered a nearly irresistible package.

Promotion made little demand on the association's budget. We made our glamorous publicity photos available to the two metropolitan newspapers, the *Citizen* and *Journal,* suggesting to their city desks that the RA was destined to become a much bigger civil service organization, with great impact. Without actually having yet recruited such a membership, I began speaking of 10,000 civil servants joining up. Under such representation, it was difficult for newspapers to deny us publicity. A radio station donated three half-hour slots a week and subsequently a half-hour time period every day. Posters, white on red, proclaimed "Join the RA Today." These cards appeared inside all buses and streetcars. The message was also plastered on billboards.

Ottawa had never seen a campaign quite like this. Even federal elections had not been run with such pizzazz. The film board set itself to making a film. Radio spots were offered by the CBC. The deluge was concentrated for one week. The climax was a free movie on a Sunday. Anyone who had signed a membership form automatically received free tickets. By the end of the week, we had 4,000 signatures.

For Sundays, I had scrounged together a film program. I couldn't get Hollywood films on loan for commercial use. Instead, the National Film Board loaned us Russian films with English soundtracks and English films with Russian soundtracks. The main feature was a drama about a Russian ski patrol. National Film Board documentaries and some short subjects from Britain rounded out the selection, such as how to build a plane, how to conserve water, and how to avoid a cold – themes you would never go to see if the films weren't offered free.

The scheme worked. When I arrived at the theatre with the film reels, there was a line-up of about 800 people. People would sign their memberships in the lobby and proceed into the theatre. We filled our first house. I rented another theatre down the street, and we started to direct the crowds there and to relay-run the movie cans between the two houses.

By the end of the day, some 7,500 people had registered as members. We had signed up 2,500 members above our 5,000 objective. Overnight, I had become a power in the RA organization. I was running the membership campaign, chalking up 10,000 members. The board was both impressed and aghast.

The government was also aghast. They had no intention of bringing in a fee check-off, but now they were committed. Reportedly, Prime Minister Mackenzie King heard about this and was very disturbed. As a politician, the development worried him; it looked like another 25¢ was coming off the poor civil servants' pay cheques. The government in Ottawa would be blamed, cursed even. He made immediate inquiries. Who was behind all this? The inquiry went to The Hon. C.D. Howe, then Rielle Thompson, who pinpointed me. I was quite uncomfortable. The issue was, now that we had all these members, when and how were we going to start giving them all these activities I had promised?

At this point, the office organization was in a terrible mess. RA had all this money coming in and no program. The massive publicity was continuing, however. RA director Roy Baxter came to me and said RA had to find a director to manage all this.

"We don't know anybody. What about you?"

I quickly said I would undertake the challenge.

"We'll have to get you appointed by the board tonight." Baxter seemed determined.

The next day, directors Kenny and Baxter appeared, wearing long, drawn expressions. My appointment had been approved, but there had been three dissenting directors.

"Out of twelve, nine were for you and three against. We hate to tell you this, but those who were against you said they were unhappy that you're Jewish."

Up to this point, I had not thought of anti-Semitism as a factor affecting me. It never occurred to me that I would have to deal with it in my career.

I asked Kenny and Baxter, "Well, how do you both feel about it?"

They said, "Terrible. We would like to have you, but with the full backing of the board."

"You can still do it, even with three people opposed," I counselled. "Call a follow-up meeting to confirm the majority vote." Once again, I became a political strategist, remembering earlier experiences at Machray School and the University of Manitoba.

"Tell the board that you acknowledge with pleasure the fact that they have elected Ed Parker director of the RA, and now President Martin Kenny would like to move, seconded by Roy Baxter, that all go on record as giving Mr. Parker the board's unanimous support." The implication, I explained, was that anyone who didn't give his support under these circumstances should resign. Kenny and Baxter worked the plan. Every hand that night went up and I was unanimously endorsed.

My next move was to resign from the federal civil service. Rielle Thompson counselled me to hold out for a one-year contract.

"You'll have a lot of fun," he predicted, "but you will antagonize a lot of people. You are going to have a lot of income from fees. Fashion a contract which will allow you to spend that income and which doesn't give the board much chance of catching up with you. Offer to go to the board and report, but make sure you have control of the executive machinery."

The RA did give me an iron-clad, one-year contract. Under it, I became an entertainment czar in Ottawa. I could do no wrong for which I could be fired. Beautiful, blonde Thora Sugrue quit the civil service to become my secretary and closest friend. I gave her a $20 per month increase over her civil service pay. She proved to be invaluable as well as attractive, and we were an inseparable RA team. The board hired a male comptroller as business manager to keep an eye on me and my spending. His major previous experience had been operating bowling alleys, and he was entirely befuddled and overcome by events.

RA rented space above Bowles restaurant next to Union Station, set up cashier wickets, and gave me a large office with a prestigious item, a carpet. My furniture was avante-garde in design. Behind me on the wall was a huge bulletin board where I tacked posters and publicity materials.

People appeared out of the air, offering to organize groups of every kind. An Olympic skier, for example, said he could organize a skiing program on a mass scale. I hired him on the spot. Group leaders were paid a nominal $5 a night. I must have hired 100 people on this basis.

Facilities were scrounged everywhere – churches, fire halls, public schools, libraries, hotel halls. When we collated the results of our questionnaires, we were both excited and appalled at the same time. Some 2,000 people wanted to take up swimming, 4,000 people wanted to take up skiing, and 1,000 signed for ballet.

At that time, the Château Laurier had the most popular swimming pool, which could accommodate a maximum of 80 people. Two public pools could accommodate a further 100 people each. The maximum grand total for swimming at any one time was 180, and we only had two evenings made available to us. A sizable problem!

The opening night of our swimming season, hundreds turned out, packing the facilities. Pool-side looked like a human ant pile, wall-to-wall people in bathing suits. So we improvised "swim bingo". Cards were handed out and the winners won the use of the pool. We played this game for hours, and at the end, most went home dry but entertained.

When it came to ballet, 1,000 would-be ballerinas registered. What we organized were gym classes. Hundreds lined up to do gym things nightly in fire halls and church basements.

I hired people on instinct and on the instant, some brilliant, some mentally unbalanced. I didn't have time to check them out. One chap whom I commissioned to teach ceramics, began his first class by throwing clay at his students. On the other hand, our instructors in weaving, stamp collecting, and bridge playing were great successes. Within three months, about 60 activities were flourishing in about 20 buildings.

Instructors were off and running after a first interview, often organizing their activities without me, knowing all I did was bless them, saying they could have any recreational activity they desired. I found them places for meetings and backed them with publicity. The weaving group met in a space just in front of my office. We were so desperate for activity space that my front office often accommodated unscheduled groups. Young leaders surfaced rapidly, and activity after activity was launched within weeks.

Thora and I were running to meetings day and night. Ours was also a romance on the run. On one of our off nights, with the place deserted, Thora and I settled down for a little amorous togetherness in the dark in my office. I had forgotten a bridge club was to meet at 8 p.m.. Suddenly the lights came on in the outer office. Out of pure panic and embarrassment, Thora and I flopped down on the carpet and kept quiet for two hours until the bridge club had finished its program and dispersed. Organized recreation was a handicap to my own need for a private romance.

My star was on the rise at this point. I had caught the eye of many senior civil servants. John Grierson would phone me every few days and ask how many members the RA had. I would say 8,000 or 9,000, and he would exclaim in wonder. People would come to me with all sorts of ideas.

All social events were advertised at a two-price system; $1 per lecture for non-members, 25¢ for members. We packed our events. Some events were even free to members. For example, I would bring in an attraction like Marion Anderson, or Cab Calloway, or any of the star acts of the day. They were usually priced $4 to the public, and 50¢ to members. RA members couldn't afford to turn down such bargains. I had the RA back everything, and we kept making money. Within five months, RA had 12,000 members, $36,000 in revenues, and profits of $30,000.

Within a six-month period, the RA drama society was performing not only on radio but on stage as well, had offered an evening of short plays, and was planning major presentations. The RA music society, with truly talented singers, had staged Gilbert and Sullivan's "Trial by Jury" in a program of diverse tidbits.

The speakers' society was holding successful, capacity meetings in a ballroom at the Château Laurier. Attendance at conventional programs had increased so drastically that new, larger venues had to be found. Bingo games, for example, were held in Ottawa's largest hall, the ice hockey rink, and hundreds had to be turned away. Whatever the RA touched, blessed or sponsored was hugely attended and the RA became a running news story in the local press.

One of the most innovative programs was a baby-sitting service for couples wishing to attend activities on regular evenings. The RA even initiated a telephone answering service, an apparent aid to greater socializing. The RA success attracted nation-wide publicity and full-page photo spreads in press throughout the country. I gloried in the wonder of it all. Even I was induced to join a sport, and I took up horseback riding for six weeks.

One of the most successful and surprisingly engaging magnets for participants was a monthly film discussion seminar organized by National Film Board writer Jeff Hurley and NFB director Robert Edmonds. When John Grierson learned that some 600 had registered for the series, he readily agreed to be the program's first speaker. I reached out for my former employer, the erudite Rielle

Thompson, to chair the event. Rielle was flattered and delighted. The resulting scuttlebutt around town ensured a capacity turn-out and a large ballroom at the Château, set up in concert fashion, had every seat filled. The questions from the floor intrigued Grierson. The audience was unusually well-informed about the work of his board and its product.

So stimulated was Grierson that, after the program, even though it was nearly midnight, he asked to be taken to the RA office for a chat with a group of us – Edmonds, Hurley, Thompson, and Grierson's lieutenants, Ross McLean and Ralph Foster. I played host. Doughnuts and coffee were brought up to the office from Bowles restaurant below our office and talk went on for hours.

Grierson wanted to learn everything he could about the RA, the basis of its audience appeal and success. What he foresaw was a technique of recruiting audiences through a club format and giving members special privileges. This, he reasoned, would entice attendance at all events and ensure box office success.

After eight or nine months, the drama club had projected sufficient programming to justify the building of an open air bandshell and theatre in the park behind the Château Laurier Hotel. We began publishing wall newspapers, huge posters with messages in large type, and plastered them on walls throughout the civil service.

RA's program was reported twice weekly in special broadcasts Our half-hour radio program was staffed by our own drama group members. The drama group had become quite outstanding. On Sundays the CBC featured us as a professional company of actors. Overnight, RA seemed to have become a special force. The ability to command audiences was power. The Canadian Army approached me with a show featuring Wayne and Shuster. The Navy also wanted to perform for the RA audience, partly for their own morale, and partly for recruiting purposes. The Royal Canadian Air Force, with probably the most outstanding jazz orchestra in the land, also wanted to perform.

My proposal was always, "Let me put a price on your tickets to the public and give free tickets to our members and we will pack the

Capitol theatre." Priced at $1 each to the public, RA members got two complimentary tickets each, a dividend of another $2 on their $3 annual membership. The Capitol theatre was packed for those shows, and I was experiencing the greatest high period of my life. The RA's audience-pulling power was now fully demonstrated.

At this point, while Kenny and Baxter were elated with the organization's results, other members who had gained prominence in the past through their association with less-glamorous activities such as bowling, bridge and field sports seemed overshadowed and disconcerted. I began to sense a mistrust of Ed Parker and his "Grover Whalen" ways. A board member's reference to Grover Whalen, the flamboyant organizer of the 1939 New York World's Fair, was meant to put me down in the eyes of board conservatives.

What now comforted and cheered me greatly was my one-year contract. The agreement assured no interference in the way I conducted the organization's programs. It had been a radical abandonment of responsibility by the board, but, at the beginning of things, no one could foresee the meteoric growth in RA membership and potential.

The box office magic of the RA brought it to the attention of the nation's press. The National Film Board produced a full-page newspaper spread of photos on the RA organization's activities and distributed the mats to all dailies and periodicals. Inquiries regarding sponsorship of performers came from the United States as well as from throughout Canada.

One of the most interesting evenings sponsored by the RA was the program offered by the Toronto-based Volkoff Ballet Troupe. Skilled in mime as well as classical dance, the young performers charmed Ottawa. Princess Juliana of the Netherlands, then resident in Ottawa, had her press officer arrange tickets for a large party. I was self-elected to greet the royal members on their arrival at the Capitol theatre and to escort them to their seats in the first row of the balcony. It was a heady experience.

Irving Zweig and I, with our large apartment as a feature, hosted an after-show party which, in the tradition of theatrical people, lasted until breakfast. Toronto friends of the Ann Cohen circle were in full attendance. However, I had failed to invite RA President Martin Kenny and Vice-President Roy Baxter. The tactical error was that no one from the RA board of directors was present, and a basis for resentment and ultimate discord resulted.

* * *

In the spring of 1944, I took a leave of absence from the RA and went off to Winnipeg. I had to plead exhaustion because holidays had not been written into my contract. Mother had finally sold the Alfred Avenue house and had moved into a basement apartment on Noble Court on the river bank around which we had played as children.

A particular drama had recently occurred around Noble Court when the Red River flooded its banks, and the water rose up to a foot below my mother's window. Many of my friends had rediscovered her at that time. They remembered she had lived on Alfred Avenue East. Flood time was actually a happy period for her. The excitement won her a lot more attention than she had enjoyed for years.

After my father's death, Rose had begun to reach out to strangers, adopting many non-Jews as friends. In the early days, my father hadn't encouraged her to speak English. Now that she was alone, her English had improved.

I had gone to visit Sam Berg. Sam was someone I had always wanted to embrace and by whom I wished to be acknowledged. He offered me a position on his Anglo-Jewish newspaper. But to accept a low-paying position of servitude under Sam Berg's tutelage after the heights I had attained in Ottawa, was not the career development I had in mind. I returned to the capital city.

Working around the clock promoting activities for the RA, pursuing my romance with Thora, and eluding the RA Board of Directors, I was bound to make one faux pas. One Friday, I took the day off and went with Thora to Montreal to attend my brother's wedding. To the directors, it seemed I was playing hooky.

When I returned to work Monday, some members of the RA Board of Directors were sizzling. Thora and I had been away the same day and without notifying anyone. This was the excuse to review all my work habits. Normally, I would come to work daily at 9:45 a.m., and then work all hours. I knew then that the board wouldn't renew my one-year contract.

Tension between me and members of the RA board was bound to surface, to be exacerbated by my success rather than failure in organizing activities. Meeting once a month and finding all the new ventures relatively exotic, board members, all of whom were long-term permanent civil servants, felt exasperated and frustrated. The board's control over my activities lay after the fact. Members could only regulate existing programs and vote or deny new funds.

In the puzzled words of Martin Kenny, board members just didn't know what Ed Parker was going to throw at them. Some mutterings began that Parker was a trade union organizer, a labour plant.

The time was approaching for election of a new board, according to the constitution. Amazingly, a simple answer was waiting in the wings, the work of a long-labouring committee. It called for democratization of the board election process. Rather than a single, large membership meeting, as in the past, when 50 or so people turned out to determine the organization's future, polling stations would be set up throughout the civil service, and a voting date set and announced. With so many new "temporary" civil servants running things, there were fresh names to challenge the veteran die hards. Excitement ran high.

The campaigning was reminiscent of municipal contests – posters, brochures, speeches. Ottawa newspapers reported that thousands had exercised their franchise on election day.

The early evening *Journal* announced the winners, fifteen "old guard" and nine new people. I really needed a majority of new people to secure me in my program.

At the first meeting of the new board, Martin Kenny lost no time in declaring that the RA would not be renewing my contract, which still had some four months to run.

My response was to appeal to the board's collective sense of greed. My tactic was to announce that I wouldn't seek nor consider an extension of my contract. I would in fact, help them find a new director, and more importantly, before my own contract year was over, I would help RA reach a goal of 20,000 members. With the lure of a further 8,000 members, the RA board happily embraced me again, waxed enthusiastic and increased my budget.

Relations between myself and members of the RA board became lyrically happy during the remaining months of my contract. Reassured that, with my leave taking in the fall, the board would gain a handle on the vastly mushroomed RA structure, Kenny and Baxter now tried to woo the Parker supporters on the board. Ron Ritchie was the leader of the new guard and it was to him that the Kenny forces turned.

Ritchie agreed to be my successor as director and would collaborate with me and understudy my vision of recreation for the civil service. In practice, Ritchie and I made a most agreeable team; Ritchie bringing up strong support for nearly every recommendation related to RA growth.

One aspiration which evolved from the old guard that was greatly aided by the new people was the proposal for a permanent RA building centre, one built especially to encompass the full gamut of organized recreational activities. The idea was an excellent keystone for the projected second membership campaign, now giving zest to all my efforts. A board committee was struck to examine sites and plan budget projections.

In the meantime, the RA had gone ahead and built an open-air bandshell behind the Château Laurier, a large stage facility which now offered entertainment to the general public every evening during the balance of the summer and into early fall.

Campaign approaches that worked the first time out in membership recruitment were reintroduced with even more flair – free movies on Sunday, large-scale picnics, outings, and dances. Newspaper, radio and billboard publicity blanketed Ottawa. It became credible that membership could be boosted to 15,000, $45,000 in fees a year and a gross budget involving revenues from all sources of $100,000.

I still had time to search out another job, but a very real employment crisis was looming. I would have to use my current success to project myself on to something bigger.

Ann Cohen, who adopted me as her protégé, declared me to be the greatest force whatever and publicized my talents far and wide. Myer Lipson, our millionaire landlord, took his cue from Ann and passed my name on to movie mogul Arthur Gottleib. Here was a character out of a Damon Runyon story. It was implied he was someone with underworld connections. Gottleib owned a large film studio in Toronto and was a friend of John Grierson. Included in Gottleib's entourage was "Two-Gun" Cohen, then in his sixties. Formerly a Jewish general in Chiang Kai-shek's Chinese Army circa 1940, he had previously helped Sun Yat-sen, the founding President of the Republic of China, by acquiring guns and equipment for his revolution during World War I.

Gottleib and Cohen confronted me one night with the staggering proposal that I become the head of their film company. At the time, I was earning about $3,000 a year. Here was a miracle proposition offering a starting salary of $14,000 a year. Lipson was to finance developments and I was to get Morten and Gudrun to join me as film makers. Lipson wanted me to represent his interests.

Gottleib invited Lipson and me to his Casha Basha hideaway resort in the Laurentians for a weekend to talk things over. Chorus girls from the Broadway musical "Oklahoma" took to soaping heads in the lake, mine included, and were ready for other games. In the evening we attended a monster barbecue which featured half a steer rotating on a spit. Gottleib never got to talk business with us that weekend. Lipson was outraged, but I found the experience amusing.

The following weekend, Myer and I were off to visit Gottleib at his home in Pickering, a small town just outside Toronto. There we met his mistress, a former movie queen. Over a seemingly trifling incident, Gottleib became furious and beat this girl in front of company. He had been a prize fighter. There and then, I knew I didn't want to be associated with the fabulous Arthur Gottleib.

Meanwhile, the RA campaign moved forward with tremendous success. A rally was arranged to raise money to build a recreation centre for the civil service. Five thousand attended a mass meeting in the local ice palace, the biggest rally in the history of Ottawa. Mayor Lewis was invited to address the gathering. We had put a proposal to him that for every dollar raised among our own members towards a building fund, the City of Ottawa would contribute a matching dollar. The province would then be asked to match each $2 so raised, and the federal government likewise to contribute $4. Governments of all levels could thus help build a super recreation centre for civil servants, a multi-million dollar recreation complex for Ottawa.

On the evening of the rally, the ice palace was packed with 4,000 people, while outside, unable to gain entrance, were another 1,000. Two very popular American bands and top-name talents were the lure. Mayor Lewis was so euphoric he promised the RA that the city would match civil servant contributions dollar for dollar.

A musician, a Dutchman called De Ridder, in Vancouver, intro-duced himself to me one day. He wanted to organize a symphony orchestra, an amenity desperately needed in Ottawa. Could the RA finance such a development? No, the RA couldn't underwrite it di-rectly, but I offered instead to have the RA buy out the entire house at his first concert and to pay him for these tickets in advance. That gave him $3,000 and put him in business. The man danced a jig in my office. And thus the Ottawa Symphony was born.

As fall approached, I worried about the termination date of my contract. Meanwhile, the RA bandshell had been built and I was emceeing big outdoor concerts. The important thing for me was to make sure of my next job. I prepared an exposition on how recrea-tion could be organized on provincial levels, how emancipating and enlightening such a program would prove if it were introduced by a dynamic government.

On Ann Cohen's urging, David Lewis, then national secretary of the CCF party, forwarded this glamorous projection to T.C. Douglas, Premier of Saskatchewan. Weeks went by with no response from Regina.

I then received an unsolicited letter of congratulation from Prime Minister Mackenzie King on the apparent success of the RA. I sent a copy of the letter along with other commendatory references to Douglas. He turned my presentation over to a young activist, Doris French, then head of the CCF youth movement. Doris passed a complimentary verdict on to Douglas, but I still received no invitation.

Ottawa Liberal MP, George McGrath, was also in touch with me at the time to help his party organize young people. Opportunities poured in upon me. Ross Cameron, with whom I had worked at the *Winnipeg Tribune*, sought me out to help organize Conservative youth for John Bracken, then leader of the Tory party. The RA success had projected me as a celebrity in Ottawa. Another friend recommended I work in Yugoslavia for the United Nations Relief Agency, and author Jim Wright talked me up with Nathen Cohen, then a 20-year-old wonderboy editor of the *Glace Bay Gazette*, a daily newspaper in Nova Scotia. Nathen wrote offering me the managing editorship of his newspaper. CCFer Morden Lazorus thought I might organize his party's next provincial campaign under Ted Joliffe. My head was spinning in a cloud of euphoria. It was the fall of 1944.

Finally, I wired Douglas saying that I had other offers and needed a reply. Back came his wire "Your appointment confirmed – When can you come to Regina?"

I had about six weeks left in my contract with the RA. The campaign I was directing had brought membership to 18,000, well on track to the 20,000 target figure. Shortly before I was to leave Ottawa, I became romantically intrigued with a very beautiful girl, the daughter of a rich, orthodox Jewish family, an Elizabeth Taylor type. Jeanette had a certain spice about her. Her fiancé was with the US Army in Europe. We met often but she made it clear that I wasn't to take our friendship beyond flirtation. Coincidentally, Jeanette was also going west. Our itineraries were not co-ordinated, but we arranged to meet briefly in Winnipeg. Thora, my office wife, I sensed, felt deeply about our relationship but hid her turmoil from me. She was a wonderful, giving person. Naively, and typical of male youth, I thought Thora would be happy for me in all things. Marriage was far from my mind. I was for friendships.

By the end of October, 1944, I was on my way to take up new challenges and open another chapter in the fortunes of a young man having the time of his life. The day came when I was off to Regina. The small group of close friends which saw me off at the railway station for Regina had a piece of exhilarating news for me – the RA had signed its twenty-thousandth member.

Once in Winnipeg, I rushed out and bought five pairs of ladies' shoes. I wanted the same style in different sizes, since I didn't know Jeanette's foot size. We met at Moore's Restaurant. I was to court her like the Prince in the Cinderella story. If the shoe fits . . . I also presented her with a volume by Omar Khayam and a single rose. She was excited, delighted, and I, in turn, was elated with her reaction. Our luncheon talk was highly animated. She expressed a great faith in my ability and was fascinated by the challenge which awaited me in Regina. I confessed I was in the dark about what I was going to do once I got there. While I was ostensibly going to introduce a physical fitness program, I was not a dedicated physical fitness buff; rather, I was an advocate of sedentary pleasures.

CHAPTER 6

THE FIRST CCF
GOVERNMENT AND
CO-OPERATIVE LIVING

I arrived in Regina in October, 1944. On leaving the railway station, I hailed a cab, saying, "Take me to the Hotel Saskatchewan."

The driver seemed incredulous, did a double-take, made a U-turn and announced, "You are there." Red-faced, I paid the fare. I could have walked across the street.

At the hotel, within minutes of unpacking, I phoned the Premier's office and reported for duty. I had no concept of how to set up a meeting with the King's first minister of the province of Saskatchewan, so I merely asked Douglas's secretary if I could have a minute or two of "T.C.'s" time right away. I had no idea where to go, to whom to report, nor into what machinery of bureaucracy I would fit.

Douglas agreed to pop out of his office to greet me the moment I showed up. He had heard from David Lewis that I could be a bit of a loose cannon if not organizationally fastened, indeed capable of being self-propelled by my own ideas and productivity. Lewis had counselled Douglas to give me a custodian who might keep me on base.

When I introduced myself to Douglas, a most affable man, he told me that I had been appointed to his department of health by order-in-council at $75 a week. I said that the sum was agreeable, although that was the amount I was already receiving in Ottawa. "Money goes further in Regina than in Ottawa," he laughingly rejoined, but agreed to see what he could do. My first cheque a month later was at a weekly salary of $80.

Within minutes of my arrival in the Premier's office, a jovial, florid, square-set man, Gilbert Darby, arrived and was introduced as my executive assistant. He and I took leave of Douglas and retreated to the legislative cafeteria for our first staff meeting.

Darby had arranged for a typist-secretary for me and himself. She would appear at 9 a.m. tomorrow at vacant offices in downtown Regina in the government insurance building – two small rooms and an outer area. Darby had been close to Douglas in all his parliamentary campaigns, and he assured me that he could reach the Premier, if necessary, day or night.

That first evening in my hotel room, I organized notes I had been preparing on my train journey. Those notes were the outlines of an ambitious, unprecedented plan for recreation for the entire province of Saskatchewan.

Darby had already informed me that the division which we were staffing was that of the physical fitness branch of the department of health, that there was already a physical fitness director waiting in the wings, a Dr. Kirkpatrick, who had not surfaced yet, since he was still in the Canadian army.

I was to be called promotional director. The title was an early forecasting of conflicts of interest and duplication of function. I had thought of myself as the head of the division and as the designated author of the Saskatchewan plan for physical fitness. After all, I was hired on the basis of a submitted proposal to the Premier.

On arrival at the office, Darby introduced me to our blonde comely, lithesome, outgoing secretary, May Drummond. I had her busy at the typewriter within minutes, transposing my notes and program projections.

With Drummond raising steam on her typewriter, my plan was to get Gilbert Darby out on the run. First, Darby and I went out to a nearby cafe for coffee and doughnuts where we conferred for the balance of the morning. I laid out my concept of a Saskatchewan Recreation Movement which would offer something for everyone in the province. Gil Darby, who wore spectacles and reminded me of the Dickensian creation, "Mr. Pickwick", seemed boggle-eyed as I talked.

I indicated a great sense of urgency. Could he arrange that I meet the Deputy Minister of Health, Dr. Davidson, by weekend? I wanted to introduce myself as a new member of his department, working for the Premier, and to lay out some of my plans before him. Meanwhile, I hoped to get my initial notes whipped into a readable memorandum which Darby and I could deliver by hand.

Gilbert spent the rest of that first afternoon setting up meetings of introduction for me with officers throughout the civil service, higher-ups who might be interested in my plans. In fact, I thought, I should meet someone in every department and that Darby should spend his time working out a schedule of introductions for me.

By 1 p.m., the office of Physical Fitness, Department of Health, Government of Saskatchewan, was in business, with typewriters going and phones ringing. Within days, the Saskatchewan plan for physical fitness and recreation was surfacing before anyone had even been alerted that I had arrived. I gave myself six weeks to produce a comprehensive outline. People in government usually allow themselves six months to several years to produce a plan.

"Relax," said Darby. "You are getting paid a salary, not a project fee."

My first rooming house was run by an oversized widow, very hostile toward anybody who worked for the provincial government. She was against the socialists. No, I said, I was not a member of the CCF, and that was true.

She gave me a room on the third floor, at the back, with all the windows facing north, a location which proved unbearably cold in the winter.

The widow's daughter, a provocative young woman, quickly became the subject and object of my nightly fantasies. Some nights, as I lay shivering in the early hours, I concentrated hard on having her visit me in my bedroom. I heard her moving about in the next room, but my wishing didn't make her appear.

It was so cold in that room that I wrote my mother, begging her to send blankets. At least three blankets on top of me were mandatory. On making my bed, the widow was consistently outraged by my initiative and would yank the blankets out from under the sheets daily and fold them. This "cold" war went on for months. I even used blankets to cover up the windows against the north wind's penetration.

Within my first week, I had met the Deputy Minister, Dr. Davidson, been toured throughout the legislative buildings, conveyed my hellos to ministers and others, and finally settled down to talks with Fred Jantzen, Curriculum Chief of the Department of Education, Chris Smith, Information Officer, Department of Health, and other key personnel in community planning and welfare. The most challenging interview was with Watson Thomson, head of adult education, a most beguiling man and soon to become my mentor.

At the Administrative level, I enjoyed early rapport with Deputy Minister Davidson, who agreed to read a draft of my plan for physical fitness and, further, to report my intent to Douglas, and to arrange a private meeting with the Premier for me when I had won acceptance of the main thrust of my scheme among those bureaucrats who might feel themselves affected.

Our strategy was to convene an interdepartmental meeting of representatives from different departments. Davidson would chair the meeting, and we would study the plan, and submit it for further consideration by selected members of the recreational community.

In subsequent meetings, representatives of the University, the YMCA and YWCA, as well as invited observers from different cultural and athletic organizations would convene to study the plan. We would not bring the plan to any vote, merely agree to consider criticisms, comments, and suggestions and to then circulate the amended proposal to some 30,000 recreational leaders in the province for further comment.

The umbrella name for our enterprise would be the Saskatchewan Recreational Movement and the SRM would, through the Regina office, provide supportive aid, certificates, adjudicators, referees and organizers where requested. To bring this concept to fruition, the advisory council would be asked to recommend that the initial budget (half provided by the federal government) be spent in a promotional and educative manner. To placate Dr. Kirkpatrick, in his absence, the council suggested that the budget include pilot projects he might organize as models to be emulated in the specific field of his specialty, calisthenics.

In my second week on the job, I had my first visitor. Ruth Hamilton, an earnest, attractive lady, mid 30s, introduced herself as a theatre booster and worker and wondered if she could volunteer to help in the formation of the Saskatchewan Recreational Association. She had learned through the grapevine that the contemplated organization would encompass the arts as part of its advocacy of physical fitness. She was open and friendly and offered to introduce me to activists in the performing arts in Regina.

She also knew an excellent amateur photographer, presently head of the local radio station. Wilf Collier, she explained, would be delighted to be involved in any publicity ventures which gave him the opportunity to take pictures.

A scheme occurred to me, and I wondered if she and Collier could form a team and set up recreational activity scenes for publicity photos. I would credit Collier and Hamilton with the work, underwrite the supplies and pay them an honorarium for their enterprise.

Within that first afternoon, Ruth had become a member of the SRM team and made daily contact with our office. In Ruth, I had found a local guide and friend, someone planning to have me visit arts, crafts, music, drama and athletic organizations in Regina, Saskatoon, Moose Jaw and throughout the province. Ruth presented me to Ellen Burgess, a grand dame of the amateur theatrical world. She in turn had me appointed a drama adjudicator for the provincial amateur theatrical festival and I began to tour the province. My evenings became progressively programmed.

Within six weeks I was given authorization by the deputy minister to publish my plan and circulate it both within the government and widely throughout the province.

I felt driven and displayed a tremendous urgency perhaps unprecedented at that time in the history of the Saskatchewan civil service. My task was blueprinting, single-handedly, a comprehensive plan for involving the people of Saskatchewan in fitness activities – social, cultural, and physical. I promised to complete the plan within six weeks.

According to my fantasy, Saskatchewan's population could be divided into three activity groups: twelve years and under, teenagers, and the Saskatchewan Recreation Movement.

I saw the Saskatchewan Recreation Movement as a challenge to the public to get organized. I would prepare literature to encourage citizens to organize themselves into a stimulating variety of activity groups in their communities. Voluntary leadership would surface for each activity – art, crafts, music, drama, and so forth. I was following the pattern set up by the Ottawa RA. For the very young, I envisioned a series of badges featuring Canadian animals for membership and achievement.

It was the first time that a formal government document was to feature a photograph on its cover. The "shot" delighted my propagandist heart. It showed people of mixed ages playing a London-Bridges-falling-down game and projected a mood of happiness. Inside the booklet, a detailed plan gave a lead to organizing every type of activity in the recreation field, from Chinese Checker tournaments to interprovincial sports and theatre festivals.

My proposed recreation plan was on schedule and delivered to the Premier for his approval within the proposed six weeks. The plan was printed as an official government paper by early December 1944.

A moment with the printer at the time produced an exchange widely circulated as humour in the bureaucracy. I had adopted American spelling forms such as "program" and "labor" instead of "programme" and "labour." The King's Printer objected until I offered a compromise: "If you will agree to take 'me' out of 'programme,' I will agree to leave 'u' in labour."

Some 30,000 copies of the plan were distributed, and overnight I had become a widely recognized personality, the author of a sweeping plan for physical fitness for the province of Saskatchewan. The SRM and I became front-page news in the *Regina Leader Post*, the *Saskatoon Star Phoenix* and other provincial dailies. With Gilbert Darby, May Drummond and Ruth Hamilton sharing platforms with me, I held a series of press meetings.

Within days of the plan's appearance, I was in demand as a public speaker, and, through new-found friends Tom McLeod and Morris Shumiatcher of the Premier's office, I was put in circulation on the social circuit. A particular friend was Frank Hanson, editor of *The Commonwealth*, who spent hours in dialogue with me explaining the Saskatchewan realities as he knew them. A special confidante was Doris French, president of the young people's section of the provincial CCF. It was to her that Douglas had turned for an opinion on my original submission, and it was with her I exchanged views on tactics regarding implementing my plan.

The Jewish groups were the least disturbed. They had the YMHA and YWHA. The group which had most effectively organized youth in the province was the Roman Catholic church. My scheme proposed that people meet in community centres regardless of church affiliations. Drama clubs, for example, would interrelate, promote festivals, and encourage talent to proceed to professional standards. Province-wide athletic tournaments would be held and championship teams would proceed to interprovincial play. The SRM would totally endorse all recreational fields.

At a public speaking engagement in Landis, a town just north of Saskatoon, I succeeded in arousing a fevered pitch of enthusiasm among the young people during a school assembly. Some of the young people invited me to address them further in the basement of their church. I came and enthusiastically projected my view of a utopian community life in which all people could find recreational outlets closest to their heart's desires.

At the end of my presentation, the priest, just out of Germany and possessing a very thick SS type accent, mounted the platform with his German Shepherd dog.

"Well Fritz, what do you think?" he began by way of thanking me. He was clearly talking to the dog. "What did you think of the talk that comes from the big city of Regina, from big government? Why doesn't the speaker show us how to organize ourselves?"

The priest's heavy sarcasm hit me hard. I was aghast. The young people, embarrassed, looked to see what I was going to do. I could not respond. Vulnerable, I returned dejectedly to the hotel to be met shortly by a delegation from the church. The young people wanted to apologize for the priest's behaviour.

My next task was to produce a magazine that would look and read like *Time* magazine. Giving myself the task of writing it in its entirety, I projected activity groups as though they were already in existence. The magazine abounded in photos of happy people participating in a gamut of activities in joyous interethnic groups. The magazine, *Saskatchewan Recreation*, was divided into children, teenager and adult sections; the teenager section included a comic book section featuring personalities of the day in fields of social endeavour.

Promotion of the Saskatchewan Recreation Movement called for no new legislation, only spontaneous and voluntary responses from interested citizens, groups, and communities. Gilbert Darby mounted a huge map of the province in our reception area. As different villages and towns offered to organize cultural and athletic programs, their acceptance of the SRM proposal was indicated with varied coloured pins on this board.

Within two months, we seemed to have had a response from most communities. Enthusiasm for the do-it-yourself recreational organization was infectious.

Dr. Cecil Sheps, a senior health department officer then committed to an educational campaign against social diseases, induced me to place an ad on the inside front cover of the proposed recreation magazine to caution readers against VD. It seemed blatant to associate curse and cure, social health versus sexual carelessness in the same publication, but Sheps was a political power in the new hierarchy and a fellow Winnipegger, and I found it impossible to deny him.

Premier Douglas couldn't quite fathom what I was doing but was pleased that I had managed to spend the $35,000 allotted, since the federal government was to renew grants on an annual basis.

Since this was the first CCF government brought to power in Canada, some of its members informed me, the agnostic, of their religion. I didn't belong to the CCF party, so they saw me as politically undisciplined. Some invited me to their homes to teach me socialism and did influence me greatly. My interest, on the other hand, was to win their support for the program I was promoting.

Douglas and his cabinet were busy from the outset doing work inherited from their Liberal party predecessors. Before it could start working on its own ideas, it had to complete the projects which the outgoing government had left in mid-process. Continuity became a first charge, whether it involved clearing roads or administrating school districts. The new Socialist government was busy trying to prove itself more efficient than its predecessors.

As a first priority, the CCF decided to organize the civil service into a union. To me, it seemed incongruous that a Socialist government would protect the jobs of partisan appointees of the former Liberal government before it had had time to bring its own sympathizers to key positions. Job security was provided to a bureaucratic force which was hostile to the CCF. This precipitous government action, however, later protected me from being fired.

* * *

I had met Watson Thomson, the newly appointed director of adult education, shortly after my arrival in Regina. During the war years, Thomson was an eloquent voice for liberalism and humanism.

One of the great broadcasts of that day was his, called "I Accuse." Thomson accused Canadians of bigotry, fighting Hitler but tolerating anti-semitism and discrimination against other minority groups at home, such as the Japanese-Canadians. He became a darling of the Jewish public and other ethnic groups.

When I met him in Regina, he was apprehensive about me. I had come enunciating a policy of physical fitness that included programs in the arts, crafts, music, drama and debate. He was director of adult-education and I had become promotional director of the physical fitness program.

In our initial meetings, he decided to be kind to me, and invited me to his home. He began to like me, saying I really belonged with him in his program as deputy director of adult education. I agreed and became his number two, his understudy, his petrol.

Watson Thomson was an exponent of co-operative living. In Winnipeg, he and his co-op group of followers had purchased a large depression-abandoned mansion for $3,600.00. Those who had proper marriages lived there with their wives. Those who didn't lived with their girlfriends. Watson could rationalize this and provide an idealistic thrust to a communal program of group sharing.

Thomson and his band of young people pioneered co-operative living in Winnipeg. They were men and women with strong humanistic and idealistic motives. To me, this Anglo-Saxon group was a new breed of people, a new experience. None, at the time, were of Jewish background. Socialistically inclined, their target was to work for a brave, new world. Self-expression and making a contribution according to one's best abilities were their ideals.

Thomson talked about sensitive relationships, honesty in love arrangements, open co-operation and communal living. His co-operative worked out what each person should do: who was to mind children, who to clear sidewalks, who to stoke the furnace, who to lead group discussions and who to lead songs.

Later I was to be one of the people who raised money to set up a Regina co-operative. My mother loaned money to help purchase a house. The group hoped she would come and live with us. She thought Thomson's disciples were all very nice people, but still she didn't understand the idea of a co-operative of members.

I became a working associate of Watson Thomson and through him involved myself deeply in the study of social and political philosophy. Thomson and I had a predisposition to end up as socialists, activists interested in working co-operatively with people solving problems in the group. I was more of an individualist, recruiting group support for my "inspirations" and activity ideas.

I was the only single person in the Thomson Regina set up. As half owner of the house, I found "co-operation" rather a strange formula for living. Wives looked after husbands, but no one specifically looked after me.

All, of course, were very concerned about me. Nevertheless, I built up quite a bit of resentment about getting a fair shake in the house. As a bachelor, I expected to use the house a great deal less, since I courted girls elsewhere. As a very private person, I didn't want to expose my romantic involvements too much.

Once a pair of lady's black panties were discovered in the co-operative wash. None of the women would claim them. Instead, they thought I had brought a bedmate in during the night. This I denied vehemently. The mystery of the black panties was never resolved; nobody ever claimed them.

There were few sexual hijinks in our experiment. Co-op living, however, did open possibilities in this regard. We believed sexual exchanges would not break up marriages. We would talk among ourselves to find out what people meant to each other. Once that was done, however, the romance was killed. Responsibility was implied, and with that, if one marriage had to be dissolved, another had to be formed.

142

This sexual aspect was very minor in my recollection, almost of superficial interest at the time. The commitment to work together on educational projects for the community was basic. By living together, three or four purposeful men with important jobs in government, education and industrial development were constantly exchanging ideas at the dinner table, working out plans during an evening, formulating ambitious social schemes.

Many people came to visit us at our co-op houses. Almost every night something was happening: a speaker, documentary films, movies, music, group studies. It was a vital home.

Still, all was not natural and ideal. I built up a personal grievance based upon a humiliating fact. In the distribution of fowl, I never once got to eat a chicken leg. In all the co-operative sharing, I sensed discrimination.

Finally, one Sunday afternoon (it got to be the biggest laugh in the co-operative) someone asked, "What's the matter with Ed Parker?" Everyone pressed me. "No one ever gives me a chicken leg," I blurted out, very much like a small boy. I had descended to the lowest common denominator of self-interest. If you live in a family, you get a square deal or a fair carving of chicken. I was human too, I was warmly assured.

Thomson was a great teacher. He didn't throw documentary material at you pell-mell to support his point of view. He related to you at your own intellectual station. He was very stimulated by the reactions of people to his concepts. His affinity for Scotch liquor made him benign and turned him into a kind of Guru personality, a leader prophet. He wasn't, however, the socialist I thought he was. He was considered at the time very radical, bordering on being a communist. It was a misreading of his point of view. Basically, he was mystical, with a feeling about humanism, wrapped up in a philosophical quest for the purpose of life. When he went mystical, I couldn't or wouldn't follow. My father had indoctrinated me against ever yielding myself to any mystical interpretation of social history.

Curiously, Thomson bore some facial resemblance to my father, which contributed to my heightened affection for him. At a later date, wishing to make a point with me, and recognizing my affection for him, he ended a letter with the term "dear son". I bridled. This was cynical. We were working associates. I wouldn't accept this form of address. In a way, it contributed to a shift in our relationship; I became much more distant. Although I didn't believe he felt I was a son, Thomson did come awfully close to becoming a father replacement.

* * *

I was very excited by what was happening to me in Regina, and I went home briefly to Winnipeg for a Christmas holiday. Morten and Gudrun were also visiting my mother. New Year's Eve, 1944, my birthday, was the excuse for a big house party. It was a happy time; all the Parkers were achieving success. I had become a "somebody" in Saskatchewan.

Back in Saskatchewan, I discovered that the professional director for physical fitness in the province, Dr. Kirkpatrick, had suddenly turned up, having just been released from the Royal Canadian Air Force. He was disturbed to find that I had taken the program off in a strange and unfamiliar direction, committing the province to the popularizing of community council organizations for recreational interests.

Kirkpatrick's approach was to concentrate on only one or two pilot projects and not to stir the whole province. His stress was on quality, not quantity. He preferred to set up an "ideal" physical fitness program in one locality and spend all his money on gymnasia equipment, team coaches and games. It was the conventional approach. The conflict led "Kirk" to offer his resignation. It would have been useful for me to have him do so, but I blundered into persuading him to stay. Premier Douglas called us both into his office. I suggested there was room for both of us in the department and Kirkpatrick agreed to remain. My mistake soon became clear to me. He would become my superior and I would find my future bleak.

Watson Thomson had a solution. "Come join me," he said. "Be

my deputy director in adult education." Watson made me heady with praise of my creative flair, imagination and propaganda skills, and I accepted.

* * *

Planning an adult education program was a challenge. My mind began racing towards practical implementations, films, film slides, radio panels, and study-group techniques to get people involved in dynamic discussions. The Thomson-Parker brainstorming came up with a program called "study-action". We would study problems and evolve practical methods of resolving needs. We would then recommend action to implement planning.

In the early spring of 1945, Thomson's division occupied a handsome structure adjacent to the Parliament buildings. Here a burgeoning little empire was at work. I became the number-two man in charge of an initial group of eighteen people. Adult education was a much larger department than the recreation division I had directed. Thomson rewarded me immediately with an attractive young secretary.

In my late twenties, in a strange job, open and a bit artless, I responded almost indiscriminately to invitations to address young people's groups. Subsequent to a speaking engagement, girls who had attended would phone and ask me to parties. My social life became very active. An overwhelming plus was that I had the use of one of the adult education cars; I was a somebody.

In those days, all secretaries, program directors and members of the legislature ate in a common cafeteria. Cabinet officers would easily join you at the table. Premier Douglas would often enter alone and sit at the nearest table with ordinary clerks and whiz kids You could talk about anything and ask pointed questions. The Douglas government was being very cautious, and I wondered out loud if he were behaving as a radical socialist after all.

Douglas explained that in his cabinet, in every cabinet, there is a left grouping and a right. The prime minister has to find his place in the centre. If he didn't find such a place, he soon wouldn't be prime minister. Prime ministers have to be pragmatists. If consensus works, he goes along with it. It was an insight into political reality which I truly valued.

When Watson Thomson had to borrow money from the bank to buy our house, the prime minister and the treasurer of the province signed our note. This was not prudent political behaviour, for it tied their financial interest with our political future. Obviously, Saskatchewan had a naive government at the time, but its leaders were very good-hearted.

Living together and working together in a co-operative manner proved exhilarating. I did develop a sense of "family", personal acceptance and security. Ideas flowed easily between us. Our hope was to canvass aspirations in all localities throughout the province.

Watson Thomson's view was that people should be helped to identify local community needs, such as literacy skills for the undereducated, basic English for newcomers, co-operative nurseries for working mothers, and greater citizen involvement in municipal matters from health services to library facilities.

To assist the adult education division accelerate its program, I was encouraged to produce imaginative literature. I reveled in the free hand Thomson gave me. First came a brochure, news-photo style, showing co-operative group activities and inviting inquiries. So welcome and popular was this material, that Thomson was able to divide the province into sixteen districts, each to be served from a regional centre and to be supervised by a field representative. Alan Johnston, many years later to become president of the Canadian Broadcasting Corporation, began his distinguished career as public servant, as a field superintendent for the Saskatchewan adult education division.

A great deal of the excitement of our work was brought home from the office to the co-op family. Mary Thomson, in particular, wanted to be fully informed. She was, in her own right, a recognized educational authority. A steady flow of new found friends from all over the province and from other parts of Canada came to the co-op house.

146

I found an excellent artist, illustrator, collaborator and friend in Irene Lehman, and we produced a brochure on how people can increase their numbers into effective social study groups, and how, by a process of multiplication of participants, soon involve entire communities.

Back in the adult educational offices, Bill Harding, our charming, soft-spoken administrative chief, had his hands full keeping track of our many projects, poking multicoloured pins into a large map of the province, thus keeping tab on those areas of greatest concentration of our field work.

Our treasurer was oddly hard-nosed. Once by way of a compliment, he declared that "Parker can think of ten ideas a day, and if one worked, that was a remarkable score." I was hurt by the remark because I didn't think any of my ideas were impractical. In fact, others interpreted the remark as a compliment. He also said few people knew how to spend budgets the way I did. To me, this again sounded like an insult, but I later understood that he had meant it takes imagination to know how to spend, to not waste public funds.

At the office, I was deputized to meet and collaborate with our field representatives and to spark their endeavours with "wit, wisdom, publicity aids and learning materials." (A Thomson quote from memory).

It was with considerable pride that I witnessed the development in several communities of well attended study-action groups. The learning of basic English language skills for newcomers and adult illiterates was a particularly successful program under the direction of Florence Gaynor. Within half a year, the division was busy coordinating the use of 16 millimeter film throughout the province. (A Bill Harding achievement).

My task was to assemble the photos and research material for the production of film strips with accompanying recordings. These were for use in the promotion of co-operative ventures in child care, regional interschool co-operation, skills exchanges and practical, voluntary programs.

As adult educators, Thomson's department exhibited missionary zeal. In our co-operative house, sweeping schemes were promoted. One of the projects close to Watson's heart was the promotion of co-operative farms. These would function much along the lines of kibbutzim in Israel. In Saskatchewan, however, they would have to be on a much larger scale with farmers each contributing a square-mile of land – 100 square miles in all. Resources would be pooled and each participant would have an equal share. Teachers, bankers, editors, doctors and lawyers would also be welcomed into the co-operative and would own equal shares, contributing cash equivalent to land value. With such resources and government loans, a model town would be built in the centre of the community and be serviced by helicopters and cars. Farmers would fly from their homes in the nucleus community to their tractors in the field. The farm would be so large that if hail damaged the crop in one corner, it would not ruin the overall investment in the entire 100 square-miles. An artist's visual rendition and film strips helped explain the concept.

One meeting in a big tent at Landis, Saskatchewan, had more than 100 farmers in attendance. About 30 indicated an interest in going ahead with such a co-operative scheme.

Present at that meeting was the leader of the CCF in Canada, M.J. Coldwell. Wearing a trenchcoat, he rose from the audience and said that since the majority in this audience were not in favour of co-operative farming, he really didn't think that the government should go ahead with it. It was a mystifying approach.

Here was the leader of a socialist political party rationalizing that if a majority in a given assembly were not in favour of a proposal, it would indicate the inadequacy of the scheme. He and I had a sharp but polite exchange. We continued our discourse later in a Chinese restaurant where we talked into the night. It was my one and only meeting with Coldwell. He thought I was a strange bird, and I, in turn, thought I could never accept the views of his party. I have never reconciled the question as to whether majorities are right.

On the announcement of the death of Hitler in May 1945, Mary Thomson encouraged me to write a propaganda monologue, "You are Not Dead Hitler." Its substance was that I didn't believe Hitler had died. If he had, I wouldn't want to believe it until such time as no one anywhere acted like a Hitler. No, I argued, Hitler was alive, in some disguise, even in women's clothes. Hitler should be suspected wherever anybody spoke out against race, colour or creed. It was a very eloquent statement. Thomson was so moved by it that the script was broadcast on the air. Watson then recorded it on a disc which we used in our adult education program.

In Regina, however, Watson Thomson was becoming restless. He wanted desperately to make a great and early impact on the province, to teach utopian socialism – theoretical social democracy. Here was a Socialist government in power that wasn't doing anything socialistic. He argued, "What is the point of being in power if you don't implement your beliefs?" That was the problem he wanted to talk about publicly.

Watson wanted to have the adult educational program do more than provide conventional services. He yearned to lay out a program for social-political awareness. After all, the people had elected the first social democratic government in the Commonwealth. In fact the British Labour party was not to achieve governmental status until after the war. Thomson felt that a Socialist government ought to interpret its mandate as encouragement to those seeking co-operative democratic solutions to all programs, even questions of international peace and order.

He kept agitating himself and his staff to come up with an answer. The approach I came up with, and which we adopted, involved sponsoring a weekly, province-wide, half-hour radio program. Its format would depict editors of a tabloid magazine evaluating hot items of news from a socialist point of view. When they decided a story required a headline, the wording would reflect its social value and not simply be based on sensational appeal. We wanted to demonstrate the realities of prejudice and bias in the make-up of a newspaper, that local editorial discretion determined whether a story was played up or down.

We called our radio program "Front Page". Following each show, I spent the entire night in my office preparing an actual tabloid. Copies were mailed to those who had written asking for a copy of the printed *Front Page*.

The second half of our radio show presented Thomson lecturing on an aspect of practical socialism. We published the lecture on the inside pages of the tabloid. By January 1946, within the first ten weeks of our show, 4,000 people had requested the tabloid.

Some in the CCF saw our activity as dangerous. The government, they argued, would be accused of producing partisan propaganda at the expense of all the taxpayers. We argued that the government had been elected to produce a socialistic program. Why should it not do something about it?

Our formation of study-action groups was enormously disturbing to some of the elected CCFers. We were responsible for encouraging new leadership to surface in the local communities, challenging MPs preoccupied with single issues such as merging school districts into larger high-school associations. In these local study-action assemblies, people with leadership ability would come forward and ask the government for specific assistance. The local elected member would then be canvassed. If he had a limited understanding of social or local problems and was elected merely because he had campaigned on a single issue, for example a better road or a new roof on the school, he would naturally resent this grassroots pressure. No one likes being told what to do.

Among the elected government members, there was much muttering about Watson Thomson's "propaganda" machine. A few party disciplinarians in the CCF began to complain that the adult education people were more socialistic than the party. These party "conservatives" made quite an issue about Thomson's "undemocratic" socialism; his agitation for change had the explosiveness to help defeat the government. Thinking our critics were reactionary, Thomson insisted we go forward with our program and I subsequently made a serious propaganda error that contributed to Thomson's downfall.

To demonstrate how newspapers "build" stories, I assembled related stories and synthesized them into single features. One such article dealt with discrimination against blacks, a serial of scattered incidents about someone being refused admittance to an ice skating rink in Toronto or to a dance hall in Halifax. I did a round-up of these stories to give the lead paragraph some punch. The feature was bannered under a hot headline, "Race Hatred Sweeps Canada." It was a gross exaggeration, the gaffe was an embarrassment to both Thomson and myself.

Called on the carpet by Education Minister Woodrow Lloyd, Thomson was told that the general conduct of his department indicated that he wasn't happy in his job. There were many political reasons why the minister couldn't support him in his program, but he wouldn't say that Thomson was politically too far to the left. Thomson was given six months severance pay. Now was the time for me to get out of sight, to go to Winnipeg for a brief holiday.

In my absence, however, Woodrow Lloyd announced my resignation in the press. The wire service carried the item across Canada. I read the story in Winnipeg. I had not, in fact, resigned. I returned to Regina to face the minister, to protect Thomson and thereby ease my deep guilt feelings and to stand by my conviction that we had been doing the right thing in our program. Fortuitously for me, a wire arrived from the Canadian bureau editor of *Newsweek*. He wanted me to blow the lid off Saskatchewan politics. I went to see Douglas.

"Mr. Premier," I announced, "as you may not know, I haven't resigned. I have been fired. You gave job-security rights to the civil service and I now want to be protected under them. I can't, under union regulations, be fired without cause. If Watson Thomson was fired because of his policies, I should not be fired for following those policies, since they were those of my superior. A civil servant does what he is told."

"In any case," I continued, "if I am fired, that could be a heck of a story to release to the press of the world."

It was a threat and I felt queasy uttering it. But I was righteously outraged by the treatment meted out to me.

"Oh," Douglas quickly said, "I, for one, never intended to fire you." Then, in my presence, he called Woodrow Lloyd and gave him hell.

"Did you fire Parker? Did Parker resign? How did such a story get into the papers? As far as I can see, Parker didn't resign," he continued. "I need him."

He then said, "What would you really like to do for us now that Thomson has gone?"

My reply was immediate. "I would like to use my propaganda skills to help you and your government. How about making me your press secretary?"

He told me to draft a proposal.

With the help of an artist friend, I drew up a visionary approach. "PR would meet VIPs at airports and train stations, show distinguished guests Saskatchewan's achievements. PR would help further good relationships with the press, assist with important releases and meetings." All this was illustrated through sketches as well as text. On receipt of my presentation, Douglas hesitated. There was really no space for me in his office, he demurred. No problem, I pointed out. There was the large entrance hall to the legislature. I would like an office built for me under the centre stairs in the hall. Such a construction would demonstrate that the government had an answer to the complaint of conspicuous waste. Public works built an office for me in the middle of that great reception area and furnished it beautifully – a carpet, chesterfields and floor lamps. My girl Friday at adult education was assigned to me.

I then manipulated the use of the Premier's car. This status symbol gained me authority by association; I had graduated in the eyes of the civil service. A chauffeur would bring the car to my home in the morning, and I would take it from there to newspapermen, visiting media people and others. Press people from all over Canada and the United States began to contact me, thus improving my standing with the Premier.

The *Toronto Daily Star's* leading feature writer, Beland Honderich, came to Saskatchewan in 1945 and settled down for ten days of intensive reporting. He prepared a most laudatory series of articles, and, as a consequence, Douglas commended me for my assistance.

Thomson and I sold our Regina house, and I moved to the home of a family of Jehovah's Witnesses. Thomson left for Vancouver in early spring 1946, and I was locked into my self-promoted job. In the House, the Liberals decided to make an issue of Thomson's leaving in order to discount the Minister of Education. Since I was still in the government's employ, I was also vulnerable, but Douglas forthrightly defended Thomson and me. The times were tense and I could probably have stayed in the government service indefinitely. But I was restive and I wrote Douglas reviewing all the things I had done for his government – organized the recreation movement, assisted the adult recreation movement, and served him in personal ways. He acknowledged my letter of resignation, saying he was very sorry that I was leaving the government.

Thomson and I had been corresponding furiously. He rhapsodized about the beauty of British Columbia and his plans in Vancouver. Vancouver was a distant land, nestled between ocean and mountains, a romantic lotus-land, a place to retire if you were lucky enough to achieve an independent income. I wanted to join Thomson in Vancouver to organize an educational movement on a national basis and to exploit the four thousand names of Saskatchewan supporters I had acquired through our radio program.

My time in Saskatchewan had been in every way a very stimulating and educational one. It was a period which spanned the latter part of the war and the beginning of peacetime, 1944-46. Regina's exhilaration on the day the war was over was expressed in the ceremonial burning of a streetcar. Out of pure high spirit and stupidity,

I lit a bonfire of scrap material in the middle of our street and then worried about burning down electrical wires.

* * *

Before leaving for Vancouver, I went to visit my mother. In Winnipeg, a visit to cousin Sam Berg's office was mandatory. Once again Sam tried to intrigue me into becoming editor of his Anglo-Jewish newspaper. But I was at the crest of my sense of personal esteem. I had been on the high trapeze of government, press secretary to a cabinet, director of a provincial health program and deputy director of a provincial adult education program. The salary I had received in Saskatchewan was $75 a week. I felt justified in asking Sam for $125 a week. He feigned shock and said he considered my attitude a great insult. He thought I was mentally unbalanced and a strain was introduced between us.

On arriving in Vancouver in June 1946, I was warmly welcomed by Mary and Watson Thomson and resided in their co-op home, a spacious house looking out towards the mountains on one side and the ocean on the other. They introduced me to a Bohemian set of writers, lecturers and social workers, people whom Watson knew at the University of British Columbia, and others who were exponents of co-operative living.

I was greeted as an arriving guru, taken emotionally and bodily into the Thomson ménage. For the first few nights, I was given centre stage and encouraged to relate in detail on what had transpired in Saskatchewan in Thomson's absence. I felt like a latter-day Lenin among émigrés.

Together we formed a new-left publishing commune to produce a journal called *Contact*. I cast the journal into an unusual format. Each copy simulated a set of proofs of newspaper clips, ready for setting-up in a paper for printing. I assembled not the finished product, but carefully executed proofs. The content constituted a commentary on peace and the current affairs of our day. *Contact* inveighed against the atomic bomb. We mailed *Contact* out to the 4,000 people whose names we had assembled in the course of our work in Saskatchewan. I would take no pay and my brother in Ottawa advanced me $200 to see me through the next tight weeks. Our vital work was noticed and drew supporters. Many leftist millionaires thought we were saying the right thing about banning the atomic bomb and sought involvement in our political education movement. Such people made generous gestures.

Vancouver certainly was a lotus-land to me. Ethnic people from Eastern Europe were the late-comers to Vancouver. Not as many had come as pre-World War I colonists as was the case in Winnipeg. The first trickle of East European families came to Vancouver between the wars, during the Depression. Unlike Winnipeg, Vancouver was not strong on folk culture, but in the forties, beginnings had been made, particularly among the left-wing, progressive groups. Since I spoke Yiddish well and was co-editor of *Contact*, I found myself booked as a speaker for large Jewish audiences. At such events, I basked in the admiration of the middle-age matrons, mostly immigrants from Europe. To them, it seemed remarkable that a native Canadian could speak Yiddish so well and even write in the language.

I also looked for opportunities to lose myself in local romances. One girl I began seeing frequently impressed me as prissy and puritanical, although strangely attractive. She was Simma Milner, later to be elected to the House of Commons as Simma Holt. When I met her, she was a feature writer on the *Vancouver Sun*. My junior by a year or two, she had been an ardent reporter on *The Manitoban* when I was editor. Ours was a re-union based mainly on campus nostalgia. Certainly I admired her work as a first-class "sob-sister". A sob-sister was a reporter with a great knack of writing tear-jerking stories about orphans, widows and victims of circumstance and society. Regrettably, from my point of view, Simma was a dogmatic Zionist, an emotional, no-holds-barred advocate of a Jewish state in Palestine. She was not as wrapped up in Yiddish culture as I was and had little in common with the Jewish folk community. To her, being Jewish meant identification with political Zionism.

155

In 1946, the issue of Zionism divided the "left" from the "right" in Jewish communities. One's attitude on the question of a Jewish state indicated whether or not one was aware of the possible range of solutions to human problems. For example, one leftist answer was advocacy of asylum in small havens throughout the world, if you could find them; for conservatives, Israel was the exclusive haven.

Like most young progressives, I found little solace in narrow nationalism. I wanted a world in which all humanity would be relatively secure. I wanted to see all immigrants, anybody on the run, made welcome in free societies such as Canada, the United States and other relatively advanced countries of the world. The political realities of 1947 did not favour an open-door policy on immigration, but this was the approach I thought public pressure ought to bring about in Canada.

From the moment Simma and I got together on a date, heated debates became the order of business. Simma was quick to introduce and pick an argument on the issue of Israel. Our non-happening romance was reminiscent of the lyrics of a song I had written in my adolescence. It beseeched:

Shut up and let me love –
What's the use of stars above,
unless you shut up and let me love when I would love you so.
Every time we're out together,
you talk about the weather,
but we'll never get together
until you run out of talk.
You talk about your evening gown,
the boys with whom you've been around,
the movies that you've seen in town,
doesn't all this talking get you down?
So shut up and let me love when I would love you so.

Now at twenty-eight, it applied to Simma every moment of our meetings. True it wasn't movies she was talking about, but Israel, Zionism and destiny.

One evening, Simma agreed to an overnight trip to Seattle in a Rolls-Royce which I had borrowed from one of our millionaire supporters. I conjured fantasies of delicious love-making. By the time dawn came, as we approached Seattle, we were into a raging battle about Zionism. We spent that entire night nursing our wounded pride, each attempting sleep, but far apart on either side of the car.

I also met Eva, the daughter of a Jewish-German millionaire, a refugee from Hitlerism who had made his money as a packing-house king and became Saskatoon's leading benefactor of the arts. Eva was indeed pretty, with fluttering eyelashes, perhaps a nervous condition. The nervous movements belied a sensible and strong person. She and I might have sparked together, but she did not share my social thinking. Thomson liked her, but was nevertheless critical of my spending so much time with her. He was wary of anyone who didn't share our orientation. When I brought people of diverse views to our house, tension would develop between us.

This tension heightened when an English girl, a well-known novelist, came to Regina. I had been introduced to her by the women's editor of the *Regina Leader Post*, Dora, a charming woman who had accepted me as her protégé. I had been a frequent guest at the home of my mother figure. It seems I fell easily into relationships with matronly women. Dora invited this blonde, young, English novelist to her apartment. I was thrilled to meet a published and successful author, and we hit it off. She had a club foot, and mindful of my own correction at birth, I was empathetic to her. She was attractive and a good conversationalist, but her outlook was negative, critical of mankind and of social reform movements. Her cause was her own individual achievement. One night at the co-op house, she proceeded to tear apart all of Thomson's premises. I defended him and my romance blew up.

Leona, a member of Thomson's original Winnipeg co-operative residence in Regina, became my secretary and a romantic interest. Our relationship was engulfed in a clumsiness, like bumping noses when we kissed. Most of our time together was spent in a printing plant at night. Trying to make love on bales of paper in the press room, however, proved to be hazardous and discouraging.

Meanwhile, our resident nymphomaniac, was cutting quite a swath through our little co-operative. Her strong appeal distracted our production schedules. Our editorial meetings reflected our domestic mayhem, something I had not experienced before. It was real-life drama based on the inability of people to level with each other, to talk things out.

Husbands and wives in the co-operative house allowed their differences to surface in the open. On one occasion, a couple arrived and separated in our presence. It was theatre in the flesh. I thought that these confrontations were too intense and dangerous. It was primitive psychotherapy, but Thomson remained calm. I learned much by observing his handling of these situations, both for my personal and later public use.

It was a desperate kind of living, but romantic in many ways. However, I found it impractical to continue to live in the Thomson co-operative because of the tensions, and I moved into a room in a basement apartment. With fall came the damp weather. I developed a terrible cold and neglected it to the point of pleurisy. Two girls I had met at a meeting had phoned to invite me for dinner only to learn that I was choked with cold. Without delay, they arrived by cab to whisk me off to their rooming house to be fed chicken soup and tucked into the largest bed in the house. The one girl would lie down beside me to warm me and to offer comfort. To the girls I was an interesting character. They didn't know what to make of me, but they were intrigued by my dedication to a better world.

From Thomson, I certainly learned how to organize adult educational projects, arrange agendas for conferences and write course outlines. Watson taught me to search for content from within a person's expressed needs. He was a great teacher and I had a great affection for him. But by November 1946, I was looking for an excuse to get out of Vancouver. My six-month sojourn had left me broke and often hungry.

A Winnipeg acquaintance, Estelle Mendes, strikingly attractive, wholesome skin, peaches and cream complexion, then came to visit me. Partly because I wanted an escape from what now seemed a rather bleak Vancouver existence, partly because I was now in debt to my brother, and partly due to a rising conflict with Thomson in regard to the direction *Contact* should take, I decided I was in love with Estelle and declared that I wanted to go back to Winnipeg with her. I had my excuse. Love, real or not, there was no place for courting except in Watson Thomson's home or in the back of the printing shop. It was a puppy-dog romance. To me Estelle was a coquette, an amalgam of many conventional interests then prevalent among Jewish girls. To marry a person of some promise was exciting to her. Easily aroused to passion, she was frightened of losing her virginity.

Love and Winnipeg were synthesized. Estelle departed for Winnipeg, and a week later, just before New Year's, I was seen off somewhat tearfully at the train station by our *Contact* family. In our minds, we were a radical band. One of the leaders of the new day was leaving. It was an emotional parting.

7

HOME AGAIN
– BUT NOT FOR LONG

Back in Winnipeg, I was introduced to Estelle's parents and vivacious sister, Dolly. Papa Mendes was a modest merchant "prince" on Main Street. Success in the second-hand merchant's area meant having an island of first-hand goods. My career to date had made him apprehensive. Consequently, I became the dubious beneficiary of lectures about "getting down to it" and maybe working in his store. I had seen myself as a national leader, a social entrepreneur, and here I was being talked to on a "how are you going to earn a living, boy?" level. While Estelle was warm but somewhat angular, her younger sister Dolly was uncritical and harboured no reservations in accepting me. I was perplexed because I was becoming increasingly aware of Dolly. I decided not to pursue this interest. Life was complicated enough as it was. I was invited to address public meetings on questions of peace, the atom bomb, war, and social justice. Estelle loyally accompanied me to the activist forums, but felt strangely out of place and uncomfortable. Our relationship was undergoing a strain. The test was not whether we could get along physically and emotionally, but whether we could accept each other's values and social expectations.

Estelle and I disengaged and spring 1947 found me moving into another kind of enterprise. Sam Berg invited me once more to his office, once more to ask me to become editor of his newspaper, once more to be faced by my unrealistic salary expectations. Sam reckoned that, since I had struggled as a pamphleteer, surely now I would come and "learn the business" and work for $50 per week. From my healthy estimate of my skills and experience, references to learning the business struck me as an affront. While I knew much about the whole communications field, in the view of local Winnipeg, relations and family friends, I would always be "little Eddie Parker".

My mother was disturbed by my attitude. She really wanted me to remain in Winnipeg. Then she spotted an opportunity. Maurice Lucow, a former high school friend, had approached her and suggested that I join him in *Town Talk*, a weekly newspaper he was publishing. *Town Talk* was the successor to the *Winnipeg Audience*, the tabloid my brother and I had run. Predicated on a similar premise, it gave considerable emphasis to show business, but its contents included a variety of community news. Maurice invited me to visit his operation and walked me through his printing plant, all the time murmuring, "Something big is to happen here in about four or five weeks." My investment would be $2,000, a good chunk of my mother's estate of almost $12,000.

On joining Maurice, I began drawing $50 a week. My major job was trying to sell advertising, something I loathed. After all the grand-scale things I had been doing, selling advertising in Winnipeg for a community paper hurt my pride. *Town Talk* was a throw-away paper, not reflective of my own publishing standards. Winnipeg now seemed an alien setting for me. It was my native spring from which I had climbed to career heights, yet I felt that I couldn't win my way back with dignity.

I tried to express myself editorially in *Town Talk*. It was difficult to create issues to be taken seriously in a throw-away paper. One was a campaign for a new bridge over the Red River near our old Alfred Avenue home. I was campaigning for a second bridge. I liked the old one; the middle span turned to let the ships go through.

Then, one day, a bookie put a teletype in our office. No charge. Nobody suspected why. The bookie made his girlfriend available as a monitor, also free. Allegedly, he wanted to help us grow as a paper. In return, his girl would phone him from time to time to read race results to him. It was a miracle we didn't get arrested. Perhaps it was just within the law. Nevertheless, it was just wrong. This was no place for me.

It was Simkin and the *Israelite Press* I had wanted to impress. After all, I was their "son", a darling of the community, proficient in Yiddish, having excelled at the university, excelled in the community, having worked as a publicist in Ottawa, and having found acceptance in high levels of government. I would have welcomed being taken into the *Israelite Press*, being told, "You have proven yourself, join us." At that particular time, if Simkin had said, "Help us run the paper, the English section," I would have settled for what would have been a very modest career target.

In 1947, I found Jewry involved in an electoral ritual, a biennial event. First started ten years previously, it was to choose ten candidates from a slate of forty as Winnipeg delegates to the Canadian-Jewish Congress being held in Montreal. It was a form of Jewish-Canadian mock parliament. Mildly interested in all this, I recalled that my father ran for such an honour in the first election and lost by a small margin. That defeat had brought a great sadness to our family; it seemed unfair. True, my father was not a Zionist, and most of the people who were elected were. As an individualist and an independent socialist, his lack of social affiliations worked against him in the vote, although he enjoyed a large personal following as a writer.

In my case, I was a bit of an anomaly in the Jewish community. Although I was highly publicized as a talent during my childhood and college years, few knew what I had done since college. I was sponsored by a left-wing youth group and this worked against my apolitical appeal. But such sponsorship gave me quite a machine to help build support for me. Since I was a co-owner of *Town Talk*, Morris Lucow agreed to donate up to a page of advertising in my support. Advertising does pay. Although four-fifths of our circulation was gentile, when the votes were counted, I was the sixth person elected. This was a popularity contest for me in Winnipeg. Although it didn't prove anything, it did mean that I would be given travel allowance to get to Montreal. From there I would be on my own. My promotional instinct took over. I wrote Joseph Atkinson, publisher of the *Toronto Star*, and asked for an assignment as a *Star* European correspondent. His reply was most cordial, offering to buy stories and to give me a letter of identification. This inspired me. With $1,100 in savings, I was ready to take off.

My mother and *Town Talk* were up in the air. I persuaded them that the paper could not offer me a living. *Town Talk* undertook to repay my mother her initial investment on my behalf. The principals, however, didn't live up to their undertaking. After an initial $500 repayment, $1,500 remained unpaid. Nevertheless, I had disengaged from my commitments in Winnipeg. Now I was on my way by train to Montreal via Toronto. After a brief stay at the convention in Montreal, I was off to Halifax to board the *Aquitania* and join about forty young Canadian delegates or observers going to the world youth festival in Prague. This great cultural convention, sponsored in the main by communist-led countries, attracted young people from Asia, Africa, South America and the Western democracies.

* * *

Prague, Czechoslovakia, was exciting and vibrant! My credentials from the *Star* helped me move about as a freelance reporter. Even on the train to Halifax, I had time to meet and interview some of the Canadians who would be boarding the ship. I soon became part of a shared camaraderie. Homer Stevens, an Indian from B.C. became a pal. He was a dedicated union organizer for the fishing industry, a real guy, big, outgoing, tactical and shrewd. In our party were also some undergraduates from McGill, an independent, fun-loving student group.

Once embarked, Homer and three others pulled a great prank on me one night. While I was deep asleep, they raised one side of my berth so that it listed at a 40-degree angle. Then they began shouting "Boat sinking." My eyes popped open. To me, the boat seemed to be listing to one side. Terrified, I screamed, "Let's get out of here!" They then turned on the lights and roared. I decided to keep an eye on Homer the rest of the voyage.

In London, I hit if off well with the young delegates. On our arrival at the railway station, we learned that the group's housing arrangements had fallen through, and we had no place to sleep that night. My suggestion was that we phone the Canadian Salvation Army. Sure enough, the Army had a hotel, and we were all given marvellously clean rooms. One delegate, Marie, who was identified by the very big luggage trunk she carried with her, had a courting eye for me. I was slow to recognize her advances. She insisted on lending me a small radio. I was to return it before the night was out, a singular excuse for coming to her room. She said she was tired, wasn't going out on the town but retiring early to bed, professing not to be feeling well. My head was elsewhere, however, now that we were in London town!

In a small cafe, I ordered a milkshake. To my dismay it was just warm milk. With the group convenor, I found myself wandering the streets of London far past midnight. We got lost and made inquiries of a young tough who offered to walk with us. After strolling some hundred yards with us, he took some knuckle dusters out of his coat pocket. These were made of brass and worn over the fingers like a row of large heavy rings all joined together. In short, they could knock an opponent unconscious. We were very apprehensive, thinking he might rob us. I told him I was a reporter and thought his life story would make an interesting editorial feature and asked him to tell me some of his experiences. He began to relate his biography.

In fact, he walked us to the door of the Salvation Army hotel, an armed escort.

The Canadians on this odyssey were routed through Paris, but I had air travel arrangements to go directly to Prague since my assignment was to cover as much of the youth festival as practical. On arrival I checked into a hotel, taking up my role as a foreign correspondent.

On a subsequent day, I made my way to the Czechoslovakian radio network. There I met an English lady, Ruth, an expatriate working on staff for Radio Prague. An emaciated type, she was nevertheless warm and outgoing. She offered to put me on the English broadcast to the BBC. She would buy any impressions I had of the country. Avoiding politics. I guffed up stories about beer gardens, theatres and the old town of Prague.

In the Prague press club, I met a South African newspaperman, a celebrated Communist writer, regularly published in *New Masses*, New York. We hit it off from the start. He invited me to his home in the country where I met a number of Czech intellectuals. One, a young reporter woman, eyed me suspiciously and divined that I might be a hostile agent. This was the first time I had been confronted with such a suspicious attitude. The suspicious woman asked me who Tim Buck was and I said I didn't know. Preposterous. A Canadian would not have to be a Communist to know who Tim Buck was. Buck was a founder and the long-time leader of the Canadian Communist party and a legend in left-wing circles. The lady was testing me.

A vivacious young nurse who had been sunbathing summoned me to her side and changed the subject. Alice Compatova was open-faced, smiling, bosomy and manager of the Czech airline office in Prague. She wasn't preoccupied with proselytizing for Communism or for anything. She had proven herself an anti-fascist in underground activity. She helped me to understand that people who had collaborated, who had been for the Germans and for the puppet regime, had forfeited their franchise after the war. The current regime was elected by those people who had no Nazi-collaboration taint. As

165

a result, the election gave the Communists 40 percent of the vote, the social democrats 30 percent and the splinter parties the rest. The Communists were the largest parliamentary grouping elected at the time. Alice joined me on the crowded train back to Prague. We stood for hours in the train corridor leaning out the window as she smoked. We talked and talked. Alice kept opening her little metal box containing cigarette butts. She would roll these cigarette ends into a full-length cigarette since cigarettes were highly prized at this time. I offered to walk her home from the station.

We walked the length of the old town, and at four a.m. we sat on a bench near her apartment to kiss, embrace and talk until dawn. I didn't know how to get back to my quarters, so she offered me a place to sleep. Alice had a girl friend who shared her quarters and was still asleep in their room. Alice brought some fluffy pillows out into the corridor and I bedded down. In the morning, people passed by me, perhaps wondering who I was. Later that morning, she introduced me to her friend, a staff writer on the Communist paper, someone instinctively suspicious of me. In a way, this friend was sympathetic, but wondered who indeed I was and whether Alice had been foolish to pick up a guy and bring him home like that.

That afternoon, when Alice and her roommate had gone off to work, I returned to my hostel. I asked my Canadian friend to go to the broadcasting station with me. We simulated a Canadian-style disc jockey show. We played western records and I talked about Canada. Czech radio paid me quite well for these efforts. Those funds helped me live in high style. The Czech writers' union routinely took a percentage of my earnings, but they did something in return. They would negotiate with other markets for my stories. They would argue that my radio scripts could very well become an article for magazines or other media. As a result, I found myself earning $50–$60 a week in freelance efforts for Czech media and I enjoyed the good life, night clubs, theatres. In addition, I had complimentary tickets to many events, since I was a guest of the Prague press club.

My flow of stories to the *Star* was steady. They used them in some form, I believe, but it really didn't matter to me. I was enjoying myself.

* * *

When I first went to broadcast at the Prague radio station, I knew I was running a fever. This was to be my first contact with socialist medicine. A doctor, attached to the student dormitory, appeared promptly. A nice young man, he gave me some pills and assured me I would recover quickly if I stayed in bed for three days. We talked socially and politically. He envied me. He wanted to emigrate, but he was a patriot. Like many Czechs I had met, he was anxious to help in the reconstruction of his country. He was also worried about the resurgence of German nationalism. The Americans, he believed, were going to build up the West Germans as a bulwark against Euro-Communism. The Marshall Plan was destined to affect such a result. The Czech Communist party played on such fears. Czechoslovakia had also been offered help through the Marshall Plan. Gottwald's government refused it on the basis that Czechoslovakia wouldn't take such help if their defeated enemy, the Germans, were to receive it.

On one of my sick-in-bed evenings, Alice Compatova arrived unannounced, bearing gifts – a loaf of fresh bread, a jug of wine, cheese. She was determined to be my friend. I should have sustained my romance with Alice, but I was so busy covering whatever was going on and getting myself cluttered with dates that Alice was neglected. I also dated and neglected Ruth from the radio station, among others. Oh, the fickleness of youth!

A French girl, angular, tall and sultry was introduced to me one morning on those last days in Prague. She seemed unduly charmed by my conversation. She insisted she would like to see me off on the train to Budapest. I gave her the time and place.

In the meantime, Lydia, the official interpreter for a Soviet group, had located me and suggested we go dancing. She liked me and this was a balm to my ego. On a rooftop restaurant, a jazz band entertained an afternoon gathering. Lydia demonstrated several popular

Russian dances. Also a professional ventriloquist, she entertained me with wit and novelty. I was charmed and felt truly saddened that I was leaving that night. She responded gaily, "Be of good cheer," and that was the end of it.

The tall French girl did come to see me off at the train, and the ardour of her farewell kiss disoriented me completely.

At the Yugoslavian border, I witnessed a pathetic scene. Herded onto an open freight car were German prisoners of war. Close up, I saw them as humanity, father, brother and son. The pathos lay in their look of hopelessness. Would they ever see their homes again? My feelings were in confusion. They were Germans. They had been part of invading armies. They had obeyed Hitler's directives. I didn't really want to look at them. Yet at this moment, their personal situations were so bad that I couldn't reconcile myself to their suffering, although it was fair punishment for war offenders. I felt much more strongly about the inhumanity of their leaders who had sent them to war.

By contrast, here I was in Yugoslavia, voluntarily, to work on a youth-built railroad. In our work camp, we found our bunkhouse "shaky" and furnished with plank beds, mattressed with strewn hay to which I was immediately allergic. Up at five a.m. the first morning, I strode out determined to get a real atmosphere story. Black bread, jam and marmalade, courtesy of United Nations Relief, were our staples. There was also some kind of terrible food in cans, marked with maple leafs, fit for dogs.

The August weather was oppressive and from noon on it was difficult to stay awake. I slept a good deal of the afternoon. Others played games. In the evening, visiting singers and dancers entertained around camp fires. Mornings we were out at dawn. Day one convinced me I didn't have the strength to push a rough, heavy, wooden wheelbarrow up the ramp, even half empty. The project director quickly transferred me to tamping down the road bed. I worried that the rail would buckle where I had tamped. I imagined a train pile-up as a result of my inadequate efforts. Finally, the camp committee determined that I was more intellectual than physical. I could sit on a hill and keep count of the wheelbarrows. Bored with the counting after three or four days, I told our group leader, "You know I am a journalist, I have to go to my next story. Good-bye." Before leaving, I traded a shirt for a jar of honey and a gym shirt for bread.

Provisioned, I was on my way to Belgrade, at least I thought so. I got on a crowded train, not south to Belgrade, but north to a very strange area. When I got off the train, there was just a cinder path. I knew enough to stay calm. After some hours, I spread my raincoat on the outdoor cinder platform and pretended to sleep. People walked gingerly around me, staring at me from a distance. It wasn't very long before another train came by, going in the opposite direction. It was empty and I got into it. At this point, I didn't care where it was heading. I took my shoes off and fell asleep, only to be awakened by someone poking a board under me.

Awake, I realized someone was sitting on the other side of the board. He had made a seat for himself. All around me were veiled Moslem women. The one seated next to me had her veil up. No great beauty, she had enormous breasts, one bared, sort of poking at me. The nipple area, looking like an egg-yolk, stared at me. She was breast feeding an infant. In the oppressive, swarmy togetherness, I couldn't find my shoes. When I finally made myself understood to someone, I discovered I was on a shuttle train. I had been travelling back and forth between two stations.

Once in Belgrade, I registered in a modest little hotel. By this time I had grown a short beard and sported a tam. I looked, in my view, raffish. Belgrade had no Canadian embassy, so I made myself known to the American embassy. The officials were leery of this bearded and strangely garbed Canadian. The ambassador, however, liked me and gave me the use of a car and chauffeur for a tour of the countryside. The driver negotiated the purchase of a dozen hard-boiled eggs, and we set off on a round of cultural sites and monuments.

On my visit to the embassy, I met a young, pretty, Yugoslavian interpreter who showed a bright-eyed interest in me. She suggested we go off to see monuments by moonlight. When we did, she seemed very skittish and nervous as though we might be discovered. She showed me a place where we could buy a blackmarket meal. What she wanted was to get out of the country. She proposed marriage almost on sight and offered to dissolve it once in Canada. When I told her that I was not up to such an agreement, she was afraid I would report her and cause her dismissal.

Meanwhile, back at my hotel, there was a coquettish young girl running the elevator. We poked at conversation in basic German. She asked would I like to take her out. That evening, she walked me to a restaurant offering only lobster. She had never eaten this delicacy and asked if she could take some home. Saying good-bye at her door, she invited me to come the next evening and have dinner at her home. Her parents would be away, she implied. I arrived early for the anticipated rendezvous delight. From the park where I sat, I saw her turn into her house. I waved and she returned the signal. But she didn't come out to get me, and I didn't know her apartment number. I don't know whether we got our signals crossed, but my romance got fouled up again. The next day she did not report for work.

I moved into a university residence sharing a room with someone from the United Kingdom. Showers were unsegregated, boys and girls, separate but open cubicles. If you walked by and saw a girl in one, you were to take no notice and proceed to an empty cubicle. Rather unconventional, and disturbing to a westerner.

Belgrade was a dusty and uninspiring city, not as open and friendly as Prague. I made my way to the government offices, where I persuaded the trade minister to send samples of their wines and liqueurs to me in Canada. I was re-united with some of the Canadians I had met earlier, young people coming back from camps and side trips. We formed a party and travelled together by train to Dubrovnik by way of Sarajevo, a Moslem city, scene of the incident which had led to World War I.

Dubrovnik, a moated city, was beautiful, but wasted on me. I had contracted yellow jaundice on the railroad project, but didn't recognize the malaise.

By sloop, I managed my way up the Adriatic Coast to Rijeka. There I wandered about for two or three days, killing time until my ship would sail. I managed my way into a symphony concert where I spotted a gorgeous girl. I had seen no one like her on my travels. She was truly beautiful. This was Ilene, an American, later to be my wife. At the concert, she was accompanied by a young Canadian of Yugoslavian origin. We found ourselves again in the same company on the ship sailing home to New York.

Most of the passengers were young Americans and Canadians returning from Europe. There were debates, shows, and arguments. Since I had no expressed political position, I served as referee and arbitrator. The *Radnik* would take 28 days to get to New York by way of Algiers and Bermuda. Evenings saw a great deal of romantic interchanges in the odd nooks and corners of the ship.

The Yugoslavian sailors were very much aware of our North American girls. Some of the more venturesome co-eds would curl up to sleep on deck at night. The sailors would come and lie down next to these girls. Rumour went that one co-ed presented herself one night in the Captain's cabin without clothes. The captain, it was said, ignored the girl, but the first mate took pity on her and befriended her that night. Love was evidencing itself everywhere. Couples would be discovered behind bails of rope, in nooks and even in life boats. One chap, Archambeau, sporting a biblical beard, had sequestered a maiden in a life boat one night. To the amazement of a few passengers strolling the deck at 3 a.m., he appeared like an apparition out of the life boat. He had wrapped himself in a bed sheet and appeared like a heavenly host carrying a virgin in his arms. The story circulated for days. One frightened, older woman ran about the boat screaming. Some of the students detested Archambeau's beard and his patrician manner. Despite his affectation of nobility, he was constantly begging cigarettes. He was always scrounging something, but in the process, it seemed he was bestowing a favour in letting you give him something.

One night, while Archambeau was deep asleep, a couple of frustrated lads shaved off half his beard, pinning him down when he awakened. Archambeau was furious. He was going to sue the ship, to sue us all. Hastily we set up a mock trail. I became the defender of the ship and its passengers. Archambeau argued his own case. About a hundred youths showed up for the hilarious spectacle. My role brought me more favourably to the attention of the beautiful Ilene Vlahov, who by this time was spending less time with her French-Canadian artist.

Our ship docked at Algiers. Before disembarking for some sight-seeing, the captain warned us about the Casbah. We knew of the Casbah, since it had served as a site for a popular movie. Naturally, we had to visit this den of intrigue. I fortified myself with a bit of chain in the event I was assaulted in the narrow streets of one of the world's most dangerous cities. Algiers was a wide-eyed adventure. Women, both exotic and repellent with various marks on their faces, heightened my awareness of strangeness. Beggars, prostitutes, hovels and the din of people contributed to a sensation of being transferred back in time. We were assaulted by the heavy scents of cooking and the stench of toilet gutters in the streets.

In the modern core of Algiers, we had seen upper-middle-class women who, while of Moslem faith, wore little silk handkerchiefs to cover their faces. In the working-class section of the city, the Casbah, women wore heavy black veils, only their eyes being visible. While on a tour of a palace, I found myself momentarily alone in a cavernous room. I had a premonition I might become imprisoned. A small Algerian boy befriended me and became my guide. He later robbed me of an extra dollar. "Pay me now," he demanded, pressing the knife into my skin about a quarter of an inch. I quickly accommodated him.

Even at twenty-nine, I was still at the stupid age when I would show off in a burst of post adolescent exuberance. Since I was in the company of attractive young girls, I thought I would rouse the natives with my impression of a barking dog. Within seconds I was surrounded by shouting Algerians. They would have killed me. Apparently, simulating a dog is a great insult to an Arab. They thought I was implying that they were all sons of a dog. My guide earned his keep when he fast-talked the mob out of violence, explaining that I was from a strange country and had no malice towards them.

Back on our ship, the next day saw us passing the Rock of Gibraltar. It was a poignant moment. The left-oriented students staged a memorial ceremony commemorating the victims of the Spanish Civil War. It was quite moving. Here we were passing Britain's fortress. Beyond was Spain, to the north. We wanted to communicate, to telegraph a message of solidarity. "You too will have a democracy, slavery is not forever." These were the sentiments the kids were writing and sealing in bottles, throwing the bottles to the ocean in the hope that they might land on a Spanish beach. The gesture was a romantic expression of idealistic youngsters.

A distinct personality on ship, I developed an unusual role for myself. I had socialist sympathies, but I was really incapable of appreciating Communist party discipline. I was also cynical about social democrats who were really too discursive for my sense of direct thinking. Nevertheless, I was persona grata with the young Marxists on board. I was the old man at twenty-nine; most of my companions were twenty and twenty-one. I found myself as chairman in the role of arbitrator at meetings where we tried to hammer out a unanimous response to the New York press. I was anxious to file stories in my own right, so I had a motive in participating. Since I seemed apolitical, my role as "sage" made me a celebrity on the ship.

The night we moved into the Atlantic, a masquerade dance was scheduled. Lack of imagination prompted me to borrow a girl's skirt, and I made myself into a frowzy washerwoman type. Playing clown was fun until I spotted Ilene, glamorously dressed as a siren in silk pajamas and brandishing a long cigarette holder. Her shipboard steady was not around. The two had quarrelled. I was in the wrong costume for what I had in mind. I rushed back to my bunk and transformed myself to "me". Dancing and promenading that evening was very romantic for me. Ilene was only eighteen and an American. To her, a Canadian was glamorous. We talked words of love and embraced. Within a day or two we would be in New York, and Ilene wanted me to call and meet her parents. I waved good-bye to her from the ship as she joined her parents at dockside. I then hurried to a hotel and slept for fifteen hours. When I awoke, I didn't feel very rested; my thought was to go home to Winnipeg. Feeling ill, I discounted contacting Ilene, a romantic image already receding in my mind as do peripheral romances. But I rather liked her and fortunately I had her address.

* * *

I returned by train to Winnipeg in late fall, emaciated, at my lowest weight in years, sporting a chin beard and still wearing my tam. I looked like a displaced person. I was to spend the fall, winter, and early part of spring 1948 with my mother at her Noble Court apartment.

About six weeks after I had returned to Winnipeg, customs informed me that my shipment of Yugoslavian spirits was being held in New York. The state trade commissioner in Yugoslavia had honoured his promise to send me some liqueur and wine as a gift in return for some complimentary PR in Canada. The Manitoba Liquor Commission would admit the bottles only if I paid the tariff. The thirty-six bottles were assessed at about $5 each. It took $180 to clear the shipment. I didn't have the funds, so I borrowed the amount from my mother, who stored the shipment under my bed. One scant taste of cherry liqueur set off the latent yellow jaundice I had been suppressing for months.

I had felt ill on the ship, but I had controlled my sickness with the help of an East European confection, halvah, an oily, sweet sugar, high in peanut value. I had seen it made in Belgrade. A confectioner, who spoke English well, had enthusiastically packed two tins with halvah. When I couldn't face such shipboard delicacies as mashed pig's brains, the halvah was a welcome substitute. The havlah was to be a gift for my mother, but by the time we had reached Milwaukee I had consumed the entire supply.

Our family doctor informed me that the body required lots of sugar to combat the illness and he prescribed extended bed rest.

The halvah had apparently saved my life. I was so enervated that I took to lying down rather gladly for about five or six weeks.

Once settled, I assumed the role and image of a dedicated author. The role was a rationale for not having a specific job and for being in Winnipeg. My chances of gaining a journalistic position looked bleak. Workers at the *Winnipeg Free Press* and the *Winnipeg Tribune* were out on strike, and public opinion was sympathetic to the strikers. The morning paper, the *Citizen*, did not carry enough overnight news to compete without strong editorials. Winnipeg had little night life and only petty crime. It became wearing to see photos of car collisions on the front page every second day.

During this period of personal disorientation, I encountered a strikingly beautiful girl, Luba Pleskow. I had seen her with a male companion in a north-end cafe, but I was not aware of her status. Smitten, I made inquiries over a period of a week and learned that she had entered the hospital for an emergency appendectomy. This gave me an opportunity to introduce myself through letters in which I affected the form of a minuscule human, a Tom Thumb. In this literary pretense, I could take erotic and fanciful artistic liberties, assuming I was sitting on her shoulder, kissing her cheek, or nestling between her breasts. It was a gamble that Luba would be flattered, and she was. She called me and we arranged to meet when she was back home. She was the most forthright person in romantic or sexual terms I had met. I was infatuated.

I had to remind myself that I often used the excuse of falling in love to motivate movement. Perhaps a spirit of derring-do would afford me with a reason to go back to Ottawa, to my area of triumph. I needed to get my career back on track. My face-saving excuse of being in love was effective and I decided to go back and tackle Ottawa.

A cheerful parting with Luba at the train station made my mother think she was in the presence of a possible daughter-in-law. Morten and Gudrun invited me to stay with them and Luba was to join us at a later date. I was to have a romantic summer in Ottawa.

* * *

Prior to Luba's arrival, I went job hunting, but I was too shy to really go the rounds. Gudrun touched a raw nerve when she criticized me for having too much ego to canvas for a job. I took instant offence. She introduced me to a local civic politician. He grandstanded by walking me to the *Ottawa Journal* and speaking to the managing editor on my behalf. Within the hour, I had a job as a reporter. The managing editor later said, "You could have gotten this job a lot easier if you had come in yourself. It was your record and reputation that made you an obvious choice."

The summer of 1948 was strange. When Luba arrived in Ottawa, we found ourselves having little quarrels and my ego was sensitive to critical remarks. We made up on the basis of affection, but intellectually we were having problems.

Luba was idealistic, socially radical and open. She was sensationally successful at parties. She was so attractive that, at an Indian Embassy reception, a chargé d'affaires decided he was in love with her. Even though I was her boyfriend or fiancé, he was not put off and came courting Luba at my brother's apartment. He spent the evening trying to outmanoeuvre me.

The desk assigned me as a member of a team covering political conventions. First came the Conservative leadership convention. George Drew was the front-runner for the leadership. Rumour had it that John Diefenbaker was going to make it a contest. Up to the weekend prior to the opening session, no one knew whether Diefenbaker was going to run or not. Friday prior to the Monday opening, the *Journal* ran a speculative story that Diefenbaker might yet throw his hat into the ring. Meanwhile, back at his hotel, Diefenbaker refused to meet the press.

That Friday evening, not having a meeting with Luba, I wandered through Peacock Alley, off the Château Laurier hotel lobby, and found an expansive Diefenbaker greeting people. I walked up to him and introduced myself as a westerner from Winnipeg. Could I congratulate him on entering the leadership race. This was a ploy. True, I was from Winnipeg, but I was professionally, not politically, interested in him. Diefenbaker opened up and talked to me as though I were a delegate who could vote his way, welcoming me deeply. Then I pointedly asked him if he was going to run. He said he would and began to tell me why. At this point, I confessed that I was a reporter on the *Ottawa Journal* staff. He grimaced. "I don't think you are going to treat me kindly. I think your paper is committed to George Drew." I was a westerner, I reiterated. I would love dearly to try and be fair to him. He decided to give me his story, the full story. I wrote furiously in a hand I could hardly read and rushed back to the *Journal* with a scoop. I was the only reporter with firsthand confirmation that George Drew was going to have a rival.

The night desk got excited. They decided to run my story under the main banner line. The next morning I revelled in the big byline scoop. It was Saturday and I was not on duty, but I went to the office anyway. To my surprise, the afternoon edition didn't carry an inch of my copy. The city editor called me to his side and said, "You are in bad odour. Better go and see Grattan O'Leary." O'Leary shouted that the last thing he wanted to do was to have Diefenbaker in the headlines. His paper was supporting George Drew and here we had given his opposition a break in the next-to-last issue before the nomination.

Monday morning, at the opening of the convention, Diefenbaker called the *Journal* and protested the killing of the Parker story. O'Leary decided to reassure him. To prove he wasn't prejudiced, he would assign Parker to cover Diefenbaker, an assignment to nowhere. However, I began to dog Diefenbaker's footsteps. At one point, I sat at George Drew's table during a convention dinner. His very brilliant and attractive wife Fiorenza watched over him with a hawk's eye. Drew related to me that he had visited Mussolini's grave in Italy and couldn't help being moved. This was really a gaffe, just after the war and talking about visiting a fascist's grave. Whatever else Drew was, he was not a man of great tact nor to my way of thinking someone to admire. This Mussolini reference was dynamite. I was prepared to run with it, but knew the *Journal* would kill the copy. Fiorenza tried to distract Drew at the table. She drew attention to their table number, seven. Drew removed the card and put it in his pocket, saying that it would bring him luck.

As a further chastening, the *Journal* assigned me to cover the fortunes of a most hapless leadership contender, the third candidate, Garfield Case. Case's claim to fame was that he had beat Canada's foremost military man, General Andrew McNaughton, in a recent by-election for a seat in Parliament. Case's bid for the leadership was treated as a bit of a clown act. Told by my editor to get Case's speech in advance, I found the candidate embarrassed. He had no written text, so I sat down with him in his room and wrote a pitch for him. The telephone rang as I concluded. It was George Drew ordering Garfield Case to withdraw. There was no room for discussion. Case would not be addressing the convention after all. Case was dejected. That was the end of his political relevance.

My running copy from the convention won me back into the good graces of my editor and I was asked to help cover the Liberal party convention which followed the Conservative shindig by a few weeks. It was the occasion when Mackenzie King turned over the leadership to Louis St. Laurent. It was pretty tame, but I was more at home here because of my association with C.D. Howe and the Liberal government.

I spent most of the summer of 1948 covering such events as the Ottawa Royal Winter Fair for which both my allergies and attitude were entirely unsuited. I certainly seemed the least knowledgeable person to be assigned to report on horses, cows, and farm produce. However, I did come across one bizarre story. I was in the midst of a crowd when a bull got loose and began charging about. Some quick-witted policeman shot it and I, in Hollywood film style, rushed to telephone the story to my copy desk.

Didn't I find out how heavy the bull was?, I was challenged. That hadn't occurred to me. The rewrite man's scorn energized me and I followed the story of the carcass right through to its delivery to a butcher shop. I fell short of naming the steak and roast buyers. The desk, however, hardly commended my diligence and zeal.

I received a rare pat on the back from the city editor for coverage of an AA meeting. I had reported the evening in a telegraphic, staccato style, in two- or three-word sentences. The editor apparently empathized with drinking problems and was moved by the story.

Another story of which I felt justly proud got me into hot water. It was a feature article reviewing a case in municipal court where an Irish war bride was suing for maintenance support. I interviewed this fiery woman in the court corridor and noted her humorous comments about her "good time Charlie" of a husband. The night editor should have known better than to publish out-of-court comment. The managing editor became livid and gave me hell for risking libel action against the paper. As punishment, I was subsequently assigned to rewrite and to obituaries. The *Journal* had originally hired me to write exposés based on my experience with the CCF government in Saskatchewan. They hoped I would volunteer revelations about Liberal party scandals. This, I could not do; I was incapable of hatchet-job writing. Such angling of stories bothered me ethically.

One morning at the end of the summer, I found a notice on the *Journal* assignment board which stated that, since I had been hired to help out during the summer, my services would no longer be required in the fall. I had never been fired before. This was a real jolt. Under the circumstances, my romance with Luba blew up and she went back to Winnipeg. I didn't want to admit it, but my days as a Prince of the Carnival were over. I would go to Toronto, put down roots and start my career and life in earnest. I planned to join forces with Al Stark, a friend of a remote cousin.

Alan Stark was my idea of a gigolo. He pasted his black hair severely back and emulated Hollywood's version of a Latin-American lover. He would seemingly glower and brood, a mating stance to attract the girls. He and his friends were to help me forget the disappointments of my career, to begin a new life as an expatriate Manitoban, to count no more on living a charmed life simply because I was born a New Year's baby.

CHAPTER 8

RYERSON – THE EARLY DAYS

I arrived in Toronto in the fall of 1948. Stark suggested we live together in his apartment and start a public relations practice. I didn't know how. With very little money and not much hope, we began our little public relation bureau, working out of the Stark apartment.

Our apartment was the scene of many wild parties. I was enmeshed in social activity in a world of actors and began to look forward to putting down roots in Toronto. An advertisement in a daily paper caught my attention. A place called Ryerson Institute of Technology was looking for a promotional director for its school of graphic arts. It had just been converted from a veteran's rehabilitation centre to a post-secondary college. From my wartime experience, I understood "graphic arts" to apply to photographers in the National Film Board stills division. I had produced film strips in Saskatchewan and thought this was what the advertiser had in mind. The title "promotional director" had to denote someone who would be able to publicize the courses. I wrote asking if they would be interested in employing someone with journalistic and public relations skills. I heard nothing for some weeks. Then late in September, Colonel Morley Finley, registrar of Ryerson, called to set up an evening interview. It was a timely call as Al and I were not prospering in our public relations endeavours. I was selling freelance stories and writing theatrical review material, picking up $50 here and there.

Ryerson was a city block of wartime training buildings surrounding the historic teacher's college "model" school. When I arrived in the registrar's office, there were eighteen candidates present, all with backgrounds in printing. When it came my turn to meet the examining committee, I plunged blindly, dropping political names like George Drew, John Diefenbaker, T.C. Douglas, and C.D. Howe. The committee was impressed.

Two weeks later, I was told the committee had narrowed the candidates down to two and I was one. Howard Kerr, the principal, had a gut feeling he wanted someone who wasn't a printer. The other candidate had typographical and some journalistic background. Since I was personally uncluttered, Kerr favoured me. I was invited to meet the Deputy Minister of Education, who asked me a few questions about Winnipeg and the West. Kerr's decision was known to him. He told me that he wanted me. This was quite a surprise and a great boost to my ego. I had a complex about my work for the first CCF government in Saskatchewan, but Kerr wasn't too concerned. It was a period at Ryerson when the administration didn't want to know too much about one's background. All kinds of talented people who had something to live down found themselves acceptable at Ryerson. Out of a seemingly "looney legion" of talent, Principal Kerr fashioned skilled teachers.

I inherited a school with seven printing instructors and a $500,000 printing plant. I was finally fulfilling my earlier ambition to operate a printing plant.

On my first day on the job, Rennie Charles of the English department befriended me and took me on a guided tour of the campus and the school of graphic arts. What a bonanza! I was in charge of an up-to-date printing plant with a capacity to produce books, posters, and newspapers. Years later, I challenged the lithography department to blow up tiny Polaroid shots to massive-sized posters and the letterpress department to print a four-colour portrait of H.H. Kerr on newsprint for the *Ryersonian*. I was determined that the day would come when I would teach journalism to printers.

There were only four full-time students in the printing management course in 1948; another thirty or so were on part-time courses left over from the post-war veterans' rehabilitation programs. Within a year, news of the journalism option at Ryerson attracted forty undergraduates to the printing management course, all of whom were interested in the writing experience.

Ryerson had about two hundred students and a hundred instructors. Kerr wanted the instructors to participate in all aspects of extra-curricular programming. He wanted to make the campus look instantly alive. At our first Christmas dance, Kerr pounced upon me and my date as though we were destined to marry and to become a current calendar event. When I was first interviewed, I sensed the thrust of the question about my single status and said I was thinking of getting married. From that point on, the faculty thought my date was my fiancé and Kerr kept inquiring how my engagement was coming along. At one point, at that dance, Kerr asked me to walk around the dance floor with him and told me he wanted to develop a Ryerson campus paper. We would call it the *Ryersonian*. I was overjoyed.

My ego was restored that winter of 1948. I found myself in a new world, a new institute, just as I had during the war years in Ottawa when the RA was being formed. I would no longer return to Winnipeg. I had finally shaken off my self-image as Winnipeg's "Prince of the Carnival".

Kerr and I had hit it off from the start. I could do no wrong. I overflowed with suggestions and Kerr would back me up, knowing that many of my schemes would bring public attention to the institute. The other instructors cringed, fearing the limelight and seeking to extricate themselves from what they considered to be circus acts.

They were leery of the Kerr-Parker gambit, since I was gung-ho for extracurricular immersion of faculty people.

Kerr agreed with my suggestion to offer a separate journalism course which included subjects such as advertising, layout and editing and with a heavy concentration of graphic arts studies. With this instant and positive response to the offering of a journalism option, he authorized me to employ an additional journalism instructor. I reached out to my college pal and journalistic rival, Earle Beattie, who took to students and teaching with a relaxed joy and involved languor.

The principal's office windows faced the School of Graphic Arts. I would sometimes fudge my time of arrival, being a night person, but Earle would do me one better. He would sometimes enter his classroom via the fire escape to avoid Kerr's apprehension. Beattie's gambit didn't always work and I was often summoned to Kerr's office to discuss the problem of punctuality of my staff. Other schools, whose quarters were behind the principal's office, had staff members with similar idiosyncrasies. Still, we were in the line of sight.

Whenever the question of staff discipline arose, the principal would invite Morley Finley to sit in on the discussion. The other directors and I thought Kerr was always mindful that a dispute could be appealed by some dissident director some day and that Morley was a necessary witness for the administration.

What Morley did contribute, through his urbane, relaxed manner, was a sense that this or that crisis would pass. There was no point in pressing argument to the level of absurdity. A great smoother of troubled waters, he would make Kerr's rough insistences on compliance with front-office dictates understandable through his companionable laugh and shoulder-shrug of fraternal sympathy and understanding.

When I hired a second instructor in journalism, Ted Schrader, full of vim and punctuality, the contrast with Beattie and myself was stark. Earle successfully argued the rights of his seniority and we seemed to escape a crisis on the question of never being late for class. Other questions, such as journalism instructors fraternizing with students over beers at Steele's restaurant, kept Kerr staring sternly across the roadway at the Graphic Arts building. Journalism instructors were viewed as "mad artists" at Ryerson, me included, and some allowance was made in exchange for the assumed colour and glamour.

In 1951 Ryerson innovated an instant tradition. Kerr, consorting with Douglas McRae, the erudite head of the architectural school, elected to have a full academic procession from the main building to the gymnasium on graduation day, spring 1951. McRae owned a clay lamp, presumably found on an archeological dig in Greece. The lamp was thrice blessed by the principal and declared a Ryerson symbol and artifact, the ancient lamp of learning. By McRae's prescription, the lamp was to be borne on a purple or red satin pillow by Jim Handley, then assistant bursar. Handley was selected for his military bearing and precision in walking. The faculty at large was to be gowned in total medieval splendour.

That first graduation pointed in the direction that Kerr wished Ryerson to grow, towards university status and a marriage between technological skills and arts.

In the early years, directors meetings were held every second Saturday morning at 10 a.m. and lasted until 1 p.m. There was some feeling that Kerr, somewhat sadistically, enjoyed having these meetings go through without a break, a trial by bladder so to speak, for staff members.

Dr. Grant Hines, Director of the School of Industrial Chemistry, saw merit in having liberal arts subjects taught to journalism and broadcasting students, but wondered if they should be prerequisites for diplomas in courses in chemistry. He was strongly supported by the trade-oriented schools of fashion, mechanical technology, retail merchandising and photography. On the fence but sympathetic to Hines, were the director of electronics and restaurant and food processing department. Kerr adamantly opposed Hines. Standing with Kerr were Col. Finley of the registrar's office and directors of English, social sciences, graphic arts, business, architecture and interior design departments.

Hines, an articulate and literate educator with an eye on the principal's succession, thought Ryerson should reduce the academic road blocks to management status in some fields. Kerr, however, was resolved to capitalize on any development which would move Ryerson forward to recognition of its courses as degree-worthy.

The ensuing debates at board of directors meetings were masterful exercises in special-case pleading. Kerr was mesmerized by Hines' ability to cast doubt on the efficacy of teaching literature to furniture designers. The stand-off did permit me to timetable subjects in the liberal arts and gave Kerr the rationale for building departments in languages, human relations and the like.

* * *

Cy Steiner, Director of the School of Interior Design, and I became great pals and would steal off the campus during a spare period, meet in Tops restaurant on Yonge Street and discuss Kerr's latest dictum. Cy found the principal to be a conundrum. On the one hand, he was for progress and change, any development which would put Ryerson ahead of university-level exploration. On the other hand, he felt secure only when faced with forms he could recognize.

Kerr preferred antique furniture over modern, failing to recognize that antique was not invariably synonymous with beauty, but mainly evocative of the familiar, the known as opposed to the unknown. Cy believed that to stand by old forms instinctively and emotionally was to give oneself the security an orthodox Hebrew might have when donning a prayer shawl.

Kerr wanted to be certain that industry would support the interior design school as modern and that the departments of education would appreciate the ensuing product as useful land acceptable. To help Cy make friends with the Queen's Park politicians, Kerr had the "furniture school" offer a chair or table as a present to a senior civil servant.

Despite any misgivings he might have, Kerr took me up on my glowing account of my undergraduate experiences at Manitoba and directed me to organize a stunt night. Imagine a performing choir of graphic arts instructors singing the Whiffenpoof song! My staff decided to incriminate me in a stunt of their own. Those were the days of liquor prohibition at Ryerson. At an event held in the new gymnasium, a group of instructors grabbed me, held me down and forced me to swallow the banned liquid. I avoided breathing in Kerr's direction all evening.

An event which involved my friend and associate, Dr. Hines, was the fall field day on the back parking lot at Ryerson. The highlight was a chariot race. Students made vehicles designed to raise chills of suspense. Kerr thoroughly enjoyed the role of judge. He also seemed inordinately proud when Dr. Grant Hines, representing the faculty, won the pie-eating contest one year.

I directed a production of Jean Anouilh's *Antigone* in 1954 to communicate the conflict between youthful idealism (the students) and pragmatic authoritarianism (Kerr). Kerr saw no contest. *Antigone,* in his view, was foolish to question the realities of court politics and the life of a royal and favoured niece and princess and to court disaster by standing up for principles.

Kerr was respectful of trade unions and made a point of saying that my job as head of a school of printing was particularly delicate, since as many as four trade unions were represented in our shop. He was most apprehensive about Jim Davidson, the crisp, letter press instructor. We were to instruct Jim to stop using a spittoon, but rescinded the order when we learned that Jim was keeping a diary of our daily administrative transgressions against his union.

The man who kept the buildings renovated and expanding was the chief of maintenance, George Hitchman. "Me and H.H." was the way George liked to indicate the nature of the power structure at Ryerson.

To my everlasting shame, I chose to be obsequious to George and was rewarded by having an extension built as an addition to the graphic arts building. Regrettably, I couldn't convince George to build handrails for the steep stairs leading to the second floor addition. When I finally fell down those stairs, raised a bruise on my bottom the size of a watermelon and showed this injury to Finley in the men's washroom, George was moved to compassion and built one rail. "Enough is enough," was his classic comment. George once shared confidence of confidences with me and led me to his office down rickety stairs into the deep basement of the third building. "H.H. never comes here," he said. Here, George and his staff could have a nip of rye and scotch and no one would be the wiser. Except, Kerr. . . He knew!

The principal faced opposition regarding a tie-and-shirt school dress code. Kerr was right, but the rationale was, "Wear the right haberdashery. Do it or get kicked out." Some of us thought that had Einstein been an undergraduate, he would have been turfed out for not wearing socks. Kerr's visual prejudices included beards on men and long hair for girls. In view of general public prejudices of the time, he was mainly right.

The only beard on campus was that of Max Rosenfeld, an exciting lecturer whose "free" lunch-period talks packed the auditorium. Kerr wanted him fired. The girl with the longest hair was Joan McCormack, a campus queen candidate, journalism scholarship winner and all-round popular student. Kerr was certain she wouldn't land a job looking like that, but she became one of the first TV newscasters for CFTO.

Kerr's attitude to education and training was pragmatic. He had in mind the institute of the future, the Shangri-La that would await tomorrow's youth once a full-scale polytechnical centre, like the Massachusetts Institute of Technology, was realized. Boston's M.I.T. was his favourite prototype. As a consequence of his preoccupation with 'what will be,' he had little feeling for injustices suffered by current undergraduates.

To receive larger budgets from the department of education at Queen's Park, he instructed the registrar and directors of schools to wink in some years at the grade 13 prerequisites, which he himself thought necessary if Ryerson were to rise to university status. We would then admit borderline cases. In another year, we would turn them down. When the pursuit was the acquisition of college-level instructors, Kerr would prescribe strict adherence to admittance requirements and a higher failure rate in the undergraduate years. He sought, in every way, to impress Queen's Park with our need for better-qualified teaching resources.

On one occasion, the editor of the *Ryersonian* had published an article critical of the department of education regarding Ryerson's need for new buildings. Kerr, afraid that the daily press would attempt to contact the editor to follow up the story, had him kidnapped and held prisoner in the boardroom. Another time, Kerr hoped to appease the deputy minister by having one of his staff bake a terrific cake for him. We did get our million-dollar budget that year, so his Seaforth, Ontario, political sense must have been right again.

After I had been teaching for four years, Kerr ruled that all staff without teaching certificates would be required to attend four consecutive six-week summer sessions at the Ontario College of Education to qualify as masters in their field. What an ordeal and usurpation of staff holiday time!

Instruction was based upon precepts involved in teaching manual arts at the public-school level. History involved kindergarten discoveries of Pestolazzi and the elementary methodology left most of my craft teachers buffaloed. Coffee breaks, two each morning, were elongated to 30 minutes, and I joined Mac Tobin's human understanding group. Our talks were around love and marriage, most useful insights which we could subsequently impart to students so diverted.

Overall, Howard Kerr was a man to be honoured. He was courtly, sensitive, warm, and welcoming. This cordiality and consideration was best exemplified in the company of his quiet spoken, entirely engaging, attractive wife, Bea. In the early years, the two opened their home to staff receptions and dinners and contributed a sense of importance and fellowship to academic colleagues.

One morning in April 1955, I endured a serious confrontation with him. Kerr was on a cost cutting campaign, anxious to demonstrate to provincial educational minister Dunlop and Deputy-Minister Althouse, that he could run a fiscally tight educational ship. At the time, in addition to my duties as a school director and my overseeing responsibilities for students, staff, equipment and course content, I was also lecturing sixteen hours a week on newspaper management and advertising. Kerr thought I should add four additional lecture hours to my schedule to teach a new course in political science. I had come to him for more staff and equipment. In the stand-off, I received more equipment and less staff.

Kerr sensed my frustration and declared that I would never find another job as good as the one I had. I left his office muttering, "I'll show him. . ." It was in this mood that I opened my morning mail and noted an unimpressive envelope from Technical Mine Consultants Limited, Toronto. I thought its correspondence of little consequence, but its one paragraph content was the key to an 'Alice in Miningland' experience and a completely unforeseen, oblique and enveloping career move.

Within the seven years that I was director, the school's diploma courses in practical journalism and printing management grew to incorporate arts courses in English, French, history, economics, industrial relations, political science, typing, photography and news broadcasting. By my final year as director, 120 students had been attracted to journalism and 80 to printing.

CHAPTER 9

THE URANIUM BOOM
OF THE MID FIFTIES

Joseph H. Hirshhorn and Franc Joubin were the uranium kings of the world in 1955, but I had never heard of them. I was rooted in the part of the world in Toronto centred around Dundas and Yonge streets. My commitment had been to the Ryerson Institute of Technology on Gould Street, as Director of Graphic Arts and founder of courses in printing management, journalism, and advertising.

Joe Hirshhorn's mining empire was headquartered in the Bank of Nova Scotia building on the corner of King and Bay streets. Franc Joubin was its managing director. Under the inspired guidance of geologist/prospector Joubin, Hirshhorn had promoted the formation of companies poised to exploit the vast uranium deposits in the Blind River/Algoma area of Ontario. His organization, Technical Mines Consultants, had some fifty companies under its aegis, among them iron, copper, gold and silver properties of considerable promise.

Hirshhorn, a financial celebrity in 1955, had first come to the attention of Bay Street with his procurement of a gold producer in the

Timmins area, Preston East Dome Mines Limited, in 1933. With Yankee flair, Joe had on arrival in Toronto purchased a page advertisement in the *Northern Miner* and proclaimed himself a messiah for the Canadian mining industry.

The letter I had received from Technical Mine Consultants was brief and to the point. Would I please contact writer Harry Buckles, P.Eng., with regard to a matter of some interest. I decided to learn something about Technical Mine Consultants in advance of phoning. I called my graduate, journalism student, John Soganich, a writer for the *Northern Miner.*

John was instantly enthusiastic. I had been contacted, he exuded, by the "hottest" mine finders on Bay Street. He agreed to visit me in my apartment that night and brief me properly.

The next day I was in touch with Harry Buckles who, in a low, almost conspiratorial voice, asked me to meet with his chief, Franc Joubin, that afternoon. I was to learn subsequently that the volatile vortex of a mine finding operation made it mandatory for most technical people to be circumspect and secretive. I had no teaching commitment at 3 p.m. that afternoon, and the appointment was set.

Bay Street, the Bank of Nova Scotia Building, the nineteenth floor; this was all a new world. Within minutes of my arrival, Joubin's gracious, soft-spoken, Japanese-Canadian secretary appeared, asked me to follow her across the hall to an unmarked, small office, separate and nondescript compared to the outer office and adjoining boardroom.

Franc Joubin personified "quiet": a faint smile, a firm handshake and a polite excuse while answering his phone. I heard mumbled phrases about drilling, uranium values and instructions to proceed as agreed. When he finally turned to me, Joubin was direct, to the point. Would I be interested in becoming the public relations officer for the J.H.H. interests in Canada?

Joubin surprised me by saying that he had had my background researched and considered me right for the job.

"But I know nothing about mining," I blurted.

Joubin beamed. "Excellent," he said. "You won't be second guessing those of us who do."

"I am unfamiliar with the stock market, with Bay Street."

"Joe will be glad to hear that. He'll be able to trust you."

So far, I could do no wrong.

"I have worked for a social democratic government, the CCF, in Saskatchewan." This would certainly prove to be anathema to a free enterpriser.

"Good," he said. "We have an operating uranium mine in northern Saskatchewan and some excellent properties in gold, silver and copper at Lac La Ronge. You know the mines minister, Brockelbank?"

My head was swimming. I nodded affirmatively.

"You have also worked in Ottawa with the Rt. Hon. C.D. Howe. As you know, Howe negotiates our uranium contracts with Washington. Your present employment with the Ontario government will work well on behalf of our provincial interests here. You are just what we want – apolitical."

Joubin then began to describe Joe Hirshhorn, but felt that I should not make up my mind regarding this career change until I met the legendary dynamo. Joe was currently distracted by a personal embroilment and was getting scandal-sheet treatment in New York and Toronto. A former secretary was suing him for a tidy sum, charging breach of promise, ignoring the reality that he was reportedly happily married to a beautiful New York painter, Lily Harmon. Joubin wanted to know, what did I think.

"If Hirshhorn is as wealthy as I have heard," I opined, "then I would predict that this transient notoriety cannot hurt him in his business dealings. His personal life may be another matter. This publicity will not prevent the chairman of the Bank of England rising from his chair and greeting Hirshhorn warmly."

Joubin seemed pleased. "Joe would appreciate that comment."

The interview impressed me as theatre, unreal. I was relieved when Joubin said that he would call me in a week or two and set up a meeting with Hirshhorn. My thoughts were in a whirl as I walked

The publicity directorate for the Department of Munitions and Supply, Ottawa, January 1943. Seated (left to right): Leslie McFarlane, Rielle Thompson, myself. Standing (left to right): Achibald Newman, Fred F. Field, Theo Dorion, Phyllis Poland, Gordon Garbutt, and Nolin Trudeau. (NFB Photo)

Norval Gray and myself, photographed April 25, 1943 in Ottawa. (Provincial Archives of Manitoba JM 2758)

(Right) Directing RA promotional activities during the war.

Members of Tommy Douglas' team responsible for implementing the Saskatchewan Recreation Movement, Regina, 1945. Left to right: G.C. Darby, myself, Dr. J.B. Kirkpatrick, Major Ian Eisenhardt, Premier T.C. Douglas. (Wilf Collier, Regina, Saskatchewan, Photographer)

WITH A FULL FIRST YEAR in Journalism and Printing assured by the excellent registration, MR. PARKER points up questions now relevant to preparations for welcoming a second year in Graphic Arts.

Watson Thomson, Director of Adult Education for Saskatchewan, and his son, Colin. His was an eloquent voice for liberalism and humanism.

The Ryersonian, *December 1949 issue.*

(Below) Showing Mother the University of Toronto campus in the 1940s.

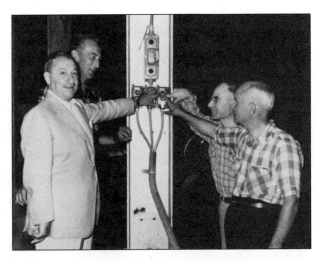

Pronto Uranium Mines was an incredible discovery, no more than a mile and a half from the Trans-Canada Highway, just 17 miles east of Blind River, Ontario. Left to right: Joseph H. Hirshhorn, promoter, Paul E. Young, Mine Manager, Franc R. Joubin, mine discoverer, and William H. Bouck, lawyer-president, placed forefingers in unison on the start-up button, and, to everyone's relief, the mill started up. (National Archives of Canada PA187449)

Some 500 guests joined company officials for the opening ceremonies at Pronto Uranium Mines Ltd. on August 28th, 1955. Left to right: W.H. Bouck, Mine President, J.H. Hirshhorn, Mrs. Hirshhorn and Franc R. Joubin. (National Archives of Canada PA187447)

Newly married, Ilene and I attended the Buffalo Nuclear Conference, 1955.

The amazing Franc Joubin autographed this photo during my tenure with World Mining Consultants Limited. (Canadian Television Films "Still" Division)

Arriving in Elliot Lake mining country by float plane. Circa late 1950s.

*A contrast in styles. My employers, Joseph Hirshhorn and Dr. Franc Joubin.
(National Archives of Canada PA 187446)*

The Ottawa opening of Joseph Hirshhorn's personal art collection. Left to right: Governor General Vincent Massey; Alan Jarvis, Director of the National Gallery; Brenda and Joseph Hirshhorn, and Mrs. Alan Jarvis. (Photo by Newton, Ottawa)

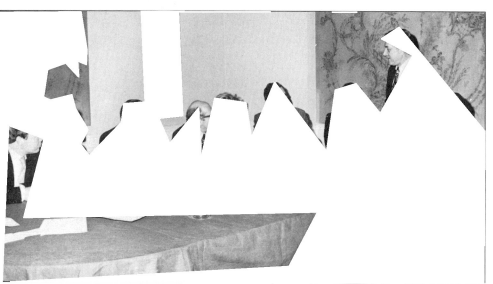

Ilene (second from left) and I (far right) as Canadian hosts of the International Public Relations Association Conference. Circa 1960s.

Mr Uranium, Joe Hirshhorn

by Ed Parker

What follows is an excerpt from a memoir of Mr Uranium, Joe Hirshhorn written by Ed Parker, who served as public relations officer for Mr Hirshhorn's interests in Canada from 1955 to 1956. After that, Mr Parker spent seven years with Rio Tinto and then opened up his own public relations firm. This is the first of a 2-part story.

Joe Hirshhorn's mining empire was headquartered in the Bank of Nova Scotia building, corner King and Bay streets, in Toronto. Franc Joubin was its managing director. Under the inspired guidance of geologist prospector Joubin, Hirshhorn had promoted the formation of companies poised to exploit the vast uranium deposits in the Blind River/Algoma area, Ont.

Joe Hirshhorn

Hirshhorn's organization, Technical Mines Consultants, (TMC) had some 50 companies under its aegis, among them, iron, copper, gold and silver properties of considerable promise.

Hirshhorn, a financial celebrity in 1955, had first come to the attention of Bay Street with his procurement of a gold producer in the Timmins area, Preston East Dome Mines. That was in 1933.

With Yankee flair (Hirshhorn was a New York-based promoter), Joe had on arrival in Toronto purchased a page advertisement in The Northern Miner and proclaimed himself a messiah for the Canadian mining

greeted, striding toward my desk. "Have you had breakfast? I'll buy you a meal."

Walking, or in fact trotting, alongside the diminutive Hirshhorn, was an experience. We headed for Child's restaurant, then located on King and Yonge streets, southwest corner. Hirshhorn ordered the works and the total bill for both was under four dollars. He left a dollar tip.

I was fascinated that Hirshhorn had dug into a pants pocket and produced a thick wad of bills, held together by a broad elastic band. Noting my mezmerization, he explained," I always carry a large roll in my pocket, in case I need it

An article I wrote for The Northern Miner *reminiscing about the Hirshhorn days.*

The original public relations team – left to right: Bill Freedman, John Black, Marian E. Bogard and myself. (Feature Four Ltd. Photographers)

Off to Ireland with the staff for the opening of Northgate Mine.

Montreal during the early 1970s: André Beauchemin, my lovely wife Ilene, Claire Beauchemin and myself. (Photo from André Sima Association International Press Service, Montreal, Quebec)

Ben Viccari and companion, Ilene and myself, at a Rosedale Theatre Fund Gala evening, during my Presidency of the Toronto Arts Theatre Club. (Toronto Telegram Photo)

home. The next day, I was back at Ryerson, teaching. All was normal again. Seemingly.

* * *

Two weeks later, the call came at ten p.m. It was from Franc Joubin. Hirshhorn would be in Toronto in the morning, and a meeting had been set for nine a.m.

I came early, spick and span, proudly dressed in a new suit which had been purchased in a dim light at Henry Faber and Son on Yonge Street, the theatrical tailors. I was uneasy about my decision to wear the unused garment, a bit flashy, a slightly fluorescent light blue.

Hirshhorn's immediate comment on meeting was, "Where did you get that suit? Harlem?"

I was momentarily offended, but there was a twinkle of merriment in Joubin's eye and I noticed a sly wink. Hirshhorn grinned broadly as he chomped on a cigar and spoke with machine-gun rapidity. He insisted that I see his oil paintings stacked against walls in every office and the "way-out modern" sculptures in his boardroom. He drew my attention specifically to a large, five by four foot canvas, painted solidly black save for a chalk-like white dot in a corner. He wanted to know my reaction. What did I sense? I skirted the question by saying that I hadn't quite seen any work like it in my life.

Across the boardroom table, I shook hands with Sam Harris, the canny New York barrister who had served the U.S. interrogation team at the Nazi trials at Nuremberg. Harris began to interview me methodically – where was I born; where was I educated; what was my first job.

Hirshhorn's patience was quickly stretched thin. "Go ahead, I am listening," he encouraged, as he began to use the two phones in the boardroom.

Hirshhorn had a telephone console built into the desk in his own office, with lines connected to two dozen investment houses. As I laboured on in my recitation, Hirshhorn continued to make calls, muttering, "buy," "sell," and "I'll get back to you" to a succession of contacts.

The great man was taken aback when I asked to use one of his phones. I wanted to call Ryerson and ask to have a class cancelled.

He could not contain his impatience. "How much do you want, kid?"

I mentioned a figure, twice my current salary.

"I can get someone from New York for two thirds," he dickered.

"The man from New York might not be worth it," I volleyed. "Much of his time would be spent explaining why an American was brought from the States to deal with Canadian newspeople, an obvious disadvantage."

Joubin chortled.

"Well," said Hirshhorn, "we'll meet half-way. Talk it out with Joubin. After all, we don't want you earning as much as he does."

Harris, Joubin, and two others who had joined the group roared with laughter.

Calling out to Lena Greenwald, his secretary, for coffee, Hirshhorn was suddenly caught up with a euphoric urge. "I feel felonious today," he announced. To my surprise, he produced a pitchman's straw hat, plopped it on his head, took a Charlie Chaplin cane off a stand and did a vaudeville buck and wing. Everyone applauded.

I had met my future and been inducted as publicity officer of Technical Mines Consultants (TMC) by my new boss, the Runyonesque character with the multimillion-dollar promotional flair, Joseph Herman Hirshhorn.

What a strange world this TMC hive of geologists and engineers seemed to me! Various staff members would pop into each other's rooms for hurried meetings, telephone calls, and daily reports. From associated offices or from the field came a plethora of technical people whose names I was in a panic to learn quickly.

Harry Buckles, the chief engineer, was my reassuring reference point. I knew we would be friends when he explained that the hole in his fedora was made by a poorly targeted bullet. Tall story teller or not, I liked Harry.

I was writing two or three news releases a day on pure faith that the information I received was accurate and that what I composed reflected the engineer's understanding and intent. I had no idea about diamond drilling programs, assay results, mineral values and feasibility reports. My naiveté was clear to the mining press; reporters without exception were kind to me on the understanding that I would be candid with them.

"When it comes to technical reports," Franc Joubin advised, "issue nothing without first clearing with me." He explained that I could be mislead by a layman's reading of results.

Within a few days, I found myself hurried into Hirshhorn's office by his aide, Steve Kay, and told to release diamond drilling results with regard to an off-shore Lake Huron exploration program. Kay said Hirshhorn wanted the news out immediately. It was undoubtedly accurate. Still, I waffled, cleared the text with Buckles, and waited for Joubin, who said he would speak to Hirshhorn. Joubin had thought a news release at this time would prove premature.

Indeed, I felt very insecure those first days on the job, so much so that I took to arriving in the office earlier than the suggested 8:45 a.m. rule. I was there at eight a.m. that second week when Hirshhorn arrived one morning by cab from Union Station. I could hear him loudly initiating calls to Hong Kong, Berlin, New York, London and Paris. I clicked away at my typewriter. Hirshhorn took a breather and heard the noise next door.

"Hi, kid," he greeted, striding toward my desk. "Have ya had breakfast? I'll buy you a meal."

Walking, in fact, trotting, alongside the diminutive Hirshhorn was an experience. He was bawling me out. "Why didn't you do as Kay had asked?" he demanded. "Whatsa matter, kid, has Joubin seduced ya?"

The latter comment ended the harangue and was delivered with a wink and a twinkle of the eye. We headed for Child's restaurant, then located on King and Yonge streets. Hirshhorn ordered the works and the total bill for both was under four dollars. He left a dollar tip. I was fascinated that Hirshhorn had dug into a pants pocket and produced a thick wad of bills held together by a broad elastic band. Noting my mesmerization, he explained. "I always carry a large roll in my pocket, in case I need it for a quick get away."

He seemed to chuckle all the way back to the office. On arrival, the TMC staff was in an uproar. The switchboard operator was frantic. "Mr. Hirshhorn you have calls from Hong Kong, Berlin, Tokyo, Berne..." Hirshhorn had set the stage for his entrance.

JHH swooped into his outer office where groups of brokers and investors from the U.S. and Canada awaited him. He beckoned them all into his office where he took his position at his console of phones and, chomping on his cigar, obscuring enunciation, began to bark orders and advice to his callers. "It's sexy. Buy some."

A red cap from the King Edward Hotel appeared and was ushered into the Midas presence. "Take this brief case and that painting to my suite at the hotel. Gentlemen, what d'ya think of my art?"

With staff rushing in to consult him, Hirshhorn was the legendary epitome of busy-ness. Phones ringing, buy-sell orders, coffee being commandeered and dictation being taken. By the time he got around to speaking to his visitors, most had excused themselves to hurry to phones and buy shares of the companies whose names they had overheard.

On the phone, his voice would drop to a confidential whisper. "Buy," he would advise in rapid-fire mumbling. His recommendations variously included Rix Athabasca, Anglo Rouyn, Plum, Peach, Pronto, Spanish, American, Panel, Buckles, Preston, Perlite, Oceanic, Pater, any number of companies in which he was involved. Hirshhorn's Toronto office operation was like activity on a Hollywood movie set, particularly when he was present and in charge.

The Hirshhorn–Joubin uranium bonanza was enjoying daily news coverage as I settled down to my press officer's job in the summer of 1955. In addition to the local financial and mining press, the "boom" development of the Algoma mining region was receiving attention in the national and international press. Plans for a town at Elliot Lake, a provincial highway to replace the original "ox" road pioneered by Harry Buckles, and "presto" housing developments were revealed in a succession of bulletins.

Time and *Newsweek* carried feature stories on Hirshhorn and

Joubin. *Life* magazine had a photo of Joubin in prospector's garb on its cover and a Hollywood producer toyed with the possibilities of a film treatment of the great Algoma uranium discoveries. References to the Blind River mining bonanza were included in press stories on Canada throughout the world, particularly in France, England and Germany. Share transfer sheets from the registering trust companies revealed that Hirshhorn's companies had considerable investor followings in many countries.

Toronto-based reporters from a host of newspapers – *Financial Post, Northern Miner, Globe and Mail,* the *Star,* the *Telegram,* Canadian Press, *Financial Counsel* and Dow Jones – introduced themselves to me. Hirshhorn gave each one a royal welcome and a story angle.

Franc Joubin encouraged me to find an opportunity to have each reporter meet with him or his subordinates to have the technical material vetted by the professional experts. According to Franc Joubin, some order in the dispensing of information to the public was taking shape and Hirshhorn was beginning to defer to conventional techniques for publicizing developments. The TMC press releases had ceased to look like shopping flyers and were taking on the appearance of unadorned and tightly composed information bulletins, a fulfillment of Joubin's goal. Press clippings of stories dealing with TMC, its properties and its principals poured into our offices in such numbers that it became impractical for us to continue to receive them as part of a *Financial Post* service.

One day, I chose to dump a month's clippings on Hirshhorn's desk, proof that I was an eager beaver at my job.

"I am impressed," Hirshhorn told me, "but all this doesn't call out any magic on your part. Now, if you can get me a spread in *Fortune* magazine, then I'd know you were a true public relations specialist."

Notice in *Fortune* was most coveted by Hirshhorn's peer group in the United States, and mention of the uranium king in this prestigious publication had eluded Hirshhorn. He confided that he had engaged his good friend, Ben Sonnenberg, the legendary public relations man in New York, to work on the problem. I felt challenged and dismayed.

I had no particular legerdemain to demonstrate, no "in" with *Fortune*. All I could do was write to the publisher and briefly identify Joe Hirshhorn as the uranium king of the world, tell of his humble beginnings as a messenger on Wall Street, his becoming a millionaire at 19 years of age, his expertise at forecasting stock market behaviour in 1929 and bailing out with four million dollars before the crash, his subsequent impact on migrating to Canada at age 35 in the dirty '30s, the remarkable teaming with Franc Joubin in the early 1950s, and the testing of the far-out "Big Z" theory of the 100 square-mile uranium swath in northern Ontario's Algoma region.

Six weeks after writing to *Fortune*, I received a phone call from New York from Emmett Hughes. Hughes had been President Dwight Eisenhower's speech writer. Prior to that he had been the publisher of *Fortune*. Now he had returned to his former publication and was given a choice of possible stories on which he could work.

My letter was among four other proposals he was examining. He was fascinated with Hirshhorn's interest in art and chose to do an in-depth biography of the "little king". What followed was most pleasant for me.

Hughes came to Toronto for a week. A fascinating man in his own right, he and I spent many hours and mealtimes collaborating on his article. He interviewed Hirshhorn and his associates at length and had a leading New York photographer take pictures. The editorial result was a twelve-page spread in *Fortune*, complete with four-colour photos of Hirshhorn and his most-prized paintings.

Hirshhorn, an ambition realized, was elated and had me phone a news vending agency immediately to order 100 copies of *Fortune* for instant use. He had already bought out the twelve copies at the King Edward Hotel and was busy handing them out to those in Toronto who might be impressed. "Get copies over to Bill Bouck, John Aird, all my lawyers," he ordered. "Got to give one to Charlie Burns, Burns Brothers brokers, kid."

Joe then received a call from Ben Sonnenberg.

Hirshhorn winked at me. "Sonnenberg, you old bastard, I got the publicity all myself. I don't need you." Laughter, then, "I'll get back to you, Ben!"

Then he said to me, "Well, what are you waiting for? Order 500 more copies."

* * *

Hirshhorn's comings and goings were not often known in advance to his staff. The rise of the sound and tension level emanating from his office indicated that JHH was in town, conducting court. He would spend three to four days in Toronto every two weeks. He found a way to make contact with me early. I was included on his list of people he would call at their homes past midnight, sometimes as late as two a.m., and demand, "What's happening?"

Early each day, he passed all his nuisance letters onto me for acknowledgement. "Most of these," he said, "are begging letters. I used to ignore them, but then people would actually travel great distances to come and see me on the off-chance that a personal meeting would melt my heart. I can't take that."

The letters were primarily pleas from the sick and destitute. On occasion, the writers would include photographs. One, a self-styled Austrian countess writing from Vienna, sent a batch of glossy photos of herself in the nude and in the most accommodating poses.

"Look at these, kid," Hirshhorn smirked. "Don't get caught encouraging this kind of thing or we'll be set up for blackmail."

Blackmail and kidnapping were very much on Hirshhorn's mind, but he suppressed his anxieties to move freely on Toronto streets. Hirshhorn encouraged me to give work to his secretaries. Janet Ritchie offered to do my personal typing, just to be busy when Hirshhorn was not in town.

I found myself writing letters on behalf of actors and artists who came by seeking help with their projects. I could not hold out any prospect of bringing their interests to Hirshhorn's attention, but I could speak glowingly of them to others in correspondence. Al Saxe, a co-director of the Actors Studio of New York, and Joan White, a prominent British actress, were thus helped in establishing themselves in Toronto.

199

Canadian broadcasting and acting star Lorne Greene, then prominent in the Stratford Festival, came by one morning, and Hirshhorn agreed to see him.

"What can you do for me?" was Hirshhorn's expansive hello.

Greene's rejoinder to Hirshhorn's opening line of banter stymied the interview. "I can help you spend your money," Lorne answered jovially, having in mind a film project in which he was interested. Hirshhorn glowered. He was not amused and the interview was soon terminated.

"People shouldn't come to me for money, but for ideas, promotional strategy," he complained to me later.

Hirshhorn, when annoyed, would chomp on his cigar and turn his attention to his telephone console. He would start making calls, a signal for those present to leave. I learned to creep out of his office on such painfully disruptive occasions.

* * *

My office was carved out of the centre of the TMC complex. It really provided a short cut to other offices for staff on the run. My area had two doors. JHH could save time by entering from the outside corridor, cut across in front of my desk in a diagonal line and exit through the door facing the receptionist. In this way, I had a communication advantage over most staff.

Willy nilly, I saw the boss more often than most of his senior colleagues who were hunkered down out of sight in their less-accessible offices, some in other buildings. Hirshhorn's compulsion to say something as he whizzed by gave me a dot and dash impression of what was happening in the world of art and mining.

From Hirshhorn, I learned that half a dozen exploration projects were coming to a boil – a large industrial mineral find in Alberta, a copper deposit of size in northern Saskatchewan, a huge low-grade iron deposit in Ungava and the incredibly encouraging uranium properties near Blind River, Ontario.

With his penchant for Ps as the first letter of names of his lucky companies – Preston in the Timmins gold mining area and the Peach syndicate in the Algoma uranium region – Hirshhorn would mutter Pater, Pronto, Panel, Plum, Perlite as part of near-inaudible tips to favoured visitors. Of these, Plum Uranium Mines Limited seemed to be the most disappointing in drilling results at the time. Joubin's advice to me was to say to inquirers that a plum is a slow, ripening fruit. Hirshhorn was not greatly amused when I repeated the witticism.

No sooner had Hirshhorn, in passing, uttered "Good news, kid," mentioned some company, and disappeared, than I began to hunt for details from Harry Buckles, Don James, and Tom Griffis. I would then attempt drafts of news releases. Franc Joubin would check my work for content, accuracy, and timing.

It was an exciting period. The duplicating machine was noisily at work each day, and the postage machine was busily addressing hundreds of envelopes containing progress reports on various programs which were bagged and mailed to domestic and international press, analysts, and interested investors.

Since I was scrounging clerical help daily, Franc Joubin decided to grant me my own secretary, Jeannie Maltby, an earnest dedicated assistant who would keep her husband, Jim, waiting in our outer office for hours each evening as we processed the day's "hot" drilling results. Hirshhorn was also drawn to my area by the whirl and bustle of our printing production. "Attaboy, kid," he would encourage.

The uranium king also found it convenient to use my office as a holding station for his visitors, cronies, and favoured investors. With my naiveté, I had little to tell them. Most had known Hirshhorn for years and were prepared to regale me with stories of how they were "in" on the big play two years ago, when Franc Joubin's geological detective work had led them to 100 square miles of uranium potential.

Pat Cuzack, a genial geriatric from the U.S. was one such visitor. Lounging in a chair in front of me, Pat would explain how the initial investors in Hirshhorn's Peach syndicate found themselves participants in nearly every subsequent mining play of TMC. With the eye-popping diamond drilling outline of undreamt of wealth – millions of pounds of commercial grade uranium oxide – the Peach stock in weeks multiplied in value up to one hundred times its original purchase price of one dollar a share. Converted by now into shares of newly spawning uranium companies, the original investors were on their way to earning millions of dollars. Cuzack's broad smile and wink indicated that he had made a killing.

Paul Westerfield, another American, had his summer fishing lodge on the Spanish River, smack in the middle of the uranium rush. The development of Spanish American Mines by TMC and the subsequent Hirshhorn deal with Westerfield also made millions.

Having such happy speculators around the office contributed to the theatrical atmosphere of stock market buoyancy and sustained the mood of great expectations.

Visitors with celebrity status, such as former U.S. Secretary of State Dean Acheson, received Hirshhorn's personal guided tour of TMC past my desk and into the general office area. I stood respectfully at attention when such events happened. "Parker keeps me out of the headlines," Hirshhorn declared as he hurried Acheson along.

I always looked busy when visitors came through. My trick was to buy a paperback book, tear off its covers, and then dispose of each page read as though searching some document.

With few exceptions, Hirshhorn's visitors towered above him. He was about five feet two inches. Acheson had his arm around Hirshhorn's shoulders, a gesture JHH detested, given the height difference.

Lord Bessborough was another six-foot-tall visitor. A former Governor General of Canada and the Queen's uncle, Bessborough was chairman of the British mining group, Rio Tinto, the Rothschild dominated company providing Hirshhorn with the $50 million or so capital necessary to round out his financing of the first three of his seven Algoma uranium mines. JHH was in a most expansive mood in his presence.

"I want you to meet Lord Bessborough," he effused to me. "He's my illegitimate son." The British aristocrat was 80 years old at this point; Hirshhorn, 58.

Bessborough smiled his "how d'you do," then burst out laughing when Hirshhorn added, "He's a real royal bastard."

I was taken aback by this banter, but the two men had obviously achieved the proper rapport, and the moment passed easily.

Edward G. Robinson was an exception to the height disparity regarding visitors. He and Hirshhorn were a matched pair. The Hollywood screen star was appearing at the Royal Alexander Theatre in Toronto and was paying his old friend a courtesy call.

"We're twins," enthused JHH. "We were raised in the same Hell's Kitchen in New York, real dead end kids. We could have both ended up in Sing Sing. Instead, I am a financier and Eddie is Hollywood's Little Caesar."

Robinson seemed only mildly amused. Edward G. Robinson, a world-famous celebrity was already widely recognized as a fine art collector. "What do you think of Joe's collection," he asked, his speech theatrically immaculate in contrast to Hirshhorn's Brooklyn accent.

I muttered something about it all being overwhelming.

Hirshhorn quickly picked up on the theme. "Well, Eddie and I, we both believe in supporting contemporary artists, eh, kiddo?"

Robinson said something courteous on leaving me. Both men then drew strongly on their cigars, comrades in total unanimity, and moved along to view other paintings strewn around the various TMC offices.

* * *

My arrival on the TMC team provided the switchboard reception desk with an answer for unheralded visitors. I was thus introduced to dozens of freelance writers, painters, speculators, promoters of miscellaneous projects, and to some genuinely interesting people. I was like a prospector panning for gold. I found several fine personal friends among the traffic flow.

Ann Sugarman, an aristocratic lady in her sixties, came looking to buy some uranium ore samples. She had developed a stone polishing skill and wished to experiment with uranium bearing rock to see whether it was suitable for lapidary jewellery work. During our talk, I found that she and I were distant cousins related through Winnipeg family connections and I offered to see how I could help her.

In the meantime, I used the excuse of trying out a new Polaroid camera to gain a few moments with Franc Joubin at the end of the work day and to tell him about Ann. The celebrated geologist was in his shirt sleeves, deliberating over some results. It was painful for him to pose for photographs. He frowned and tried hard to concentrate on the sheaf of papers in front of him on his desk. I tried to be unobtrusive as I flashed away. I found an opportunity and reported Ann Sugarman's visit and her request. The grim visage gave way to one of pleasure. Quickly, he looked up and smiled, "Give her this." He reached for a large grab sample on his desk, then handed it to me. It was, he assured me, high in uranium oxide content. "A gift."

Ann was delighted and some weeks later presented me with a beautifully polished and mounted uranium chip, an ornament for my desk.

One pert, winsome widow from Quebec would come daily at three p.m. for nearly three weeks to try to meet Hirshhorn. I had interviewed her and found her personality and accent beguiling. She believed herself fated to live a short life and was determined to make a million dollars, to taste life to the full and to provide for her children. She was certain that JHH was to be the deus ex machina in her life. Joe Hirshhorn would guide her investments, and she was sure he could help her realize her financial and lifestyle goals.

After three weeks, she announced that she was running out of money and had to return to Quebec City, but would leave a forwarding address. She had hoped that JHH would call at her Toronto hotel. As a last desperate attempt to make something of her initiative, she asked me to take her to dinner. I was terrified of compromising involvements and declined. Her look of sardonic disbelief haunted me for many years.

Hirshhorn thought I had handled the situation well. "I don't believe in affairs," he confided. "I guess I am old fashioned." Gone was the memory of his involvement with his former secretary. I didn't know at the time that JHH was in the process of a divorce settlement from wife number two, Lily Harmon, the painter. Rumour had it that the divorce arrangement involved a one-time payment of $4 million. Hirshhorn seemed in no mood for extramarital levity. I was yet to hear of his current involvement with a Manhattan socialite named Brenda.

* * *

One day, an old acquaintance, Jack Seigel, showed up unannounced at the TMC office. I had first met Seigel casually during the war period in Ottawa. He had been working at the National Film Board in graphics when I maintained publicity liaison with the board on behalf of the department of munitions and supply. I was delighted to greet him.

He was an immaculately groomed young man, sporting a hand-shaped bow tie. Jack twitched a great deal and spoke nervously of his career as an artist and his desire to come to the attention of Joe Hirshhorn. He was diffident, shy and tentative in manner, but did prevail upon me to look at some of the samples of his work. He had brought along a large leather-covered portfolio. He hoped that I would interest myself in his work and intercede on his behalf with Mr. Hirshhorn. I ducked out of my office and asked Hirshhorn's secretary for a favour, to find a moment when I could bring Jack into the JHH presence.

Hirshhorn was in an expansive mood, standing behind his desk, his cigar at a jaunty angle. Things were going well today. His aide, Steve Kay, who shared the "old man's" office, was busily chatting up two visiting firemen from New York.

"Let's see what you've got there, kid," Hirshhorn beamed at Seigel after I had barely managed an introduction. "Go ahead, spread your stuff out on the carpet," Hirshhorn encouraged the nervous artist.

Hirshhorn was obviously taken with Jack's ability. "I'll take that, and that, and that." Hirshhorn, like a kid in a candy store, was obviously having a great time, involved in his favourite diversion, contemporary art buying. "Tell you what, Seigel," he offered. "I'll underwrite your living costs for a year, but I must have your best works for myself. I'll come around regularly to see if you are working and to keep you honest."

Jack, to whom Hirshhorn was an entirely new experience, was unsure whether he was to take the quip as a joke. He nodded nervously.

Then, Hirshhorn, in an aside to me, winked and said, "Get all the necessary information on this guy; his address, phone number and sex history."

Jack blanched.

"I'm just kidding," Hirshhorn reassured him, laughing, and then wrote out a cheque for $5,000. "That will keep you going for a while."

This was 1955. $5,000 was a viable annual income for a near-starving artist. The interview was over and Jack was now beside himself with joy at his good fortune.

* * *

Ron Krantz, a freelance writer with the CBC, dropped by to introduce himself one day. He was writing children's TV shows, but had recently sold his potential as a planner to the current events program department. An outdoorsman, he had romped around Blind River, Ontario, heard tales of the uranium rush, and was intrigued with the Franc Joubin-Joe Hirshhorn story. Ron wanted to create two programs; first, a straight Joubin discovery story, and then the tale of the amazing New York master of financial legerdemain, Joe Hirshhorn.

I regaled Ron with the already garnered lore on Joubin – how he was known for his sobriety and quiet wisdom. How he preferred to drink tepid tea in the bush, and how he engaged himself at night by reading the transcript of the anti-Nazi Nuremberg trials. Joubin identified himself with the mine finders, the geologists who brought ore bodies to light, rather than with operators who managed the mines and directed labour who turned out product economically at risk to their safety and health. Thus he contributed tangibly to a nation's wealth.

After completion of the first program, Ron's producers wanted something entirely different by way of show production in Hirshhorn's case.

The CBC was experimenting with new formats and hoped Hirshhorn could be interviewed live on camera in his King Edward suite. Joe McCaulley, warden of Hart House, would conduct the interview from the Jarvis/College street studio. Hirshhorn agreed, provided he would be asked about his celebrated art collection. He was preoccupied with the need to find a permanent home for his art treasures.

In the telecast, Hirshhorn proved, to be an ideal subject – genial, relaxed, and easy – talking rapidly and naturally, blowing cigar smoke at the camera and laughingly apologizing to McCaulley if it got in his eyes.

Hirshhorn was McCaulley's best subject. Taking the cameras on tour of his suite, Hirshhorn made a point of showing off his Jack Seigel "masterpieces". Seigel, Hirshhorn asserted, was Canada's greatest, most talented living artist. It was a preposterous claim, but it came from someone whose commendation could only do the artist good. When the show concluded, Hirshhorn could hardly wait to phone Seigel. "Well, kid, what did you think?"

To Hirshhorn's amazement, Seigel was distracted, seemed agitated. He had worked up a great deal of anxiety regarding the way his work was displayed. He had given no thought to the great publicity boost. "My paintings were hung badly," he wailed. They were seen crooked."

Incredulous, Hirshhorn felt cheated of the praise he was due. From that day forward, Hirshhorn's enthusiasm for Jack Seigel and his work waned and the art lover's passion towards this hapless talent cooled.

In the meantime, Ron Krantz had scored a great personal success with the Hirshhorn program and he and I became close friends. High in Krantz' mind was the temptation to write an hour-length television play for General Motors Presents with a character such as Joe Hirshhorn as the subject. He wanted me to collaborate. I felt that this venture might impinge on my loyalty to my employer. In the end, I agreed, provided we fictionalized events and I was allowed a pseudonym as co-author. When the finished play, "The

Blackwood Deal," was telecast in the fall of 1955, to my great surprise and relief, no one at TMC found it reminiscent of the Hirshhorn character.

* * *

A college friend, Liz Trott, associate editor of the *Monetary Times*, called to renew contact, to tell me about the unusually arresting man in her life and to invite me and Ilene, my bride of two months, to dinner at Angelo's.

Eli Borowski impressed me as larger than life, an eccentric, buoyant character made nearly incomprehensible by his mouth-full-of-marbles type of speech and his European guttural accent. He was loud and overwhelming, but if Liz loved him, then he was okay.

After directing the waitress to serve us her "best spaghetti" and demonstratively hugging Liz, Borowski quickly disclosed his interest in meeting me. He was, he explained, a biblical scholar turned dealer in artifacts and antiquities. His inventory included invaluable objects, often unearthed by mid-Eastern grave robbers and other unsavoury characters and then smuggled into the international art market. He had found a profitable role for himself at the end of the process, dealing with private buyers and academic institutions. He wanted me to introduce him to Hirshhorn, whom he would turn into the world's great possessor of biblical art treasures. Borowski was florid, perspiring with excitement and enthusiasm.

I suggested that he call Hirshhorn directly and that he might say that we were newly acquainted through a mutual journalistic friend.

The next day, Hirshhorn burst into my area to tell me of this self-proclaimed expert on archaeology whom he had invited to his hotel suite that evening. Could I be present?

Borowski, the effusive giant, and Joe Hirshhorn, the pint-sized dynamo, took to each other on sight as only an odd couple can, both talking a blue streak, neither quite listening.

First came a tour of the Hirshhorn art scattered around the rooms. Then, in a moment of grandstanding, Hirshhorn made a gift to me of a Doc Jones print.

In the living-room, both men sat down boy-style on the carpet and began to do business. Borowski unwrapped objects which he conjured up from a small valise. The men began to finger the treasures: Here was a perfectly preserved horse's bit, made of brass, typical of those used by cavalry thousands of years ago; the intact vase predated the rule of Persian kings; the beautifully ornamented serving dish glorified male sexuality and probably was from Babylon. And so it went, on and on.

The small cylinder was the seal of a vanquished king, made around 3000 BC. Borowski noticed Hirshhorn's obvious fascination and made a grand gesture. "It's yours. A gift."

Hirshhorn insisted on paying for it. Borowski refused, but instead sold Joe $20,000 worth of other items. The two traders, absorbed in the pleasure of their commerce, agreed to put these purchases on display at the Royal Ontario Museum within weeks.

The next morning, Hirshhorn felt that perhaps he had lost his professional cool, that he had bought a line from Borowski. Hirshhorn's aide, Steve Kay, asked me to check out "the good doctor," see if Borowski's references stood up. After two or three calls, I was able to clear Borowski.

Yes, he was known to Ted Heinrich, director of the Royal Ontario Museum. He was spoken highly of by a Dr. Albright of an American university, a man whom Borowski had described as "the Einstein of the archaeological world." Borowski, in turn, was described as the Duveen of the art treasure trade, a reputable international wheeler-dealer in the art black markets of the world. Apparently Borowski's specialized scholarship attested to the validity of the items sold.

Hirshhorn was stimulated by his purchases, impressed with Borowski. Now came Borowski's big play for Hirshhorn's involvement.

Borowski had an option for a few months on some sixty-seven interconnecting ivory fragments which were once part of the erotica decorating a royal bed several centuries before Christ. The set could be purchased for a nominal $500,000. Would Hirshhorn help the Royal Ontario Museum acquire this supreme art treasure?

A special dinner was arranged in Hirshhorn's honour at the exclusive York Club with Dr. Sidney E. Smith, President of the University of Toronto, as toastmaster. Hirshhorn was declared a life member of the museum. He, in turn, turned over $1,000 for the honour. He actually peeled off a one-thousand-dollar bill from his pocket wad. All went swimmingly with much laughter, cognac and cigars. Hirshhorn offered to lend the half million dollars needed to secure the purchase to an ivory acquisition group without interest for a few months. He insisted that local donors provide the dollars needed to make this gift to the ROM. He would contribute a share.

When the smoke settled, no local money was forthcoming. Within a few weeks, the project died. A disillusioned Hirshhorn was no longer open to Borowski or Ted Heinrich and was becoming increasingly critical of Canadians as art supporters.

* * *

In the fall of 1955, four months after I had joined Technical Mines Consultant, the first of seven uranium mines, Pronto, developed under the Franc Joubin management, received its official opening. Pronto Uranium Mines was an incredible discovery no more than a mile and a half from the Trans-Canada Highway, just seventeen miles east of Blind River, Ontario. The Pronto celebration reminded me of the wartime hoopla I experienced when the Department of Munitions and Supply celebrated the completion of the first Lancaster bomber made in Canada at Malton, Ontario.

For the Pronto weekend party in the bush, I had managed to interest major Canadian press, radio, television and film sources, leading New York newspapers and magazines, and several international publications, including the prestigious *Financial Times* of London, England. More than fifty media representatives were accommodated. A special CPR overnight train to Blind River with sleeping, dining and observation cars was chartered to leave Toronto on Friday at midnight and held over on-site to return on Sunday evening.

Some five hundred guests toured the new plant at Pronto. The wives of mine-staff members threw a gala reception in the afternoon at the office site. Excited laughter and hubbub prevailed. Paul Young, mine manager, Franc Joubin, discoverer, Joe Hirshhorn, promoter, and Bill Bouck, lawyer-president, placed forefingers in unison on the start-up button, and, to everyone's relief, the mill started up and the first batch of uranium oxide was in the making in the Algoma region.

On Saturday evening, everyone was assembled in the Blind River Legion Hall for a camp caterer's banquet deluxe. Congratulatory speeches were euphoric with bullish stock market optimism, Hirshhorn beaming and promising yet greater mining wonders.

The Rio Tinto group of London, England, and major financiers of the venture were present. Rumours were already circulating that a deal was in the works. Jimmy Scott of the *Globe and Mail* had heard that Joe Hirshhorn was going to sell his controlling interest in all his Canadian holdings to Rio Tinto London for some $130 million cash and stock, an astronomical amount at that time. Scott made me promise to check.

Hirshhorn merely grinned when I spoke of the inquiry in hushed tones in the smoking car. He beckoned me to join him at a table in the dining car, away from the Rio Tinto Canadian consultants. Conspiratorially, head leaning towards mine, he asked me to speak of other things. The man loved being mysterious. He muttered, "Barbi Lake. Barbi Lake. Tell your family to buy Barbi Lake."

On Wednesday, I found two notices in my mail at home; one, a purchase order of 5,000 shares of Barbi Lake stock, and two, a sell order at double the purchase price. It was a transaction in the name of my wife's little daughter, Tia, and constituted a present from Uncle Joe. Joubin smiled enigmatically when I told him about the boon. "That's Joe's way of saying he was pleased with your work on the opening."

Joubin confirmed that there was a major transaction in the works and that he would be leaving TMC. In unguarded moments, Franc Joubin, chortling, would report Hirshhorn's early meetings with the Rio Tinto board of directors in London. He had been inducted as a member.

Ebullient Hirshhorn would upset the fixed "stuffy" seating arrangements by taking a chair near the head of the board table, thereby creating a disconcerting disturbance of rank, resulting in an exercise of musical chairs.

Joubin also relished the story of how the British charmed Joe with their pride and customs, afternoon tea and inviolate weekend withdrawal from business. The fact that they would now embrace him as one of their own beguiled Hirshhorn. He was flattered to be invited to participate in their investment circle and beamed when it was suggested that he be knighted and called "Sir Joseph". Joubin wondered who had outpromoted whom when he learned that Hirshhorn had taken back some Rio Tinto shares in the overall exchange for his Canadian holdings and that he was now a major participant in Palabora Copper Mines, a large, but chancy, South African venture.

In 1954, I had received word that my mother's health was failing; she was not expected to live for more than a year. She had come to visit her boys in the east in 1955, her last trip. She had spent the summer with Morten and his wife in Ottawa, and was to stay with me and my wife, Ilene, in Toronto that fall.

Around Christmas she did not feel well. We took her to a doctor in Toronto, and he recommended she go back to Winnipeg immediately. I had purchased tickets for her to see the Ice Capades and asked him if it would be all right. He thought the suggestion irrelevant and academic when she might only live another two or three weeks. The doctor's attitude implied, "What good would Ice Capades be to her?" I took her anyway, and she enjoyed the show immensely and had a great laugh at a clown who threw snow at her.

That night, mounting the steps to our porch, she slipped and fell. She suffered no injury, but it was a portent that things were not going too well for her. In a day or two, we put her on the plane for Winnipeg. Within a week she was in hospital. A week after, she had died. We never really found out the cause of her death.

Her funeral contrasted with my father's rather markedly. Some twenty or thirty people were present – neighbours, Mrs. Berg, Schloime, Ester, and their children.

One day, in the spring of 1956, some thirty lawyers representing the British group, the Hirshhorn group and other associates met in crowded confusion, mulled over documents and milled throughout the TMC offices. The moment of truth had arrived. Signatures were affixed to contracts. Hirshhorn stood in the centre of this hubbub, searching for a momentary respite. He spotted me inconspicuous in a corner of the boardroom. "Parker," he called out imperiously. For the moment, I gained in importance. "Come with me."

I followed him out of the office and down the corridor to the men's washroom. After a quick glance under the cubicle doors to assure himself that no one was present in the room, he began to laugh uncontrollably, tears flowing, doubling over with glee. "Imagine," he challenged me. "Here I am, a little kike from New York, doing business with the Queen of England!"

Startled by his seeming self-deprecation, I reminded him that it was not the first time in history.

"Ya, I know," he agreed, turning solemn. "Disraeli and Queen Victoria."

Joe would become a minority shareholder in a new holding company and chairman of the board. Joubin would become a special consultant on worldwide ventures to the London company, working out of his own private office in Toronto. Joubin was also going to serve the United Nations as a global geological consultant, working out of New York for specific periods. Hirshhorn's deal ensured that the present TMC staff would stay in place for the time being and that I would be sold like a slave with the plantation to the Rio Tinto Mining Company of Canada Limited. Hirshhorn conceded that the new British management didn't have a clue what they were going to do with me. Their idea of public relations, he observed, was to hand out a synopsis of their annual meeting to half a dozen favoured newspapers and to have two "cosy" writers in for lunch in their board room once a year. "You'll have to educate them," he said mischievously. "I'll keep in touch." Hirshhorn would operate out of three offices – one at Rio Tinto, another privately with Steve Kay as office manager in Toronto and a third as his own in Manhattan.

* * *

The concept of a memorial bearing his name and encompassing most of the major art possessions he had accumulated over a lifetime had long niggled in Joe Hirshhorn's mind. I had heard him speak rhapsodically of such a project on my first visit to his glass-encased summer home on the shore of Lake Huron near Blind River. His guest that weekend was Philip Johnston, the famous American architect.

Johnston had brought with him a scale model of a nine-floor building which encompassed the Hirshhorn concept of a skyscraper in the wilderness. It would be the centrepiece of a new town, called Hirshhornville and was to house all the mining company offices in the area in addition to Hirshhorn's world-class art collection. Joe foresaw it as an irresistible tourist draw to the Algoma area.

One of those caught up with the excitement of the model unveiling was a genial personality, Henry, the local federal Member of Parliament. We spent some time together speculating on how to get federal and provincial government support for the program. In the fashion of a promoter, Joe envisioned having the cost of the building raised by sources other than himself. Land accommodation would be made by the Ontario government; Ottawa grants would match uranium company contributions towards building costs and so forth.

It was a wild concept, and I sensed that whether it was practical or not, it would command wide media attention. It subsequently did in *Time*, *Newsweek* and various Canadian publications.

Algoma MP Henry said that he would introduce me to Alan Jarvis, then head of the National Art Gallery in Ottawa. At a subsequent luncheon, the three of us got along famously. Alan learned that I had been taught history by the Rt. Hon. John Pickersgill, the secretary of state and cabinet minister responsible for the National Gallery. Jarvis suggested that Hirshhorn invite Pickersgill and himself to his home in New York to have them view the "proud collector's" art and to persuade him to allow some of his pieces to be featured in a special show at the National Gallery.

Hirshhorn was delighted and included Ilene and myself in his guest list for the weekend. He put us all up at a favourite hotel, introduced us to his curator, Alan Lerner, and then took everyone dining and dancing. It was an occasion to introduce us to his latest fiancée, a Manhattan socialite whom he planned to wed on completing his divorce contract with his second wife. Between dancing and drinking, Pickersgill and I reminisced about the days at United College.

In the end, a deal was struck. If Governor General Vincent Massey would sponsor the show, Hirshhorn would send whatever art Alan Jarvis selected to Ottawa. A second show would follow at the Ontario Art Gallery in Toronto. Hirshhorn hoped that he might sell Ottawa on building a Hirshhorn centre in Canada's capital. The Canadians hoped that Hirshhorn would donate his possessions, no strings attached, to the National Art Gallery.

Joe, his wife and I comprised the party staying at the Château Laurier Hotel in Ottawa on the eve of the Hirshhorn art show at the National Art Gallery. Joe had been formally invited to the Governor General's mansion for tea. The invitation had not been extended to his wife Brenda, probably because of some uncertainty about her marital status. Brenda, laden with nasal congestion, was furious. She reminded me of an outraged Adelaide in the musical "Guys and Dolls" or an avenging Judy Holiday in "Born Yesterday."

During an early morning press meeting in the Hirshhorn suite, she burst on the scene and confronted Joe, demanding an explanation for the vice-regal slight. Momentarily flustered, Hirshhorn turned to me. "Why can't Brenda come, Ed?"

"Protocol," I quickly improvised.

"That's it," Joe exulted, "Protocol." Then, as a conditioned business reflex, he muttered "Protocol Mines Limited – not a bad company name." The press people laughed and the incident passed unreported in the Ottawa newspapers.

Hirshhorn's art involvement was news even in Canada's financial press. On my advice, John Kieran, then with the *Financial Post*, hopped on the overnight train to Blind River one Friday, an occasion when he could be sure to meet Hirshhorn in the dining car. As a result, the *Fi-*

nancial Post had a scoop, a full-page visualization of Hirshhornville, Algoma, on the Trans-Canada highway just south of Blind River.

Joe had me order five hundred reprints of the *Financial Post* article immediately, even though he had no clear view how to proceed with the promotion. The publicity was duly brought to the attention of his British associates and, by them, to the notice of the directors of the Tate Gallery in London.

On subsequent trips overseas, Hirshhorn speculated that his collection would be better displayed in London, Paris, or New York. Still, no one offered to set up a special building in his honour, bearing his name. A proposal was made to start a Hirshhorn wing in the Tate Gallery. Joe relayed his dealings to influential friends in Israel. They offered to help raise money for a Hirshhorn building in Tel Aviv. But the approaches were too convoluted, too tortuous for Joe Hirshhorn's sense of getting things done.

At this point, he was able to interest U.S. President Lyndon B. Johnson's wife and daughter Lucy to visit his estate in New Haven, New York. Excited by what they had been shown, they rushed back to the White House and insisted that Lyndon offer to build a Hirshhorn museum in Washington. The rest is art history. Despite protests from some in congress that Hirshhorn, a stock promoter, was being elevated to fame in the U.S. Pantheon, the project was realized and the Hirshhorn Museum and Sculpture Garden has proven to be a much-attended attraction in Washington.

My wife Ilene, a fine painter in her own right, and I had occasion to visit the Hirshhorn building. We pondered why the sculpted head of Joe Hirshhorn on display in the building's foyer was measurably smaller than his actual head. "Obviously," quipped Ilene, "a case of overcaution. They didn't want to show Joe with a swelled head."

* * *

I enjoyed and appreciated Joseph Hirshhorn. Perhaps his diminutive height aroused affection, although I didn't dare put my arm around him, tempted as I was by conviviality, when we walked down a corridor together. Perhaps my fondness was based on the fact that I knew him in "theatrical" terms, as an extrovert character in some play. Little or nothing of his reputed sharp dealings in the stock market was known to me. I had arrived on the scene when he had already had it made. I had none of the bitterness of his family or close friends, who thought him ruthless and insensitive to their needs in either domestic terms or in the business world.

I went on to serve The Rio Tinto Mining Company for seven years and then opened my own public relations practice in 1962.

PUBLISHER'S EPILOGUE

Ed Parker was one of those rare individuals whose special magnetism reached out to change forever countless persons with whom he was acquainted. Thanks to a mutual friend, I first met him over lunch as his guest at The Toronto Board of Trade Building. We warmed to each other from the start and in no time he was rattling off the names of prominent Canadian friends from all walks of life, persons he felt certain would share his immediate enthusiasm for my publishing activities at the time. This meeting and many more to follow were to prove personally and professionally invaluable.

A few years prior to his passing, on March 29, 1988, Ed asked me for my opinion on another book publisher's assessment of his auto-biographical writings. He appreciated my comments and began to suggest that perhaps I would care to publish his memoirs. I readily assured him of my interest, but as fate decreed Ed's declining health and my own hectic schedule prevented the publication of his story within his lifetime. Fortunately, thanks to the interest and encouragement of Ilene Parker and family, this Publisher was to eventually re-enter the picture, now resulting in the 1993 publication of *I Didn't Come Here to Stay*.

One of my great pleasures in life has involved extensive historical research, and wading through the accumulation of writings, notes, correspondence and photos that Ed Parker left behind has suited me to a "T". The man knew everyone from statesmen to corporate giants, from potters to painters to poets. Ed's contacts with a host of diverse and memorable personalities... Margaret Laurence ... John Black Aird... Doris McCarthy... William Withrow ... Arnold Edinborough, went far beyond the final typed pages he left behind. Alas, those recollections end with the beginning of his Public Relations company in the 1960s and we hear nothing from him concerning his close association with the late Edmund C. Bovey and the Northern Ontario Natural Gas Company. But Celia Davies, former Executive Assistant to Mr. Bovey, recalls how Ed Parker's significant role increased with the company's growth and evolvement. Like so many others, she especially remembers how Ed made work fun and how hilarious it was for her colleagues and herself to be around him.

It should be pointed out to the reader that Parker's notable achievements continued into the '70s and '80s These included his role in 1977 as Executive Editor overseeing the preparation of reports by The Royal Commission on the Northern Environment in Ontario and his long association with York University, where he taught Creating Writing until 1983.

At one point in their married life, Ed and Ilene owned a delightful "Cover Story" house in the small Ontario community of Hastings. Unlike Ilene, for Ed the restoration of this sizeable old residence and the never-ceasing grounds work held little appeal, as his main activity was to saunter into the nearby village store in search of the Toronto newspapers. On those occasions when there were house guests comprised of his York University students or other writing friends, Ed was in his glory. Otherwise, he yearned for the beat of the big city.

Ed continues to be remembered and missed by an astonishing number of people and in many different ways. The following recollections by a select few provide insights into the essence of Ed Parker.

Syd Perlmutter, Ed's first cousin

Ed was the family historian, always primed to reveal humorous, sad or revealing stories. Once started, information, interpretations and ideas flowed unendingly it seemed. He impressed as the consummate universal "reporter and commentator".

Walking and talking with Ed was intriguing. Many evenings in the late 1940s, Ed and I would walk round trip from Alfred Avenue East in North Winnipeg (we were neighbours) to Childs Restaurant at Portage and Main. I always looked forward to these occasions. I was a student at the University of Manitoba. Ed was always interested in my education and future. These walks and stimulating talks provided many hours of "continuing education". My father was a teacher. Ed saw the logic to extend the family tradition with my continuing studies in Education at the University. He encouraged my early acting interest and involvement in the Winnipeg Theatre scene after the War.

In the summer of 1956, Ed Parker informed me of a search for a person to head the Radio and TV Arts Program at the Ryerson Institute in Toronto. By this time I was fully active as a teacher for the Winnipeg School Board, a stage actor and director and a performer for CBC Radio & Television. Fortunately this was the combination Ryerson required. In words of the old cliche, "the rest is history".

Did Ed Parker prophesy a dream for me? He did much more – he made it real.

Harry Gutkin, President,
The Jewish Historical Society of Western Canada

I remember Ed, and I remember his father Harry Parker, who sat permanently stooped, and stooped even as he stood, an occupational hazard from sitting day in and day out at a linotype, while working for Dos Yiddishe Vort, *The Israelite Press*, at 165 Selkirk Avenue East, in Winnipeg. He was, as well, a prominent essayist, whose acid pen satirized events in his own community. I knew Harry well before I knew Ed well. By 1940, Ed worked as the stage and screen editor for the *Winnipeg Tribune*. This meant that he had free passes to stages of the Playhouse and the Dominion theatres, and the screens at the Metropolitan, the Capital, and the Lyceum theatres.

Ed and I became friends in the middle forties when he first went to work as Deputy Director of Adult Education for Tommy Douglas, in Saskatchewan, to help him usher in the New Jerusalem. Then he went on to found and direct the Journalism and Graphic Arts program at Ryerson, and I recall the enthusiastic group of young visionaries he had gathered around him. Later, in the fifties and sixties, when his idealism was spent, and he was by then ensconced in a plush suite of offices in the higher regions, as a public relations major domo for the mining entrepreneurs, I would visit him, and behind closed doors we would pursue utopias yet a-boring. Most of all, I recall a relaxed Ed, and his charming wife, Ilene, during my rare visits to Vesta Drive.

Ilene Parker, Wife

Ed's image of himself was as a creative innovator.

He loved the English language, the spoken word. His ideas came best conversing. One could almost see this strange chemistry occur when he spoke and new innovative ideas would pop out. It was the creative process in action, sheer "magic". This was enhanced by his golden voice, retentive memory and open, winning smile.

Ed was very generous of himself and his ideas. His own performance standards were high. He drove himself, often becoming his own worst enemy. When Ed sensed his energy waning, he decided to pull back in gradual stages from the public relations practice. Wanting always to give his very best, he gradually withdrew from the public scene, when he felt this was not achievable.

Ed Parker with his family. Seated, left to right, Ilene, granddaughter Pilar, daughter Tia, daughter Ara and son Ivor. Standing behind are son Josh and Ed.

As his physical resources diminished over the years due to a large slow-growing tumour later detected, he became unhappy with himself because the periods of "living", being "on high" were less frequent and he was beginning to lose contact with the outside world.

Ed was a very private person who adored his family. We entered into our union in 1955 with a child each from previous marriages. Another girl and boy completed our family several years later.

Elizabeth Lancaster, Former Student

Lunch with Ed made you feel "up" for a week because of his humour, intelligence and spontaneous ideas on any subject. He would seize upon an idea you had just expressed or a topic in which one was interested and there would be an immediate explosion of creative possibilities from him as to how you could achieve success.

I first met Ed Parker through business around 1970, at which time he was operating his own Public Relations Company. He had just been contracted to serve as the Public Relations Director of my husband's new business in Toronto. Later on, as a participant in his Saturday morning Creative Writing course at York University, among the many wisdoms of his imparted clearly, the chief one that I remember most was when he said "When you can write about sex, you have freed yourself of the corset-strings that bind you and you can write about anything."

. . . and finally a letter from Ed to his former student, February 5, 1970
Elizabeth, Sweet Majesty, Greetings!!
Your good wishes for the New Year and now your letter have contributed greatly to my cheer here in my strange exile. In fact, I was delighted! My purpose was to escape the winter and to be in temperatures where I would be tempted to take long walks, and in an environment where I wouldn't be bored silly in the evenings. Well, the weather has been 20° below normal, December and January, with unheard of snowstorms last week. Ugh. Brr.

The strip, well it's fun when there are visitors, but once you become a quasi-resident you become jaded. Ilene, who has been with me for January and how has returned to Toronto for two months, (and back in April), is actually looking forward to all the involvement in Toronto despite the cold. So, you see in some way I envy you your locale. You are involved.

I began conducting my course in Creative Writing at the University of Nevada three Saturdays ago, and with 30 participants, that activity will bring me new friends, and certainly some more realistic involvement. The class differs from those in Toronto, not in the basic humanity of the stories, i.e. love, marriage, divorcemorphanges, – but in the particular vocations of the participants, gamblers, dealers, former call-girls. Makes for a mixed cage of wounded lions and tigers.

Which brings me to your own beautiful and creative communication. I was so pleased with it, that after ingesting the personal communication, I couldn't resist marking the copy as I do in class, in order to find a poem in the poem. I return the letter to you (since you have no copy) just for your amusement. Maybe you will really start writing this time.

I welcomed the news of you and yours, and look forward to a catch-up meeting in the spring.

Much affection,
Ed

* * *

As an appropriate postscript, I am pleased to report that THE EDWARD PARKER MEMORIAL AWARD was established in July 1989 by his family. The award in the amount of $1,000 is presented annually to the most promising print journalist in the first year of a two-year program at the Ryerson School of Journalism. The first recipient was Michelle Lalonde, in October 1989. Ed would be delighted!

Barry L. Penhale